Literature of the 1980s

The Edinburgh History of Twentieth-Century Literature in Britain
General Editor: Randall Stevenson

Literature of the 1980s

After the Watershed

Joseph Brooker

Edinburgh University Press

For Peter and Margaret Stray

© Joseph Brooker, 2010

Edinburgh University Press Ltd
22 George Square, Edinburgh

www.euppublishing.com

Typeset in 10.5/13 Adobe Sabon
by Servis Filmsetting Ltd, Stockport, Cheshire, and
printed and bound in Great Britain by
CPI Antony Rowe, Chippenham and Eastbourne

A CIP record for this book is available from the British Library

ISBN 978 0 7486 3394 4 (hardback)

Contents

Acknowledgements

This book was written with the support of a Research Leave grant from the Arts and Humanities Research Council of Great Britain. I am grateful to the AHRC for this vital assistance.

It has been a pleasure to work with Edinburgh University Press on this project. The Edinburgh History of Twentieth-Century Literature in Britain was first introduced to me by Jackie Jones, who has been a crucial influence on this series and an unfailing source of clarification and information for me as a contributor. I have been fortunate to work with Randall Stevenson as General Editor. Having read and commented on my initial proposal, he also offered detailed comments on every chapter of the completed book. While his expert advice on the work has been tremendously useful, writing this book has also brought me access to Randall's regular updates, usually wry and stoical, on the fortunes of St Mirren FC.

I wrote this book while working in English and Humanities at Birkbeck College, University of London. I am once again grateful to my colleagues for the creative and supportive atmosphere that they have fostered. Steven Connor, Esther Leslie, Mpalive Msiska, Gill Partington, William Rowe, Laura Salisbury, Lynne Segal and Carol Watts are among those who have most enriched the conversation about the literature of the contemporary period and recent past. I wish to give special thanks to Roger Luckhurst, an exemplary colleague who over several years has been supportive of my work in general, and of this research project in particular. Thanks also to Julie Crofts for textual information.

I have benefited from the support, advice and encouragement of both my parents, Liz and Pete Brooker. My father also gave particularly valuable assistance in seeking illustrations. I am grateful to Alan Denney for the use of two of his photographs, and to Alasdair Gray for the use of an image from *Lanark*. My brother Will also gave advice on images. I have enjoyed sharing reminiscences of the 1980s with him, ever since the days when we experienced them together. I dedicate the book to my grandparents, who have survived not only the 1980s but everything else since James Joyce published *Ulysses*.

Other friends, over a number of years, have also discussed this period with me. From the academy they include Claire Feehily, Finn Fordham, Andrew Gibson, David James, Nola Merckel, Kaye Mitchell, Nigel Parke, Paul Sheehan, Tony Sweeney and Scott Thurston. Beyond it, I have savoured the writing and conversation of Travis Elborough, Tom Ewing, Alistair Fitchett, Tim Hopkins, Peter Miller, Chris Roberts and Mark Sinker. Stephen Troussé has shared distinctive shafts of illumination and recollection about the period over fifteen years of friendship. But the most formidable memory of the 1980s I know is that of Michael Jones, who can still recite every Everton result and Wirral bus timetable from the decade. For this and many other virtues, I salute him.

JB
March 2010

Illustrations

General Editor's Preface

One decade is covered by each of the ten volumes in The Edinburgh History of Twentieth-Century Literature in Britain series. Individual volumes may argue that theirs is *the* decade of the century. The series as a whole considers the twentieth century as *the* century of decades. All eras are changeful, but the pace of change has itself steadily accelerated throughout modern history, and never more swiftly than under the pressures of political crises and of new technologies and media in the twentieth century. Ideas, styles and outlooks came into dominance, and were then displaced, in more and more rapid succession, characterising ever-briefer periods, sharply separated from predecessors and successors.

Time-spans appropriate to literary or cultural history shortened correspondingly, and on account not only of change itself, but its effect on perception. How distant, for example, that tranquil, sunlit, Edwardian decade already seemed, even ten years later, after the First World War, at the start of the twenties. And how essential, too, to the self-definition of that restless decade, and later ones, that the years from 1900 to1910 *should* seem tranquil and sunlit – as a convenient contrast, not necessarily based altogether firmly on ways the Edwardians may have thought of themselves. A need to secure the past in this way – for clarity and definition, in changeful times – encourages views of earlier decades almost as a hand of familiar, well-differentiated cards, dealt out, one by one, by prior times to the present one. These no longer offer pictures of kings and queens: King Edward VII, at the start of the century, or, briefly, George V, were the last monarchs to give their names to an age. Instead, the cards are marked all the more clearly by image and number, as 'the Twenties', 'the Thirties', 'the Forties' and so on. History itself often seems to join in the game, with so many epochal dates – 1918, 1929, 1939, 1968, 1979, 1989, 2001 – approximating to the end of decades.

By the end of the century, decade divisions had at any rate become a firmly-established habit, even a necessity, for cultural understanding and analysis. They offer much virtue, and opportunity, to the present series. Concentration within firm temporal boundaries gives each volume further scope to range geographically – to explore the literary production and shifting mutual influences of nations, regions and minorities within a less and less surely 'United' Kingdom. Attention to film and broadcasting allows individual volumes to reflect another key aspect of literature's rapidly changing role throughout the century. In its early years, writing and publishing remained almost the only media for imagination, but by the end of the century, they were hugely challenged by competition from new technologies. Changes of this kind were accompanied by wide divergences in ways that the literary was conceived and studied. The shifting emphases of literary criticism, at various stages of the century, are also considered throughout the series.

Above all, though, the series' decade-divisions promote productive, sharply-focused literary-historical analysis. Ezra Pound's celebrated definition of literature, as 'news that stays news', helps emphasise the advantages. It is easy enough to work with the second part of Pound's equation: to explain the continuing appeal of literature from the past. It is harder to recover what made a literary work news in the first place, or, crucially for literary history, to establish just how it related *to* the news of its day – how it digested, evaded or sublimated pressures bearing on its author's imagination at the time. Concentration on individual decades facilitates attention to this 'news'. It helps recover the brisk, chill feel of the day, as authors stepped out to buy their morning newspapers – the immediate, actual climate of their time, as well as the tranquillity, sunshine or cloud ascribed to it in later commentary. Close concentration on individual periods can also renew attention to writing that did *not* stay news – to works that, significantly, pleased contemporary readers and reviewers, and might repay careful rereading by later critics.

In its later years, critics of twentieth-century writing sometimes concentrated more on characterising than periodising the literature they surveyed, usually under the rubrics of modernism or postmodernism. No decade is an island, entire of itself, and volumes in the series consider, where appropriate, broader movements and influences of this kind, stretching beyond their allotted periods. Each volume also offers, of course, a fuller picture of the writing of its times than necessarily-selective studies of modernism and postmodernism can provide. Modernism and postmodernism, moreover, are thoroughly specific in their historical origins and development, and the nature of each can be usefully illumined by the close, detailed analyses the series provides. Changeful, tumultuous and challenging, history in the twentieth century perhaps pressed harder and more variously on literary imagination than ever before, requiring a literary history correspondingly meticulous, flexible and multifocal. This is what The Edinburgh History of Twentieth-Century Literature in Britain provides.

The idea for the series originated with Jackie Jones in Edinburgh University Press, and all involved are grateful for her vision and guidance, and for support from the Press, throughout.

Randall Stevenson
University of Edinburgh

Introduction: After the Watershed

In 2004 Alan Hollinghurst won the Booker Prize for his novel *The Line of Beauty*. The book's reconstruction of London life in the 1980s focuses on the household of an ambitious Conservative politician. On the morning of the 1987 General Election, his dissident daughter and lodger discuss the effects of the last eight years of Conservative government. They conclude on this note:

> 'Well, it'll soon be over.'
> 'What? Oh, the election, yes.' Catherine stared out into the drizzle. 'The 80s are going on for ever.' (2004: 393)

Catherine is psychologically unstable, and the drizzle has perhaps come out in sympathy with her. She means that the decade's end is still not in sight; that the world it has announced seems without end; that she can see little prospect of the downfall of the father she resents, and the views and interests he represents. But the line suggests a slyer significance too. Looking back from seventeen years later, Hollinghurst is playing with hindsight. In one sense he gently mocks and frames the feeling that the 1980s would last for ever, from a moment when they are long gone. In another, he leaves the post-millennial reader to wonder if they have ever ended. Readers may reflect that the world around them is the product of the 1980s, or at least that it shows profound continuities with that decade. They may also feel that the very act of writing this novel, and its critical and public success, are signs of an inability fully to leave the 1980s behind, or leave them alone.

This book describes and discusses British literature in the 1980s. It considers different genres: the novel, short stories, poetry, drama, screenwriting. Instances of these modes of writing are gathered around themes. A primary aim is to attend to the specificity of the literary texts. But I also aim to inform the reader of the historical and social contexts that shaped writing in this period, and to which writers responded. It is necessary to do this in part because the 1980s are indeed distant. Their last days are now over two decades away. But the book is also written with a conviction that the 1980s have been important in shaping the world we inhabit in the early twenty-first century.

This book's chapters are organised around five major headings. Chapter One considers the literary establishment of the period, noting the transition between generations of writers. Chapter Two turns to instances of dissident, working-class and regional writing. Chapter Three assesses trends associated with postmodernism. Chapter Four addresses representations of nation and ethnicity; and Chapter Five records the impact of feminism on literature. Before those, this Introduction aims to restore historical and cultural conditions. My account of the politics and social conditions of the 1980s leads into a discussion of the cultural and ideological climate, a crucial context for creative work in the period. I assess the changing connotations of the concept of culture itself, and focus on the fate of the Arts Council as a key instance of cultural policy's shifts in relation to broader historical currents. Finally I turn to the modes of production, distribution and representation of literature, particularly the novel. These analyses will prepare us for the more detailed discussions of literary texts in the chapters ahead.

Consensus and Beyond

Any period can be described in many different ways. What is most important about it depends on the angle of vision, how far back one stands, and what one is looking for. But discussions of British life in the 1980s are not randomly diverse. A dominant theme persists; pervasive, almost inescapable. This is the influence of the Conservative governments that administered Britain for the entire decade, and the attempts they made to alter British society and its historical trajectory. One word gathers these themes: Thatcherism. Thatcherism is not the only fact about Britain in the 1980s. But it is the central one, which will interact with and inflect any other story – for instance, the story of feminism and gender relations in the period, or the story of publishing. We must thus reckon with Thatcherism now.

To appreciate its importance requires historical perspective. Thatcherism is widely seen as an intervention in the pattern of British governance, society and economy that had been established since the Second World War. The conditions of war were formative for post-war Britain. The perception of collective action and national unity, the realities of rationing and state planning for strategic purposes, were already germinating a new social dispensation before the end of hostilities in 1945. Writing in late 1940, George Orwell had announced that social revolution was necessary if Britain was to prevail against fascism (Orwell 1982). The revolution did not take place. But extensive social change and reform did. The immediate and iconic event was the landslide victory of the Labour Party in the General Election held in July 1945. Over the next six years, Clement Attlee's Labour government instituted important structural changes in British society. It established the welfare state of provision and support, funded from general taxation rather than paid for by individuals at the point of need. The welfare state included a system of social security, covering pensions and sickness and unemployment benefit. It expanded the free secondary school system and sought to increase the social range of those going to university. In 1948 the Health Minister and Labour left-winger Aneurin Bevan established the National Health Service. The state also sought to remake the physical landscape of Britain. An extensive programme of building and social housing included the creation of New Towns like Stevenage and East Kilbride. A 1949 Act aimed at the protection of the environment was echoed by the maintenance of public parks as a 'green belt' or 'urban lung'. Meanwhile, following and endorsing the centralised planning imposed by wartime conditions, key elements of the British economy were nationalised, brought into state ownership. These included the Bank of England, coal, civil aviation, Cable & Wireless, the railway and canal networks, the electricity supply and the production of iron and steel.

Some of these developments were controversial at the time. But when the Conservative Party returned to power from 1951 to 1964, it did not seek to reverse many of these key policies. An implicit agreement emerged that both major political parties would manage this new dispensation. This scenario has come to be called the post-war 'consensus' or 'settlement'. 'From the late 1940s to the mid-1970s,' states David Marquand, 'governments of right and left alike adhered to a form of liberal collectivism, sometimes known as "Keynesian social democracy"' (1996: 6) after the economist who had inspired it, John Maynard Keynes. That mode was not identical with the dreams of the Labour left in 1945, let alone the revolutionary left; nor with the instincts of the Conservative Party. It was a compromise between Labour and Conservative parties as they adapted to historical circumstances. By the early 1950s at the latest, Marquand writes, the consensus 'had become the lodestar of the two front benches in the House of Commons, of the Whitehall mandarinate, of the leaders of organised capital and organised labour and of the academic and journalistic apologists and interpreters of this nexus of interests' (1996: 7). The consensus implied that, as Keynes had argued, markets must be allowed and encouraged, but were insufficient of themselves to generate stable and just societies. It was desirable for government to intervene in the market, and to extend the public realm of state provision and citizenship. It was agreed that social and economic equality were valuable goals, and that the state should where possible work towards them.

The point extended also to culture. Attlee's government had instituted a programme of cultural institutions and arts organisations that almost rivalled its work in economic and social policy. Again, peacetime innovations were partly rooted in wartime expediencies. The wartime Council for the Encouragement of Music and the Arts became the Arts Council in 1946, strongly under the influence of Keynes himself. The idea of funding for the arts in Britain, of government subsidy for theatre and other creative forms, dates above all to this moment. Numerous other institutions were also created or financially stabilised: the opera houses at Sadler's Wells and Covent Garden; the Royal Ballet and Manchester's Northern Ballet Theatre; Scottish and regional orchestras. The National Theatre was established in 1949 at the Old Vic, and at last gained its permanent home in London's South Bank in 1976. The BBC's Third Programme, later Radio 3, commenced broadcasting in 1946, providing classical music and lectures. It is readily apparent that most of these developments were in the realm of 'high culture' and arts whose audience was traditionally a minority. Critics have pointed out that the main beneficiaries of state-subsidised culture since the war have been middle class (Mulgan 1996: 201). Ideas of culture and its value have shifted significantly since the 1940s. But this programme of 'cultural welfare', as Alan Sinfield has called it, was intended to make advanced cultural achievement available to the widest possible audience. Culture was treated as an improving force, a social good that should be widely distributed rather than diluted or adapted to supposedly lower tastes.

To be sure, British society was rocked by challenges and crises through the 1950s and 1960s: the Suez crisis of 1956, the development of the Cold War, the emergence of youth cultures and the pressures of America's war in Vietnam. But it is widely agreed that through to the mid-1970s, the post-war consensus was intact. Who or what dismantled it is a matter of some debate. Patricia Waugh, for instance, argues that the crucial year of transition was 1976. She points to a sense of crisis and fragmentation on all fronts, from violence in Northern Ireland and racial tensions across England to the highest unemployment figures since the war (1995: 14). At the Labour Party conference of that year, Prime Minister James Callaghan and Chancellor Denis Healey argued for a change of economic direction that would eventually be considered the beginnings of 'monetarism' – a word more usually associated with Conservative policy of the 1980s. The novelist Irvine Welsh has angrily recalled: '"Tory misrule" or "monetarism" or "Thatcherism" . . . all these things actually started in 1976, not 1979, when the Labour Government expressly went to the institutions of multi-national capitalism with a programme for the domestic economy based on those principles' (Redhead 2000: xix). Just as the post-war settlement was effective because of its adoption by both parties, it may be argued that the break with that settlement was also a bipartisan affair. But there is no doubt that the determined, decisive and iconic break was that made by Margaret Thatcher's governments from 1979. Without this political and ideological force, the transformation of British society would have been very different. What it might have looked like must now be a matter for counter-factual historians. Thatcher described her victory as a 'watershed election' (Campbell 2003: 47). Over the next decade she managed to make this assessment look justified. This book will consider what happened after that watershed.

Thatcher was the political figurehead of a transatlantic movement that came to be called the New Right. The Conservative Party has an age-old reputation as the unthinking person's party, tactically pragmatic rather than introspectively theoretical. But during the formation of Thatcherism, its weather was made by intellectuals and policy gurus. The New Right traced its intellectual origins back a long way: from the twentieth-century Austrian political philosopher Friedrich von Hayek, through nineteenth-century economic liberalism, and at least as far back as the eighteenth-century British economist Adam Smith. More immediately, as an intellectual movement it had germinated in the post-war 'Chicago school' of American economics, dominated by Milton Friedman. This was a source of inspiration when, in the mid-1970s in Britain, a number of think-tanks began to organise a renewal of social and economic thinking on the Right. The Centre for Policy Studies had been set up by Thatcher's predecessor Edward Heath. But after her accession to the Tory leadership in February 1975 it became dominated by the radically right-wing thought of Keith Joseph and Alfred Sherman. The CPS became a greenhouse for the cultivation of a new Conservatism. Other think-tanks – the National Association for Freedom, the Institute for Economic Affairs – added to the intellectual ferment. To an important extent, these bodies were populated by untraditional Tories. They were not just intellectuals or would-be theorists; they were also of petit-bourgeois origin, self-made men committed to enterprise and commerce rather than traditional privilege. In 1977 the CPS produced a policy document entitled

Stepping Stones, which proclaimed that the Conservative Party needed to stop seeking 'peaceful co-existence' in the management of decline. It was a signal of the New Right's impatience with the post-war consensus, and an attempt to switch Britain on to different tracks.

Margaret Thatcher was elected prime minister in May 1979, in the wake of a season of industrial unrest that had damaged the Labour Party's electoral prospects. At the time it was not necessarily apparent that she was about to transform the nation, or to set her stamp on it for the next eleven years. The most remarkable fact about her was her sex. Even the departing Labour premier James Callaghan declared that 'for a woman to occupy that office is a tremendous moment in this country's history' (Campbell 2003: 1). If anything, this made it difficult to believe she would endure – let alone that, as Hollinghurst puts it, her decade would go on forever. Thatcher's first years in power were spent dealing with economic recession, while employment figures ascended towards the three million mark which many considered politically unsustainable. What most drastically transformed her fortunes was the Falklands conflict of 1982. The successful despatch of a British task force to recapture the South Atlantic islands from an Argentinian junta stirred popular support. A year later, Thatcher won her second term with a much increased majority of 144. Thatcher's second term was also marked by struggle, most notably in the year-long industrial dispute with the National Union of Mineworkers from March 1984 to March 1985. The government's defeat of the miners' union was Thatcher's most defining domestic triumph. It signalled the subjugation of organised labour in its most potent form, and spelled disarray and disaster for the traditional forces and tactics of the political Left.

The Labour Party was already changing at this point. Neil Kinnock's leadership was beginning the process that would eventually issue in Tony Blair's New Labour. But the new model Labour Party could still not defeat Thatcher in 1987, and she became the first prime minister of the twentieth century to win three consecutive general elections. Her third and final term takes us to the end of the decade. While her parliamentary majority was reduced from 144 to 102, her social triumph was becoming apparent. By the decade's end Britain was already a significantly different place from the country she had taken over from Callaghan. In November 1990 Thatcher was ousted from the Tory leadership, and replaced by her apparently unassuming chancellor, John Major. The timbre of British politics has never been the same since. But the end of Thatcher's reign did not necessarily mean the demise of Thatcherism – even if she was ambitious in declaring, a month before leaving office, that 'Thatcherism is not for a decade. It is for centuries' (Johnson 1991:

Figure 1   Send Her Victorious: Margaret Thatcher celebrates election victory in Downing Street

250). Arguably, for the first twenty years after her departure, Britain continued within parameters that she had established.

Some assert that Thatcherism's intellectual coherence has been overestimated. The conservative commentator T. E. Utley complained in 1986 that the concept was 'a monstrous invention', and Thatcher a brilliant pragmatist whose virtue was her lack of the kind of elaborate theory more usually associated with the political Left (Utley 1991). To be sure, all governments must respond to external events, and – as with the Falklands – Thatcher's often managed to thrive on unexpected difficulties. But hers were also, to an unusual degree, ideologically driven, intellectually determined and politically focused. Indeed, this focus and drive are a difference between Thatcher's administrations and those that had preceded it: they mark the desire to intervene and transform an existing settlement, rather than merely to manage it. Labour's former deputy leader Roy Hattersley judges that 'In 1979, no less than 1945, the result was decided by men and women who wanted to reject the established view of society, who believed that a new and clear ideology was necessary to end an era of failure and injustice' (1997: 61). Thatcher herself was in no doubt about her opposition to the hitherto prevailing consensus – or to any consensus. At the 1981 Conservative Party conference, she scornfully declared:

> To me consensus seems to be the process of abandoning all beliefs, principles, values and policies in search of something in which no one believes, but to which no one objects . . . [It is] the process of avoiding the very issues that have to be solved, merely because you cannot get agreement on the way ahead. What great cause would have been fought and won under the banner 'I stand for consensus'? (Campbell 2003: 122–3)

Let us consider, then, the specific ways in which Thatcherism challenged the legacy of the post-war settlement, and proposed alternatives.

Our Duty to Look After Ourselves

The twentieth century, proposed the New Right, had become a battlefield between socialism and its opponents. Margaret Thatcher saw her great contribution as defeating socialism in Britain, and by extension across the rest of the planet, and thus securing human liberty. The ultimate enemy, from the post-war period to the end of the 1980s, was the Soviet Union. But Thatcher and the New Right considered democratic social and labour parties as part of the same problem: less actively malign, but still deeply debilitating. Communism, she has announced, 'enslaved the East, while its first cousin, socialism, impoverished much of the West' (Thatcher 2003: 2). A central motif of socialism, on this view, was the prominent role of the state.

The state, argued the New Right, had grown too large in modern democracies. It was not a good in itself, and potentially impeded individual effort and liberty. State intervention and involvement in industry, business and daily life was the thin end of a wedge which sloped up to the USSR. The state should be as small and unassuming as possible. In the United States, 'smaller government' was a popular slogan. In Britain, too, the government purported to aim to diminish its role in social life. In particular, the government was to avoid excessive management of the economy. Freed from the state's fussing hand, the marketplace would correct itself. In social-democratic 'corporatism', government was assumed to be involved in an active, tripartite relationship with labour and capital. The New Right led a retreat from this approach: the government should remove itself from industrial negotiations, leaving these as far as possible to trades unions and employers. More than this, the state should divest itself of its own industrial holdings. State-owned industries – telecommunications, gas, British Airways – were privatised, and sold off in share options to the public. Private monopolies too were subjected to deregulation, notably when franchises for independent broadcasting were sold in 1990. The doctrine, which would have a long afterlife, was that the private sector was more efficient than the public, and that the pressure of competitiveness would drive down prices and ensure better value and more effective service. The market was thus enshrined as the model for social organisation. These policies commenced during the 1980s; but Thatcherism's success in redirecting British society was demonstrated in subsequent years as further industries and areas were subjected to the market. Some, like railways, Thatcher herself had not dared to touch during her period in office. Privatisation had the added benefit, for Thatcher's governments, of passing responsibility for industrial relations within those industries over to private companies, and diminishing trades unions' opportunities to confront the government.

'The single biggest intellectual error during my political lifetime,' Thatcher later announced, 'has been to confuse freedom with equality. In fact, equality – being an unnatural condition which can only be enforced by the state – is usually the enemy of liberty' (2003: 2). Too great an emphasis on social and economic equality would result in the denial of individual aspirations and the desire to be distinctive. The primary way in which governments had pursued equality was through redistributive taxation, in which money was systematically siphoned from the better-off and made available to the poorer through the provision of public services. The wealthy had often complained that such tax regimes held them and Britain back, removing the motivation for enterprising individuals to make money. Now the highest rates of tax were cut dramatically. In his budget a month after entering office, Thatcher's first chancellor, Geoffrey Howe, cut the top rate of income tax from 83 per cent to 60 per cent. In 1988, his successor Nigel Lawson took the basic rate as low as 25 per cent, while the top rate descended from 60 per cent to 40 per cent. The lower tax regime was one element of the proclaimed attempt to foster a culture of enterprise. But lower taxes usually involve a trade-off with public services. By the end of the 1980s, those sceptical of Tory rule agreed that the fabric of certain public services (hospitals, schools, public transport) had deteriorated. In October 1988 the Labour Party's policy document *Neglect into the Nineties* alleged that a lack of investment in public works since 1979 had left the nation's infrastructure creaking (Campbell 2003: 592). Polly Toynbee in 2007 recalled this legacy enduring to the late 1990s: Tony Blair's Labour government had inherited a public realm in 'shabby disrepair', in which 'roofs leaked, temporary buildings and even wartime Nissen huts took overflows of pupils and patients' (2007: 30).

This was arguably in keeping with an ongoing devaluation of the public realm, and promotion of the private. Collective provision was deemed less important and valuable than individual enterprise. Such provision as unemployment benefit and welfare payments could even actively do harm, discouraging individual endeavour and encouraging Britons to rely on handouts. Thatcher repeatedly asserted that one of her great aims had been to end a culture of dependency in Britain. In a speech in 1984 she proclaimed that her overriding legacy would be the break with 'a debilitating consensus of a paternalistic government and a dependent people' (Barnett 1984: 140). At the 1981 party conference, the employment secretary, Norman Tebbit, memorably opposed this form of dependency by insisting that the unemployed should do as his father had done and get on their bikes. Like many emphatic Tory assertions, this one was picked up and widely recycled in political polemic and satire. But the most resounding phrase of all, which has come to define the era more than any other, was offered by Thatcher herself, in an interview with *Woman's Own* in October 1987. She was asked about the causes for a perceived deterioration in Britain's moral standards.

> I think we've been through a period where too many people have been given to understand that if they have a problem, it's the government's job to cope with it. 'I have a problem, I'll get a grant.' 'I'm homeless, the government must house me.' They're casting their problem on society. And, you know, there is no such thing as society. There are individual men and women, and there are families. And no government can do anything except through people, and people must look to themselves first. It's our duty to look after ourselves and then, also, to look after our neighbour. People have got the entitlements too much in mind, without the obligations. There's no such thing as entitlement, unless someone has first met an obligation. (Keay 1987: 10)

'There is no such thing as society' has become the phrase that defines Thatcherism. Improvising in a relatively lightweight interview, Thatcher could not have expected her words to be elevated to the defining statement of her premiership. Yet she was clearly seeking to articulate convictions that drove her government. Indeed, as her biographer John Campbell points out, she made similar statements in other interviews that went comparatively unnoticed (2003: 530–1). She succinctly voiced the suspicion of the collective and public, and the promotion of the individual and private, that ran through much of the policy of the decade, and strongly affected British culture. Her statement gave offence, Campbell observes, because 'it seemed to legitimise selfishness and reduced public provision for the poor to the bounty of the rich'. Thatcher's ultimate view seemed to be that 'citizens should be allowed to keep as much as possible of their own money to spend on personal consumption, while essential public facilities like roads and railways, museums and libraries, swimming pools and playing fields were financed wherever possible by private enterprise – or private benefaction – rather than by the state'. In the end, 'the market would provide' (Campbell 2003: 533). In practice, her government did not achieve such a transformation by the end of the 1980s. It could not but compromise with the existing mixed economy and the extent of often popular public services. Not everything could be cut, deregulated or privatised at once. But her 1987 statement gave an insight into the ideal state toward which her actual governance strove.

Firm Government

Thatcherism became associated with enterprise, freedom, the iconoclastic assault on old pieties and allegedly moribund institutions. Yet it also deployed a rhetoric of authority, tradition, firm governance, national identity and security, prudent financing and family values. It was thus alternately conservative and radical, reactionary and revolutionary. It could be said that the effects were discordant. But it is also arguable that the conservative dimension of Thatcherism was a necessary counterpart to its radicalism: a strategic maintenance of images of continuity and authority during a phase of social transformation. Stuart Hall was one of Thatcherism's most swiftly percipient analysts on the Left. As early as 1978, he identified 'the key themes of the radical right' as 'law and order, the need for social discipline and authority in the face of a conspiracy by the enemies of the state, the onset of social anarchy, the "enemy within"' (1988: 44). The value and importance of family, discipline, morality and nation were reiterated, with a strong accompanying sense of their peril.

The politics of the family and sexuality comprise a significant example. The Right had created a furore around the existence of books demonstrating the possibility of stable gay relationships, accusing left-wing councils of promoting homosexuality to children. In Haringey, the chairman of the local Conservative Party thundered that 'No person who believes in God can vote Labour now' (Durham 2003: 242). Following the 1987 election, a Local Government Bill was amended to outlaw the 'promotion of homosexuality' by councils. The amendment became notorious as Clause 28, later Section 28. It represented a distinctively reactionary policy, a deliberate gesture at rolling back the relative liberalisation around homosexuality since the 1960s. The policy seemed to query the legitimacy of a whole section of British society. It gave concrete legal status to an illiberalism that had been evident in the government's rhetoric. The new conservatism took other forms too. Single parent families were suspected, both as a departure from the traditional family unit and as a likely drain on welfare resources. Progressive education was attacked, and more regimented schooling recommended. In Thatcher's third term a National Curriculum for secondary education was introduced. The prime minister herself was keen to promote the study of British history, taught through key dates and the achievements of great men. She came to think that interfering pedagogues had watered down her ideas too much, producing an insufficiently British and chronological view of history (Campbell 2003: 543).

These conservative dimensions of Thatcherism hint at something harsher still: what may be called its authoritarian aspect. The year 1984 had been an iconic temporal destination since the publication of George Orwell's *Nineteen Eighty-Four* in 1949. For the political Right, the novel could only confirm the terrors of communism against which, as the year itself dawned and waxed, Thatcher continued to take a stand. But her critics complained that Thatcher's Britain was beginning to resemble Orwell's Airstrip One. Colin Leys, writing in 1984, cautioned against the snap deployment of the term 'authoritarian' for the British government. Compared to Chile, let alone the USSR, Britain remained a relatively liberal state. Yet authoritarianism, Leys concluded, was nevertheless on the rise in Britain. The state was resisting democratic reform and accountability; new technologies were being deployed to enable surveillance and spying by the police and security services. Thatcherism, in particular, Leys proposed,

> has campaigned on an appeal to 'law-and-order', blaming the victims, scapegoating minorities, those on welfare, and the trade unions. It has introduced explicit appeals to authority ('the smack of firm government') and it has fostered chauvinism and militarism over the Falklands and the nuclear arms race. [. . .] Perhaps Thatcherism's most serious contribution to authoritarianism has been in accepting the permanence of acute social differences and giving official endorsement to a 'police view' of the consequences, which sees active opposition as misguided and ultimately seditious; and in making such an absolute commitment to the cold war and to the acceptance of Cruise missiles and all that they imply. (1984: 67–8)

It appeared that the Conservative government had a special relationship not only with the administration in the United States, but with the police forces of the United Kingdom. The most evident deployment of the police against the government's opponents was their centralised mass mobilisation against NUM pickets in 1984–5. But the intelligence services were also deployed against the government's perceived opponents: tapping the telephones of trades unions and infiltrating their offices with moles, breaking into the homes of peace campaigners, vetting BBC staff (Campbell 2003: 386). The government also visibly pursued those who were seen to undermine it through revelations or publications – as in the police raid on a BBC documentary unit in 1987, the state's vain determination to ban the former MI5 operative Peter Wright's memoir *Spycatcher* the same year, and the attempt to suppress ITV's documentary *Death on the Rock* (1988). Civil servants at the Ministry of Defence were pursued under the Official Secrets Act: in 1984 Sarah Tisdall was jailed for giving the *Guardian* newspaper a document on the deployment of Cruise missiles at Greenham Common, and a year later Clive Ponting evaded imprisonment for leaking information on the conduct of the Falklands War.

These examples confirm Leys' observation that domestic and foreign policy were profoundly connected. As the playwright David Edgar put it, with reference to both the Falklands conflict and the outbreaks of urban unrest at home: 'zapping the enemy without on the beach-heads of the South Atlantic was an effective and timely corollary to confronting the "enemy within" on the streets of London, Toxteth and Moss Side' (1984: 39–40). Surveillance, politicised policing or the pursuit of injunctions in Britain often centred around issues of defence and international conflict. The Falklands War was itself, in effect, a symbol and expression of Thatcher's traditionalist and authoritarian side. It involved the defence of an imperial holding against a Latin aggressor; it evoked Britain's heroic naval history, from Elizabethan times through to Lord Nelson. Thatcher herself sought echoes of Britain's lonely role defending freedom in the Second World War, casting herself as another Churchill. It was not difficult for a right-wing leader to win popularity among the military. Antonia Fraser reported that Thatcher was 'far and away the favourite object of sexual fantasy' for the armed forces (Campbell 2003: 138) – though the radical songwriter Billy Bragg, who joined and left the Army during her first term, fails to corroborate this fairly grotesque and implausible claim (Collins 2002: 78).

A more significant source, and more fearful symbol, of authoritarianism was the deployment of nuclear weapons in Britain. Thatcher and Ronald Reagan were seen as nuclear soul-mates. Their alliance was an important element in perceptions that Britain was closer than ever to the United States, in cultural as well as military matters. In fact she was the fiercer Cold Warrior of the two. John Campbell makes clear that Reagan's Strategic Defence Initiative was aimed at the ultimate dream of a nuclear-free world – a dream that Thatcher thought implausible and dangerous. She insisted that White House statements cede minimal ground to the possibility of disarmament. She pointed out that since the development of nuclear weapons, Europe had been at peace for decades; the deterrent was effective. But her enthusiasm for the weapons seemed to go beyond glum calculation and into a positive relish (Campbell

2003: 287–97). Nuclear weapons were a significant factor in the atmosphere of the 1980s. They provoked many artistic responses, virtually all in protest: from Raymond Briggs' *When the Wind Blows*, a cartoon book (1982) and film (1986) recording the fate of two pensioners after a nuclear strike, to Frankie Goes To Hollywood's number one pop single 'Two Tribes' (1984), whose sleeve carried details of current nuclear arsenals. Novelists and dramatists also responded, as we shall see in Chapter Five.

All this reminds us that some of the most significant transformations of the 1980s – even those that would profoundly affect Britain – took place beyond the United Kingdom's shores. In Britain, the 1980s arguably saw the replacement of the consensus that had stood since 1945. The same was finally true of the world order established in the same period. The process of *Perestroika* or reconstruction overseen by the Soviet Union's President Mikhail Gorbachev would result, by the last days of the decade, in the collapse of the entire Eastern bloc. Its symbol was the opening of the Berlin Wall in November 1989. By the end of 1991 the Soviet Union itself had disintegrated. The scale of the Cold War's thaw might make Thatcher's revolution look like a local skirmish – though she would claim, to the contrary, that her own leadership had been pivotal in hastening the end of the Stalinist bloc.

The authoritarian side of Thatcherism was conveniently exemplified in the persona of the prime minister herself. She was happy to appear unbending: determined to the point of rigidity. Her best-remembered sound-bites played up to this role. At the 1980 Conservative Party conference she famously denounced the demand for policy U-turns: 'You turn if you want to. The lady's not for turning' (Campbell 2003: 87–8). In more characteristically solemn mood, in the autumn of her political career, she spoke in the House of Commons on the prospects of European integration, culminating in the emphatically triple rejoinder 'No. No. No' (Campbell 203: 713). The effects of the persona were overdetermined by gender. As the first female prime minister, Thatcher emphasised her strength to a degree that might have seemed eccentric in a male politician, but for a woman in her position was a strategic ideological compensation. She also projected herself as a provincial housewife for whom the country's budget was to be managed like a household's. As Stuart Hall showed, such projections helped her to capture the ground of ideological 'common sense'. The 'spendthrift state' could not dispense 'wealth the nation has not earned'. The enemy of ordinary people was 'the "welfare scrounger", living off society, never doing a day's work' (1988: 144–5).

For even where the government did not produce the actual legislation that its most right-wing supporters desired, it undoubtedly produced its own rhetorical climate. Hundreds of Conservative speeches and statements contributed to this effect. It could be defined not only as a reassertion of conservative values, but as an active repudiation of the liberalisations associated with the 1960s. The enemies implied or imagined by this stance would naturally include hippies and their sub-cultural descendants, peace campaigners, progressive teachers, left-wing councillors and militant trade unionists. They also included the more sedate figure of Roy Jenkins, the Labour home secretary who oversaw a series of liberalising measures in the late 1960s. Following urban riots in 1981, Thatcher proclaimed to the Commons that 'A large part of the problem we are having now has come from a weakening of authority in many aspects of life over many, many years', ominously warning that '[t]his has to be corrected'. Jenkins' liberal judgement that 'a permissive society is a civilized society', she said, was 'something that most of us would totally reject. Society must have rules if it is to continue to be civilised' (Campbell 2003: 115). In a 1988 interview with the *Daily Mail* Thatcher again decried 'Sixties culture':

> Permissiveness, selfish and uncaring, proliferated under the guise of the new sexual freedom. Aggressive verbal hostility, presented as a refreshing lack of subservience, replaced courtesy and good manners. Instant gratification became the philosophy of the young and the youth cultists. Speculation replaced dogged hard work. (Sinfield 1989: 296)

To claim that things have declined is also to imply a superior moment from which the present has descended, and which we should strive to emulate. The exact historical location of that moment varied. In this interview, Thatcher contrasted the 1960s with the preceding decade, recalling the 1950s as 'old-fashioned', 'clean and orderly'. To hanker for the 1950s, as the moment before all went wrong, has become an emblematic move among Anglo-American conservatives. The film historian William J. Palmer has judged that America's 1980s were a replay of its 1950s, Ronald Reagan a rerun of Dwight Eisenhower (1993: ix–x). In the Conclusion to this book we will return to such contests over cultural memory.

Yet Thatcher was best known for invoking a more distant period. She first spoke of 'Victorian values' in a television interview in January 1983. Three months later, still elaborating the memorably alliterative phrase, she told the *Evening Standard*:

> I was brought up by a Victorian grandmother [. . .] We were taught to prove yourself; we were taught self-reliance; we were taught to live within our income. You were taught that cleanliness is next to godliness. You were

taught self-respect. You were taught always to give a hand to your neighbour. You were taught tremendous pride in your country. All of these things are Victorian values. They are also perennial values. (Samuel 1998: 334)

The slippages in syntax (Thatcher would characteristically move between 'I', 'you' and 'we') are matched by further slippages – between the Victorian period and the quite different era of Thatcher's own youth, and between values apparently specific to one period and those that are 'perennial'. Such considerations could not stop 'Victorian values' carrying a complex political charge and becoming another of the decade's major catchphrases. As Raphael Samuel has shown, the phrase was in part a way of 'conjuring up lost innocence': 'Against a background of inner-city disturbances [. . .] she pictured an older Britain where parents were strict, children good-mannered, hooliganism (she erroneously believed) unknown. [. . .] Victorian Britain was constituted as a kind of reverse image of the present, exemplifying by its stability and strength everything that we are not' (1998: 337). The invocation of the Victorians was politically risky: it could stir connotations of the workhouse or of 'Dickensian' deprivation. Neil Kinnock boldly told a Labour audience that the real 'Victorian values' had been 'cruelty, misery, drudgery, squalor and ignorance' (Samuel 1998: 333). Either way, the phrase stood in the public mind as Thatcher's most characteristic piece of retrospection, signalling the past with which she most wanted to constellate her present.

Contradictions of Thatcherism

Numerous critics and historians have noted the apparent tensions between Thatcher's radicalism and the rhetoric of return to historical precedents. David Edgar saw a 'potential contradiction between the two sides of the coin – Thatcherism's desire to roll back the state in the economic field, and its policies (or at least its rhetoric) on the social questions of policing, education, censorship, defence and immigration' (1984: 39). Alan Allport describes two Thatchers, a libertarian and a conservative: while one 'hacked away at the paternalistic shackles of the state, selling off council houses, trimming tax burdens and deregulating industrial monopolies', the other 'harangued the BBC for its insufficient displays of patriotism' (2003: 30). Raphael Samuel casts the contradiction in temporal terms: 'Mrs Thatcher's traditionalism allowed her to act as an innovator [. . .] while yet sounding as though she were a voice from the past. By turns radical and reactionary, modernizing and atavistic, she moved from one register to another with the dexterity of a quick-change artist' (1998: 343).

Such contradictions need not be politically damaging. As Sinfield observes, they may simply signify 'a capacity to get you whichever way you move' (1989: 297). And in a sense these paradoxes can be resolved into a larger unity. 'Victorian values' might be, not part of the contradiction, but its resolution. As Samuel shows, the term encoded not just tradition but the values of effort and enterprise. The captain of industry would once again be a social hero; the great collectivising experiments of the twentieth century (national health, welfare dependency, the Labour Party itself) would cede to a reborn nineteenth-century ethic of 'individuals and their families'. The monetarist policy that dominated her first term, in which government sought to combat inflation even at the expense of mass unemployment, she viewed as representing 'an old-fashioned horror of debt', a pursuit of 'honest money' (Samuel 1998: 333; Campbell 2003: 81). And the quest to restore Britain's greatness by vanquishing socialism and shaking out unproductive industries was of a piece with the military display of national strength to foreigners.

Yet the cultural effects and tones remained incongruous. One can grasp this by the thought that Thatcher herself was not necessarily the most representative figure for the culture and society that she helped to create. The characteristic architecture of the 1980s involved toytown apartment buildings, converted warehouses, gleaming blocks; it was best summarised by the redevelopment of London's Docklands into a Manhattan-on-Thames, whose shining towers were serviced by warrens of apartments like Piers Gough's riverside Cascades development (York and Jennings 1995: 80–9). In Hollinghurst's *The Line of Beauty*, we witness a number of buildings and environments that conjure the decade. A bank with its new 'steel and glass atrium and high-tech dealing floors'; a 'glinting open-plan' office of 'reflecting glass and steel', and accompanying flat decorated with 'vulgar' postmodern eclecticism; a Victorian property transformed into a 'monster Lego house, with its mirror windows and maroon marble cladding' (2004: 203, 199–200, 444). This was the landscape of Thatcherism; but one could hardly imagine Margaret Thatcher wanting to live in it. The people to whom such a landscape did appeal were of a different generation and temperament entirely: the young upwardly mobile professionals of the City and media. The word 'yuppie', borrowed from the United States, always at least hinted at derision or resentment (Wright 1991: 288). These were the most visible beneficiaries of Lawson's 1983–7 boom, the period in which Thatcher began to speak of 'popular capitalism' (Campbell 2003: 231).

Figure 2   Manhattan-on-Thames: the new landscape of Canary Wharf

The effects were widespread. John Campbell recalls 'cultural change at all levels of the economy, from the City of London to every provincial high street': from the deregulation of the stock exchange in 1986 to a proliferation of jobs in the service sector. He also observes that the new heroes of business were 'children of the 1960s and 1970s who used the expanding opportunities of the 1980s to realise visions nurtured in the pop and fashion industries of their youth': Richard Branson with Virgin records, Alan Sugar and Amstrad personal computers, Sophie Mirman and her Sock Shop, Anita Roddick and the Body Shop (Campbell 2003: 243–6). Some of these figures could be found in alliance with Thatcher, as in Branson's enlistment to an anti-litter campaign. But most of them belonged to a different generation, and might appear to espouse different values. Roddick's successful chain sold itself partly on connotations of environmental awareness and new age ethics, a long way from Victorian values. Thatcherism could thus find itself in inadvertent alliance with cultural codes that seemed contrary to it. In particular, as Campbell shrewdly suggests, the moods and energies of the 1960s, so reviled by the Conservatives, could find a new and profitable outlet now that the baby boom generation were middle-aged and comfortably salaried.

The paradoxes we are considering could be vividly figured by the popular music of the period. Margaret Thatcher herself did not stray far beyond the early Cliff Richard and the 'always melodious' Adam Faith (Frith 2006: 145). But some contemporary music was considered representative of her Britain. Thus, from the early 1980s on, the New Romantic group Duran Duran gained loose connotations of cultural Thatcherism, located in their glossy sound and in their ostentatious lifestyle of high consumption and excess. The apotheosis of this remains the promotional video for their 1982 single 'Rio', with the band riding on a yacht off the South American coast, wearing brightly coloured suits and lusting after slow-motion glamour models. This has gone down in British cultural memory as an emblem of the decade. Their pop rival Boy George described 'the champagne-swilling, yacht-sailing Duran Duran playboyeurism and new pop superficiality. Suddenly it was OK to be rich, famous and feel no shame. Some saw it as a natural consequence of Thatcherism'. The final complaint is hazy, but the broad association has stuck. As the band's biographer sees, such images did not express explicitly political choices, but they did catch and garishly project some deeper cultural change, in which foreign travel became more available, technology encouraged greater prominence and daring in graphics and design, and the high street became more colourfully stocked (Malins 2005: 94–6). For Simon Reynolds, the sounds and sights of the mid-1980s pop charts signalled a culture insistent on enjoyment, in which America represented 'the supreme incarnation of the modern, of the coming health-and-efficiency culture [. . .] In pop terms we're talking about MTV and videos, stadiums and nightclubs and wine bars, growing links between Hollywood and rock and between advertising and rock'. The local result was 'a Thatcherite vision of classless, "popular capitalism", of a Britain that would be more like America. Those modern figures – the yuppie, the soul boy, the B-boy – are all infatuated with the American vision of the future' (1989: 245, 252–3). The journalist Peter York would become the prime narrator of this shifting landscape, in which every high street gained a branch of Next and chain store ties were made from silk rather than polyester (1995: 63). Once again, all this is some distance from the Grantham Methodist who was supposedly making it possible. In January 1983 she delighted in visiting, not the Brazilian beaches of 'Rio', but the windswept South Atlantic rocks that her troops had retaken, described by her husband as 'miles and miles of bugger all' (Campbell 2003: 158).

Cultural Turns

Architecture, television, newspapers, pop music – these are different kinds of evidence from the literary texts that will preoccupy most of this book. They would all fit into the broader category of 'culture'. Even silk ties and wine bars might well do so. But it is worth pausing over that capacious term. In the twentieth century 'culture' had at least two primary meanings. First, the arts and creative, expressive works, including literature: this might be called 'high culture'. Second, much more broadly, the barrage of texts, images, signs, experiences and practices in a society; the 'whole way of life' in one vocabulary, the 'range of signifying practices' in another. The two senses co-exist, and need not conflict. But while the first, artistic definition remained intact, the second, anthropological sense continued to gain prominence during the 1980s. The decade was a stage on the way to the apparent omnipresence of the cultural, as the medium in which modern people consciously swim. Terry Eagleton has succinctly traced this ascendancy, in which by the late twentieth century culture would become a master concept: 'As politics were spectacularized, commodities aestheticized, consumption eroticized and commerce semioticized, culture seemed to have become the new social "dominant"' (2000: 126). By 1984 the American theorist Fredric Jameson had already perceived a change in the idea's status, describing

> a prodigious expansion of culture throughout the social realm, to the point at which everything in our social life – from economic value and state power to practices and to the very structure of the psyche itself – can be said to have become 'cultural' in some original and yet untheorized sense. (1991: 48)

Culture had indeed expanded. By the 1980s, there was simply more of it about than before: more books, more magazines, more channels, more videos. This expansion would continue. The narrator of Michael Bracewell's novella *Perfect Tense* (2001), which is in part a retrospect on the changes we are tracing, describes a world in which the Western subject is faced with 'so much of everything: sandwiches, technology, holidays, shoes, cars, records, TV channels, restaurants, you name it' (2001: 128). But Jameson seeks to articulate not just a quantitative increase, but a more qualitative change in which the items listed by Bracewell might readily be subsumed under the cultural label. In a telling example, Peter York describes how the 'Voodoo Arts' of advertising, market research and Public Relations gained new importance and sophistication in the 1980s (1995: 136–50). For businesses, film stars or political parties, media management was coming to be seen not as an indulgence but as essential. The new corporate logo, reproduced on every letterhead or menu and giving business a new semiotic self-consciousness, is another suggestive instance of Jameson's case.

So too is the mutual involvement of media and politics. This was not a new phenomenon, but the 1980s in Britain did represent a fresh phase for the presentation of politics, or what an imported American term would later dub 'spin'. The process is succinctly caught, not only by Thatcher's own dedicated work at changing her voice and televisual persona, but by the transformation of Labour's self-presentation between the 1983 and 1987 elections. Michael Foot, leader from 1979 to 1983, had campaigned in the manner of Labour politicians of decades past, favouring the hustings and the Labour club meeting. Labour's 1987 campaign, by contrast, was best remembered for the broadcast nicknamed *Kinnock: The Movie*, a soft-focus biographical sketch by *Chariots of Fire*'s director Hugh Hudson, in which the leader and his wife walked hand in hand along a rocky coastline. (Remarkably, Thatcher herself believed that this broadcast would cost her the election, declaring 'Kinnock had a marvellous programme – it's hardly worth bothering, let's give up, it's the end' [Campbell 2003: 516].) All this could be described as a gradual Americanisation of British politics. It could also be described, more generally, as an aestheticisation of politics, in which the political comes to seem part of the cultural realm as much as it does a separate and restraining sphere outside it.

We may note two other relevant engines for a burgeoning of the cultural sphere. One is the legitimacy accorded to the market by the New Right. If the market was an appropriate arena of evaluation, and competition usually a healthy development, then a commercially successful culture could be freshly validated. The most popular forms – soap operas, the tabloid press – might be suspected by cultural mandarins or by the critical Left, but if success could be measured in commercial terms then these forms could claim centrality. Moreover, culture in its narrower, artistic sense was itself challenged by this trend. Government subsidies for the arts were diminished: more than in previous decades, culture must pay its own way. The keenness to spread cultural value to all was challenged by the belief that the market should decide what could flourish. This might involve populism, the need to attract audiences by playing safe and ensuring the broadest possible appeal. It also increasingly involved sponsorship, as we shall see in the changing strategies of the Arts Council.

The market, then, was arguably a source of cultural relativisation, throwing existing hierarchies of value into question. Yet that activity was also undertaken at another level, in intellectual work on culture.

The academic discipline of Cultural Studies counts among its British wellsprings the work of Richard Hoggart and Raymond Williams, who in major works of the 1950s had sought to extend the concept of culture and broaden the prospects of cultural value. In the late 1960s and 1970s, Stuart Hall had led the Birmingham Centre for Contemporary Cultural Studies into engagements with European critical theory, as well as studies of the uses and effects of popular culture in the micro-politics of working-class lives. By the late 1980s Cultural Studies had become not only a discipline with a history, but recognisably a part of public discourse, an audible contribution to conversations about cultural value. Its practitioners might be heard asserting the crucial links between culture and power, the ideological damage done by distorted news services, or – a new trend – the potential of consumers to make their own meanings from texts, and even thereby to subvert dominant ideological strategies.

'Culture', in any case, could be girls' comics, playground chants, trade union banners, American cop shows, cereal packets. An insistence on power relations and on the contexts of ordinary lives, rather than on aesthetic virtue traditionally conceived, militated against the traditional value judgements that would have ruled some of these forms out of consideration. In a sense, social and political considerations (reactionary or subversive?) could displace aesthetic judgements (beautiful or blemished?), even as, in Jameson's eyes, society as a whole was gradually aestheticised. Many theorists, like the French sociologist Pierre Bourdieu in *Distinction* (1979), considered that aesthetic hierarchies not only were profoundly shaped by social inequalities, but actually reproduced them. The influence of semiotics also effected a certain neutralisation of traditional value judgements. If spy novels or Hollywood blockbusters worked with similar narrative structures and signifying materials to Tolstoy or Balzac, then questions of aesthetic value could be bracketed while homologies were pursued. The narrower artistic sense of 'culture' was thus placed under some suspicion, both as an ideological tool and as an implausible, arbitrary form of exclusion. At the same time, the kinds of culture about which one could speak and write in detail proliferated, and would eventually take up not only popular cultural texts but spaces, foods, objects, moods. The imperatives of the market and the visions of Cultural Studies could even form a kind of alliance, in the upper reaches of the media. Michael Bracewell has depicted an emerging epoch of style magazines and cultural commentary, whose participants borrowed the intellectual credibility of academic discourses while setting up as arbiters and harbingers of taste. Everything, he recalls

– all the bits and pieces of contemporary culture, from architecture to mineral water – had become semiotic Phenomena [. . .] In the lab of semiotics (you could imagine that it looked like the Clinique counter in a big department store) everything was significant, busily signifying something – it was all signage. (2002: 2–3)

Bracewell more than most would produce fiction from within this world.

Yet traditional forms of culture retained significant support. Britain's most important official cultural institution in the 1980s remained the Arts Council. Robert Hewison argued that it had 'a central role in defining the terms and setting the conditions in which any discussion of the arts can take place': 'the Arts Council helps to establish cultural meanings' (1987: 108). It is thus a good place to consider the fate of the arts and the politics of culture during the decade. As we have seen, the Council was a Keynesian body forged as part of the post-war settlement. It had survived through governments of both colours for over thirty years. Executives were appointed according to the political patronage of the day – at the start of the 1980s the secretary-general was still the social democrat Roy Shaw, a result of the Wilson government – yet the Council was proud of the 'arm's length' principle with which it administered funding for the arts without taking direct orders from government. In this it resembled the BBC, another national institution paid from public money yet independent of Downing Street.

During the 1980s the Arts Council undertook initiatives in favour of minority arts and equal opportunities. A percentage of funds was earmarked for spending on ethnic minority arts, and the black artist and lecturer Gavin Jantjes was appointed to the Council and charged to write the report *Towards Cultural Diversity* (Sinclair 1995: 286, 297). Like other organisations, the Arts Council was thus affected by the sustained pressures of cultural activism from the political Left. But it was the political Right that more definitively set the agenda, and the Arts Council more strikingly demonstrates this. For one thing, its leadership was remade along Conservative lines. Margaret Thatcher's first arts minister, Norman St John Stevas, insisted that the treasurer of the Conservative Party, Lord McAlpine, be part of the Council. Roy Shaw protested that McAlpine was an opponent of public subsidy; Stevas told him that the appointment 'came from a very high source indeed', meaning the prime minister. McAlpine soon tired of the Council and departed, but the episode is typical enough (Witts 1998: 371). Richard Hoggart, a veteran intellectual sponsor of post-war socialism, was vice-chairman of the Council until, in 1981, the new arts minister Paul Channon abruptly dismissed him. 'I have no room for manoeuvre,' the minister explained: 'Number Ten doesn't like him.' Hoggart adjudged that 'governmental intervention in the work of such bodies started very early in the Eighties', made worse by 'a disposition in some Ministers to be more royal than the Queen [Thatcher], to guess in advance what she might like' (Sinclair 1995: 252).

The new chairman and secretary-general of the Arts Council were men better placed than Hoggart to do that. William Rees-Mogg, former editor of the *Times*, 'gave the appearance of being a fossil', and declared that 'at its most important art is a way of apprehending God' (Witts 1998: 371; Sinclair 1995: 254). He denied that he was Thatcher's placeman, claiming instead (as if the tale were more reassuring) that Paul Channon's twelve-year-old son had proposed him as he attended the same private school as Rees-Mogg's own son (Witts 1998: 372). Robert Hewison calls Rees-Mogg 'a convinced supporter of the government's monetarist economics', and witheringly quotes Channon's own cosy account of appointing 'somebody you respect and get on with and whose views on the arts you're more likely to be more in agreement with than not' (Hewison 1987: 113). Roy Shaw sceptically considered Rees-Mogg's role 'to put the Arts Council right – to put it to the right' (Sinclair 1995: 253). The new secretary-general was an even more telling appointment. Luke Rittner had been director of the Association for Business Sponsorship of the Arts. Arts Council staff signed a petition against his arrival, a *Guardian* leader decried it and the Labour Party suggested it would be reversed if they were elected (260–1).

As in the rest of the public sector, the 1980s began with a round of cuts in arts funding. In the early 1980s the grant-in-aid to the Arts Council was frozen; in December 1980 the Council severed the grants of forty-one organisations (Hewison 1987: 114). Sir Peter Hall, director of the National Theatre, considered that in Rees-Mogg 'Thatcher had appointed a chairman of the Arts Council who was seemingly content to dismantle the subsidy structure of the previous twenty years and allow the Council to dwindle from an independent agency, fighting the cause of the artist, into a tool of government policy' (Sinclair 1995: 272). He claimed public attention for his protest by climbing on to a table at a 1986 press conference, and announcing the closure of the Cottesloe Theatre as a necessary measure in a time of reduced funding. Ken Livingstone's Greater London Council, in one of its last acts before being abolished in 1986, gave Hall a grant to re-open the theatre, thus underlining the political position-taking. Thatcher herself asked one arts minister, 'When are you going to be able to stop giving money to awful people like Peter Hall?' (274). Yet Randall Stevenson argues that it was not culturally central figures like Hall who suffered most; by the end of the decade, funds for the National Theatre and Royal Shakespeare remained disproportionately high compared to regional and touring companies, or even the Royal Court, while opera received immensely higher funds than any other art, as it had since the war. By the end of the 1970s, Stevenson notes, many small companies were claiming as much as 12 per cent of the Arts Council's annual drama budget; but in the early 1980s funding for such initiatives was cut. The socialist company 7:84 (England), its name a reference to a small percentage of people enjoying a disproportionate proportion of national wealth, saw its grant ended in 1984, and ceased work altogether (Stevenson 2004: 392, 325).

A new emphasis was placed on the cost-effectiveness of the arts. The major theatre companies and opera houses were affronted by being subjected to unprecedented financial audits. Other areas of society, like higher education, would be subjected to similar surveillance. The 1981/2 Arts Council Report was keen to assert that the arts could contribute to Britain's 'economic struggle' (Stevenson 2004: 34). The Council's 1987 booklet *Partnership: Making Arts Money Work Harder* explained that the 'cultural industries', claiming funds from more diverse sources than hitherto, had a role to play in 'stimulating the economy'. It could be demonstrated that the arts gave value for money: 'the real economic cost to the Government of financing the arts is substantially less than the actual value of the grant' (Sinclair 1995: 279–80). Staff were trained in marketing. Already fluent in the new idiom, the controller of Marketing Resources declared 'a redirection of energies into pro-active initiatives serving Council priorities' (289). John Pick, a critic of the Council, bemoaned the move 'to describe the arts no longer in their traditional language which includes aesthetic judgement, private satisfactions and spiritual benefit, but as a purely commercial benefit, to be justified by its economic benefit' (308). Anthony Blackstock, the Council's director of finance, pleaded that 'You have to talk to this government in a language it understands' (282).

The most telling development was the rise of corporate sponsorship. Stevas warned that 'Government policy in general has decisively tilted away from the expansion of the public to the private sector'; 'we look to the private sphere to meet any shortfall and to provide immediate means of increase' (Sinclair 1995: 248). The appointment of Luke Ritter from the business sector indicated an ideological shift. He himself declared the arrival of a 'market ethic' (278), and advertised that 'If prestige and the altering of a perception is what you're trying to do, then the arts can achieve that, and not necessarily very expensively' (Hewison 1987: 124). Richard Hoggart, before being removed from his post, was affronted by the sight of the Royal Opera House proclaiming 'Martini's *Traviata*': 'Poor old Verdi'. The Arts Council, Hoggart pointed out, had paid ten times as much as Martini for the production; but their support, unlike the sponsor's, could be taken for granted (Witts 1998: 177). The Association for Business Sponsorship of the Arts, Luke Ritter's previous posting, was founded in 1976: between then and 1986, in a staggering statistic, annual commercial sponsorship grew from £600,000 to over £25 million (Hewison 1987: 123). By the end of the 1980s, Bryan Appleyard considered the Arts Council transformed 'as radically as the most rabid New Rightist could have wished', and demonstrating a 'functional entrepreneurial role' (Sinclair 1995: 312–13). Robert Hewison, who had written extensive histories of Britain's post-war culture, registered his distaste for the new climate. Corporately sponsored work, as Hoggart had noted, remained dependent on invisible state subsidies; while public bodies sought to further the arts, corporate sponsors acted in the short term and with only their own interests at stake. The commercial climate, Hewison argued, led to unadventurous policy: 'heritage' work was supported at the expense of artistic experiment. Traditional defences of art had ceded ground to hard-bitten economic ones: 'We are no longer lovers of art, but consumers of a product' (1987: 129). Hewison's dismay at Thatcherism's effects on cultural value is representative of a widespread sentiment.

The Literature Department was always marginal to the Arts Council; during the 1980s it was wound up altogether, then revived. The Arts Council document *The Glory of the Garden* (1984) noted that drama, like opera, could not exist without subsidy, but that 'English literature' was 'sustained by a large and profitable commercial publishing industry', 'a basic ingredient in the school curriculum' and 'available to the public through the public library system'. The impact of funding for was thus 'highly marginal' (Sinclair 1995: 275) – except for poetry. While the public financial support for poetry was minimal next to other arts, it was significant in the context of the penury of most contemporary poets. Randall Stevenson records that in the last decades of the twentieth century poetry was read by no more than 4 per cent of the adult population (2004: 153). It was thus not entirely marginal that public funds supported initiatives including the Poetry Society and its journal *Poetry Review*, the Poetry Book Society, and some small presses. In the case of fiction, though, the most significantly shaping financial context was not that of public money, but of the marketplace.

Value Industries

One of the most sophisticated analyses of the contemporary literary field has come from Richard Todd. He sees the British book industry as changing significantly since the late 1970s, in line with other changes of social practice and atmosphere associated with Thatcherism. The end of the Net Book Agreement in 1997 allowed booksellers to determine their own prices, and contributed to retailers' ascendancy over authors or publishers as the most powerful interest in the book industry. Todd sees this as 'a theoretical terminus of Thatcherite thinking', which might not have occurred 'had British politics taken a different direction in 1979' (2006: 20–1). The number of novels published had risen steadily from a low point at the end of the war, though recession at the end of the 1980s would see prudent publishers slim down their lists again (Chapman 1993: 49–50). Publishing, notes Stevenson, became less expensive: from the mid-1980s, this was effected by computer typesetting from floppy disks supplied directly by authors (2004: 129). The new speed and efficiency of publishing meant that publishers could print a limited initial run of a title, reprinting according to demand (Waterstone 1993: 103–4). The proportion of fiction published in paperback – a long-term development since Penguin's innovations in the 1930s – continued to rise. The vast majority of what was now called 'literary fiction' was still published initially in hardback, but by the early 1990s hardback print runs were smaller. Ian Chapman, as publishing director of Pan Macmillan, recorded a 'vast change' over the decade: 'Previously it would have been reasonable to expect a sale of between 1,500 and 2,000 [hardback] copies even for the most inexperienced or untried author', where now a hardback sale of 1,000 would be difficult (1993: 52–3). The independent publisher Peter Owen lamented the diminished funding of public libraries as a factor reducing sales, and asserted that 'All publishers, including the largest, have cut their print-runs': in his case from 2,000–2,500 to as low a run as 800–1,000 (1993: 42–3). Chapman noted a prevailing attitude of snobbery towards paperbacks – 'Paperbacks are for beaches and planes; not really to be taken seriously; to be discarded once read' (1993: 49) – but several publishers were experimenting with straight-to-paperback originals, often in larger format to bridge the gap between hardback prestige and paperback ephemerality. Dan Franklin, then an editor at Secker and Warburg, considered that 'where literary fiction is concerned, there has been a revolution': most first novels, he estimated, would soon appear as trade paperbacks, with only a 'premier league' of authors selling over 20,000 copies appearing in hardback (1993: 29).

Bookselling, proposes Richard Todd, saw a 'revolution [. . .] that amounted to a dramatic extension of the book-buyer's franchise [. . .] a shake-up of the entire system' (Todd 1996: 123). Two large chains were central here. Dillons was purchased from the University of London by the Pentos Group in 1977: Tim Waterstone considered the chain to have gained vigour from 1985 after a 'dormant' decade (1993: 101). Waterstone's own chain was founded in 1982 and would become a dominant force in British bookselling. Together, Todd reckoned, they had 'utterly transformed the face of bookselling in Britain' (1996: 124). Both chains had over 100 branches by the 1990s. Their shops were typically much larger than the traditional independent bookshop: Waterstone's sought 1,000 square metres of space per store. Tim Waterstone explained that the electronic inventory system EPOS increased the efficiency of a store's orders, and was thus 'the route to ever higher sales per square foot (by means of maximising inventory quality and dependability)' (1993: 105). Yet he added that human judgement remained paramount. His chain employed enthusiastic, knowledgeable young staff, 'virtually 100 per cent graduates and hand-picked for book knowledge'. Staff, Waterstone claimed, were unusually well remunerated and turnover was abnormally low (1993: 106). Stores often remained open through the evenings and opened on Sundays: these extended hours, Waterstone averred, were of 'prime value' in maximising sales. He also noted the benefits of extra consumer services: gift-wrapping, delivery, local branch promotions, community initiatives with schools (107). Signings, tours and meet-the-author events had become far more prevalent by the 1990s. Stevenson avers that Waterstone's offered a more hospitable climate for shoppers who would have been intimidated by the specialist outlets of previous generations (2004: 132). In this sense it was of a piece with a major social shift, the erosion of older class distinctions and barriers by a levelling consumerist environment. At the same time the expansion of large chains was bad news for independent bookshops; Waterstone admits that many were forced to retire from the field (1993: 102).

In literary publishing, too, conglomeration and corporate economies of scale were a major theme of the 1980s. Stephen Brown adjudges that in the low-growth book industry, 'the only way to keep profit margins healthy is through acquisition, rationalisation and the search for scale economies (eg. through the centralisation of necessary functions, such as accounting and production, and the bulk buying of consumables, such as paper and packaging)'. At the same time, parent companies can pour resources into marketing and create synergistic publicity across a range of media (Brown 2006: 4). Publishing witnessed a dizzying series of key mergers and takeovers in this period. The academic publishers Routledge

& Kegan Paul and the drama specialists Methuen were taken over by Thomson Books. In 1986 Penguin bought Thomson, also including Michael Joseph and Hamish Hamilton; along with Longman, Penguin would in turn be absorbed into the Pearson Group. Octopus Books bought a range of presses (among them Heinemann, Hamlyn, a third of Pan) and was then itself bought by Reed International. Chatto, Bodley Head & Cape – an amalgam of three unusually prestigious publishing houses – bought Virago, a pioneering feminist house founded in the 1970s; with declining sales, the director Ursula Owen explained, Virago 'needed to stabilise' (Gerrard 1989: 22). Yet once the group was purchased by Random House in 1987, Virago bought itself out and became independent once more. Random House itself was later assimilated, along with Doubleday, to the German giant Bertlesmann. The potential for these manoeuvres to cause ideological angst became evident in one public instance. Jeanette Winterson published her first novel, *Oranges are Not the Only Fruit*, with the newly established feminist press Pandora in 1985. Pandora had been sold, along with Routledge, to Associated Book Publishers, who in turn were bought by Thomson. In 1990 Pandora was sold on to HarperCollins, now the property of the Australian news magnate Rupert Murdoch. Appalled to be associated with this 'born-again multi-billionaire', Winterson took the novel to Vintage, and explained her reasoning in a new Introduction (Winterson 1991: xv).

Corporate mergers and conglomerations may have been made for the sake of survival: Stevenson sees publishers 'huddling closer together to resist the economic chill' (2004: 146). But the climate of the late 1980s also produced extravagance. Reflecting on increased advances paid to established authors, Todd records that '[t]he caution of the early 1980s had been transformed, within the space of three or four years, to confidence leading almost to hubris'. He perceives a paradox: that 'authors, agents and publishers of serious literary fiction, many of whom might have been expected to have been hostile to the political and financial climate engendering the Lawson boom of the later 1980s, were swept along in its wake'; the buoyancy 'oddly reflected the new assurance of the Thatcherite meritocracy' (1996: 111–12). Ian Chapman likewise sees the rocketing of 'major league' advances as part of 'the "Decade of Greed"' (1993: 48). Nicci Gerrard described the new era of corporate 'transfer fees' as 'fantasy land, separating the majority of writers from the money-spinning stars'. Publishing, she adjudged in 1989, was following broader trends: 'Some writers are wealthier than ever before, others poorer, usually in relative, but sometimes in actual, terms. In a neat reflection of British life, the gulf between them is growing wider and more divisive' (1989: 25–6).

Todd and Gerrard record a series of increasingly large sums, like the £125,000 reportedly paid to Graham Swift for the short novel *Out of this World* (1988) and the transfer of Fay Weldon from Hodder & Stoughton to Collins for £450,000. In keeping with the fantastical nature of the sums, they differ over the amount Salman Rushdie received for *The Satanic Verses*: Todd records an $850,000 payment from Viking for US rights, Gerrard asserts an improbable £1.5 million advance. This last figure seems unfounded; the smaller figures were milestones on the way to the most notorious of such deals, when in 1994 Martin Amis received an advance of around £500,000 for *The Information*. Todd points out that literary fiction could not easily recoup such amounts; as prominent a title as Amis' *London Fields* (1989), he calculates, cannot have earned more than £200,000 in royalties in its first five years. Such works, he explains, must thus be viewed not simply as commercial ventures but as loss-leaders and cultural totems, expenses paid by large corporations for prestige and publicity. Gerrard concurs that the 'wilder advances' were paid not on strict commercial grounds, but 'in order to beat off the opposition and keep an author, in order to take over an author from her previous house, or in order to advertise an imprint' (1989: 26).

To an extent, then, the era of publishing mergers and high advances is part of an era of star writers – the most enduring of whom have become brands, with their backlists distinctively packaged (Todd 2006: 32). Such literary fame is not the same as immense financial reward. James F. English and John Frow, like Todd, see the Thatcher years as a crucial period in the formation of contemporary literary celebrity and publicity. But they note that the kind of fame enjoyed or endured by a figure like Amis is not a matter of fabulous wealth and ubiquitous sales, but of cultural visibility in a world that is ever more mediated and subject to commentary. English and Frow suggestively describe a 'literary-value industry' that they see blooming since the late 1970s:

> the whole set of individuals and groups and institutions involved not in producing contemporary fiction as such but in producing the reputations and status positions of contemporary works and authors, situating them on various scales of worth. The past 30 years [since 1976] have witnessed substantial growth in both areas, but the latter has greatly outpaced the former. (2006: 45–6)

One location of this evaluative industry, note English and Frow, is the academy, in which post-war writing began to be taught. By the end of the century contemporary fiction was perhaps the biggest growth area in English studies. In the field of journalism, two initiatives were especially important on the eve of the 1980s. In 1979 the *London Review of Books* was launched, funded from a combination of sales, private patronage and an Arts Council grant. The *LRB* became Britain's most consistently high-quality cultural review. Figures like Amis and Julian Barnes would write for the *LRB*, until they were prestigious enough to spend more time being written about. Their generation also significantly featured in another key publishing venture of 1979: *Granta*, a glossy journal of new writing in the format of a paperback anthology. The magazine had existed since 1889 as a Cambridge student publication, but its 1979 revival found a broader base of contributors and audience. In Chapter One we shall consider its contribution to debates about the novel.

Todd sees literary fiction after 1979 not only as increasingly commercialised and market-savvy, but also as constantly involved in the construction of a contemporary canon. The two are linked: whereas the traditional literary canon might be presented as a body of works that remains valuable despite its inaccessibility or lack of contemporary commercial potency, the canon of contemporary fiction is evidently formed partly by media and marketing exercises. The academy, again, is one source of such canon-formation, through the discussion of texts like Angela Carter's *Nights at the Circus* (1984) or Graham Swift's *Waterland* (1983) in both classrooms and critical works. But beyond the university, in the early 1980s two factors made a particularly public and lasting contribution to the idea of a contemporary canon. *Granta*'s editor Bill Buford recalled the Book Marketing Council as

> created in the characteristically eighties' belief that books should be treated like any other commodity, and that just as there was a Meat Marketing Council, urging everyone to go out and eat a British cow, so it followed there should be a comparable institution urging everyone to buy good, honest British novels.

The Council's most successful campaign was in 1983: a list of the twenty Best of Young British Novelists, all under forty years of age. A *Granta* special issue featured work from all twenty. Buford remembers how the campaign 'became, despite itself, a serious statement about British literary culture' (1993: 10–11). It also became a statement about *Granta*: as English and Frow note, this is 'perhaps what *Granta* is best known for' (2006: 47), with new lists following in 1993 and 2003.

The 1983 list is the most prominent instance of a canon of new fiction in the 1980s. But a still more public intervention was now being made each year by the Booker Prize. This had been awarded annually since 1969. Its finances came from Booker plc, a conglomerate primarily involved in food production, but the prize was administered by the Book Trust, a charity sponsored by the Arts Council. At the start of the

1980s the prize money stood at £10,000; by the decade's end that figure had doubled. The Booker is one sign of the increased sums of money that were flowing around the upper levels of the British literary world. It had produced some controversies in the previous decade, notably in 1972 when John Berger dedicated his win to the Black Panthers and denounced the corporate wealth behind the prize. But the Booker's most significant break into public consciousness was at the start of the 1980s.

In 1980 it was perceived as a 'two-horse race' between William Golding's *Rites of Passage* (which won) and Anthony Burgess's *Earthly Powers*. This has been billed as a clash of literary titans, which raised public consciousness of the prize. In retrospect it was also an episode involving veterans of an older literary era, whose best-known works had appeared in the 1950s and 1960s. The following year dramatically announced a new generation. Salman Rushdie's *Midnight's Children* won from a field in which D. M. Thomas' *The White Hotel* was also a fancied contender. At just thirty-four, Rushdie was far younger than the two favourites of the previous year. His vision of independent India also represented a change from, even a challenge to, the writing about Anglo-Indian relations which had prospered in the previous decade, in the work of Paul Scott and J. G. Farrell. Rushdie was a self-consciously post-colonial writer, whose work would do much to nourish a school of criticism and theory. He was a self-proclaimed radical hostile to Thatcher and her government. And his novel was an immense and elaborate instance of a literary mode that would become prominent in the 1980s. We shall consider what the critic Linda Hutcheon dubbed 'historiographic metafiction' more fully in Chapter Three.

Meanwhile the prize itself was winning more publicity. As Todd puts it, 'By delaying the judges' final decision until several weeks after the shortlist had been made public, Booker managed to create a potent brew of suspense and speculation' – to the extent that it became a popular subject for betting. From 1981 the ceremony was broadcast live on television, making literary judgement into public spectacle (Todd 1996: 73–4). The television coverage would come to encompass panel discussions among critics and non-shortlisted writers. Promoted by such coverage, the Booker became probably the most prominent literary event in Britain. In 1993, to mark the twenty-fifth anniversary, *Midnight's Children* was named as the 'Booker of Bookers', in a poll considering all the winners thus far. The novel's triumphant association with the prize was sealed. When Rushdie's book won the award again in 2008, it seemed to be assuming the unassailable status in Booker history that *Citizen Kane* holds among film critics.

Meanwhile a series of other prizes was initiated, or was revised and enhanced in the wake of the Booker's new public profile. Todd lists the Betty Trask Award (inaugurated in the early 1980s to reward non-experimental fiction); the *Mail on Sunday*/John Llewellyn Rhys Prize for writers under thirty-five; and the *Sunday Express* award, first given in 1988 and tending to reward genre fiction. The prestigious James Tait Black Memorial Prizes for fiction and biography continued to be administered by the University of Edinburgh. Chosen by academics, it occasionally pre-empted the Booker. Thus James Kelman's *A Disaffection* won in Edinburgh in 1989, five years before his Booker award for *How Late It Was, How Late* caused a stir for the book's ready obscenity and uncompromising deployment of Glasgow dialect. The most significant development in the 1980s, though, was the promotion of the Whitbread Awards. Separate prizes were given across a range of genres: fiction, poetry, first novel, biography or autobiography, children's fiction. From these an overall winner was selected. In 1985 the prize for that winner was raised to £17,500, making it more remunerative than the Booker. Todd notes that the Whitbread was positioned as Booker's rival: the fiction prize was often awarded to works that were seen as having been unfairly deprived of Booker recognition. That category included a novel we shall consider in Chapter Five, Ian McEwan's *The Child in Time* (1987).

In any case, the new profile of the Booker Prize encouraged a whole culture of literary awards which continued to grow rapidly through the 1990s, when new prizes, like the Orange Prize for women's fiction, were inaugurated for categories that could be deemed under-represented in the Booker lists. The culture of awards with substantial sums of money was one of the 1980s' major contributions to the 'literary value industry', and to the way in which contemporary literature is publicised and perceived. Todd proposes that the Booker Prize is 'the best-known of the awards whose prominence during the 1980s is associated in the public mind with the entrepreneurship that characterized the Thatcher decade', and that during this decade the prize became a significant 'consumer guide to serious literary fiction' (1996: 61).

It is clear that the new prominence of prize culture, in its emphasis on competition, its cultivation of publicity and media attention, and its channelling of money to winners, can be aligned with the spirit of enterprise whose promotion by government we have observed during this Introduction. It is thus quite fitting that by 2004, the prize could be awarded to a novel explicitly concerned to reconstruct those turbulent years. *The Line of Beauty* is much concerned with the winners of the 1980s, and the costs and exclusions involved in their victories. In the next chapter we shall consider other forms of success during the decade, and look more closely at the composition of the literary establishment.

Chapter One

Generations

Added Up on a Balance Sheet

Among the most celebrated fictional retrospectives on the changes wrought in British society in the 1980s is Jonathan Coe's *What A Carve Up!* (1994). Its protagonist is the stalled author Michael Owen, who in September 1990 visits his former publishing house for the first time since 1982. In the early 1980s, 'Long years ago', Michael was considered 'one of their most promising young writers' by this 'small but well-respected imprint which had run its business, for most of the century, from a Georgian terrace in Camden'. But Coe's fictional press has had to face new realities: 'recently it had been swallowed up by an American conglomerate and relocated to the seventh floor of a tower block near Victoria. Something like half of the personnel had survived the change', among them Patrick Mills, the editor who had handled Michael's fiction (Coe 1994: 94).

Coe registers some of the changes in the book business that we have just surveyed: mergers, acquisitions, the rationalisation of publishing along more strictly commercial lines. When we meet Patrick Mills, Coe describes a straitened situation for the fiction editor: 'even more depressed than I remembered him', in 'a tiny office, done out in an impersonal beige, with a smoked-glass window offering a partial view of a car park and a brick wall' (Coe 1994: 99). He describes a world in which the terms of literary success have changed:

> 'I mean, it's just not the same job any more. The whole business has changed out of all recognition. We get all our instructions from America and nobody pays the slightest bit of attention to anything I say at editorial meetings. Nobody gives a tinker's fuck about fiction any more, not *real* fiction, and the only kind of . . . values anybody seems to care about are the ones that can be added up on a balance sheet.' (1994: 102)

The authors most likely to be favoured with contracts now, Patrick explains, are those who already possess celebrity in some other field. Literature retains value, but as an extra garnish for worldly wealth: '[T]hese people want fucking immortality! They want their names in the British Library catalogue, they want their six presentation copies, they want to be able to slot that handsome hardback volume between the Shakespeare and the Tolstoy on their living-room bookshelf' (1994: 103). In Coe's comedy of manners, the repeated punchline is that Patrick himself has by now embraced the literary marketplace he loathes: he is annoyed, rather than proud, to have missed out on publishing a novel featuring 'Lots of media people being dynamic and ruthless' with 'Sex every forty pages. Cheap tricks, mechanical plot, lousy dialogue' (1994: 103).

The novel in question is by one of Coe's villains, Hilary Winshaw: a right-wing pundit whose columns are composed of ignorant bile. Her novel, we see in another scene, will be called 'Lust, or Revenge, or Desire, or something', though she would be content to 'leave that to their marketing people' (Coe 1994: 80). By the time Coe wrote his own novel, he might even have had in mind the specific case of Julie Burchill, the former *New Musical Express* prodigy who had touted herself as a highly-paid columnist through the latter part of the 1980s and published a début novel, *Ambition*, in 1989. (Coe was well aware of the progress of Burchill's generation through music and style journalism: he depicts their days at the *NME* in his later novel *The Rotters' Club* [2001: 157–60].) Burchill's heroine, Susan Street, seeks preferment at the newspaper *Sunday Best*, and is thus subjected to a sequence of tests and humiliations by the proprietor before emerging triumphant. *Ambition* was sold as a fat airport paperback: its embossed cover shows an attractive model and the slogan 'The only thing she can't hold down is her own ambition'. In the tone of this strapline and the shiny globetrotting of its plot, the work shamelessly invokes the melodramatic American soap operas *Dallas* and *Dynasty* which had introduced a vision of new wealth to large British audiences in the early to mid-1980s. Burchill was an intelligent enough writer to understand that *Ambition* was a generic work, a crowd-teaser and 'bonkbuster': as a self-styled leftist (even, when the mood took her, Stalinist), she wrote the novel with a calculated view to maximum commercial success. Self-consciously occupying a form that other authors would judge beneath them, she is thus not quite like Coe's Hilary Winshaw; but the financial and literary outcome may be similar enough. It thus says something about popular definitions of the 1980s that an unofficial website devoted to Burchill calls the book '1980s-defining'.

Seeking to excuse his eight-year absence from print, Michael Owen offers the thought that 'The 1980s weren't a good time for me, on the whole. I suppose they weren't for a lot of people' (Coe 1994: 102). This apologetic reflection stands as a quiet keynote to the book: the 1980s, Coe implies, weren't good for most people. But some did prosper; not just Burchill and those other celebrities and journalists who were encouraged to become novelists, but writers who have been better acclaimed by literary criticism, some of whom gained a kind of celebrity of their own. Indeed, as James F. English and John Frow (2006) have observed, the 1980s were a significant period in the development of the author as star and media personality, not to mention the inflated financial advances for novels that we observed earlier. In a dark mutation of literary celebrity, by the end of the decade one of its defining writers, Salman Rushdie, had acquired both unusual cultural credibility and unprecedented global notoriety. For several of his generation of novelists, the 1980s were indeed in career terms a good time, even as they decried actual events in the world around them. Patrick Mills' story of decline, in which commercial values displace or corrupt aesthetic ones, should thus be held alongside other ways of narrating the period. This chapter looks first at the literary establishment as it stood at the start of the 1980s, then at the new generation of writers whose work is more often viewed as defining the decade.

The Trend of the English Novel

To find one of the most prominent critical statements of the 1980s we must backtrack a decade from the lament of Patrick Mills in summer 1990, to the third issue of the journal *Granta*. The Cambridge-based magazine established itself during the 1980s as a central source of new writing, offering readers a regular supply of short stories, essays and chapters of forthcoming novels. It was also the source of some memorable interventions in the critical field; not least its third issue, titled *The End of the English Novel* and carrying a monochrome graveyard scene on its cover. Coe's protagonist might think in retrospect that the 1980s had been a bad time for a lot of people, but even at their outset one might infer from this publication that they were going to be an even worse, terminal or posthumous time for the English novel.

In fact the title proved to be more melodramatic than the contents of the issue. The issue contained several instances of writing that promised a healthy literary future. Its title was, inevitably, a polemic and provocation. In an editorial Bill Buford, an American who had studied English at Cambridge, surveyed the pitfalls of the present scene. At its heart was the Current Crisis in Publishing, eccentrically appearing in bold type. Robert McCrum – a young editor at Faber, on his way to being a key player in the fiction industry as well as a novelist himself – had used the pages of the main trade paper the *Bookseller* to accuse British fiction of being insular, incurious, middle-class: 'happier adding to the myths, writing about the world we have lost' (Buford 1980: 8). Buford considered that the real problems were deeper, and that writers were less responsible than publishers. Publishing had changed too little since the nineteenth century: '[T]he book, in more than one sense is a hand-made art in an economy no longer able to accommodate it' (1980: 13). Too few outlets were available for new writing, including university bookshops. Publishing houses were too timid to print numerous works in translation, thus beaching the few translations that did appear. 'How, in such a context,' Buford asked, 'can the British writer be anything but provincial?' (1980: 11). The Great British Public had been underestimated in order to serve publishers' own complacency: the success of new ventures (Virago, Picador, The Women's Press and Carcanet among them) proved a demand for 'new kinds of writing – distinct from competitive market identities' (1980: 12). New ways of publishing ought to emerge, making a virtue from the present crisis: 'Imagine a reader commissioning a writer [. . .] Or a group of readers commissioning a whole issue or even a series of issues' (1980: 15). This suggested that *Granta* itself wanted to be such a new medium for writing. It would indeed be one of the prime loci of new work and a major channel for international (notably American) voices to Britain, though the scale of change for which Buford hoped might really demand another technological revolution.

Buford cannily redirected blame from superstructure to base. The problem lay not with Britain's supposedly lacklustre, backward writers but with the industry that transmitted them, and that was probably excluding the 'embryo Conrads' (1980: 11) who were going unheard. Otherwise his article was divided between tirade and promise. The former, though energetic, was generic, the tone of the angry young man seeking to kick down a sclerotic establishment. Buford found McCrum's complaints about fiction 'familiar stuff'; his own radicalism, though more original, also has the ring of tradition. At the same time, like other such polemicists, Buford was ultimately promoting a future. The existing fictional establishment he characterised as 'that postwar, premodern variety of the middle class monologue, with C. P. Snow on one side and perhaps Margaret Drabble and Melvyn Bragg on the other (Kingsley Amis will always be nearby providing vitriolic commentary)' (1980: 9).

Buford maintained a respectful distance from this group, and ultimately proposed other virtues and newer writers. He suspected the arrival of 'a different period of creative prose [. . .] a writing which, freed from the middle class monologue, is experimentation in the real sense, exploiting traditions and not being wasted on them' (1980: 16). Across the page Salman Rushdie's *Midnight's Children* began, running for thirty pages a year ahead of its full publication, and followed by a short story from Angela Carter. Buford had found the writers to back his pronouncements; these two will be considered in detail in subsequent chapters. *The End of the English Novel* is thus, if not really a gravestone, a significant landmark in the discourse around the genre in the decade ahead.

Yet the latter part of *Granta* 3 points in a different direction. It contains a 'Symposium on the British Novel' with contributions from two academics from the University of East Anglia, professors from the United States and Canada and, most challenging, the avant-garde writer and theorist Christine Brooke-Rose. Almost by definition, their accounts of the state of the novel look back. They say little about several names that are now heavily associated with the 1980s, and who will feature significantly in this book. Brooke-Rose asks about the viability of an experimental tradition which passes through Beckett and American metafiction. From British Columbia the expatriate Frederick Bowers scorns the British novel, in rather traditional terms, for 'its conformity, its traditional sameness, and its realistically rendered provincialism [. . .] local, quaint and self-consciously xenophobic' (1980: 151). The three other critics refer primarily to Malcolm Bradbury, Angus Wilson, Doris Lessing, John Fowles and Iris Murdoch. At the outset of the 1980s, the current canon of fiction, unsurprisingly, centres on novelists who have been publishing through the previous decades, most of them since the 1950s.

Isn't That Enough?

Early in the twenty-first century, Philip Tew (2004) argued for a clear distinction between 'post-war' and 'contemporary' writers. The two categories, he proposed, had once been identical but now designated different periods. The second category, in Tew's view, included at its earliest those who had begun to publish in the 1970s and become prominent in the 1980s. Richard Bradford joins Tew in writing of 'the novelists who began to establish the territory of contemporary fiction' as 'the ones who started their careers in the 1970s and who have made their presence felt over the past three decades' (2007: 11). That generation will figure prominently in what follows, though it is still barely emergent in the *Granta* symposium. We should also note, however, the persistence of Tew's 'post-war' generation – in fact generations plural. They would include the many who made their names in the 1950s and 1960s, becoming a kind of canon as they won loyal readerships and began to be discussed in critical works. In the novel their number would include – supplemented here with their dates of birth – William Golding (1911), Anthony Burgess (1917), Iris Murdoch (1919), Doris Lessing (1919), Kingsley Amis (1922), John Fowles (1926), Alan Sillitoe (1928). In poetry the most celebrated figures were Philip Larkin (1922), the so-called laureate of the welfare state, and Ted Hughes (1930), who was acclaimed for bringing myth and animal energy back to an English poetry that had become urbanely conversational. In British drama the founding legends for post-war tradition are Samuel Beckett's *Waiting for Godot* (1955) and John Osborne's *Look Back in Anger* (1956), respectively announcing new forms of social realism and of minimalist exploration. Major new dramatists flourished thereafter: Harold Pinter (b. 1930), Arnold Wesker (1932), Joe Orton (1933), Tom Stoppard (1937), Shelagh Delaney (1939).

Almost all the writers just mentioned were still alive in the 1980s (Orton's murder in 1967 producing the exception), and still writing and publishing. D. J. Taylor's polemic *A Vain Conceit* (1989) considered several of them – Fowles, Amis, Murdoch – to be central to the decade; in fact that persistence accounts for some of Taylor's impatience with Britain's literary scene. The writers just mentioned span a couple of generations and write from diverse perspectives. Their careers often involve intellectual and political journeys: Murdoch's from existentialism to Platonism, Amis' from communism to conservatism, Pinter's growing explicitness about politics after more enigmatic beginnings. Even Larkin, who cultivated a persona of grudging resistance to change, had to shed an early attachment to Yeatsian symbolism and a first vocation as a novelist to fix his image as the hermit of Hull. They cannot, then, be treated as a unified group in form or theme; just as a chronological set of writers whose most pathbreaking works had preceded the 1980s, even though some of them remained prolific. Some did not. Long literary careers wax and wane through several phases, and not all these writers produced their most significant art in the 1980s, even when they still had major, acclaimed work ahead of them. Pinter, for instance, would return to the stage in new work and productions throughout the 1990s, but the 1980s were his least productive literary decade, though he did channel his energies into political activism – for international causes like that of the Iraqi Kurds, and more locally as a central figure in the literary world's opposition to Margaret Thatcher.

But some of the oldest figures remained as productive as ever. The incorrigibly fertile Anthony Burgess, for instance, produced a series of ambitious historical novels, notably *Earthly Powers* (1980), a black-comic retrospect on the first four-fifths of the century; *The Kingdom of the Wicked* (1985), which narrates the birth of Christianity; and *Any Old Iron* (1988), which sends its characters across the Atlantic on the Titanic and into both world wars, while also inventing a modern fate for King Arthur's sword Excalibur. Like Burgess' other historical novels, *Any Old Iron* features fictional cameos from real world-historical figures, including Churchill, Stalin and Anthony Eden. Burgess' historical imagination thus continued to paint on a giant scale, and from great learning as well as his extensively international personal experience (from military service through Malaya and Borneo to tax exile in Monaco). His late work shows a renewed concern with religion: most evidently in *Earthly Powers*, whose protagonist Kenneth Toomey is engaged, on the basis of his skills as a bestselling author, to assist with the canonisation of the late Pope Gregory. The history of twentieth-century calamity that Toomey produces casts the Pope's liberalism as misguided. As Patricia Waugh observes (1995: 95–6), the novel's implied view – that reforms in the Catholic Church mistakenly relinquish traditional severity for dangerous laxity – can be seen as consistent with the rest of Burgess' oeuvre. Long a lapsed Catholic, Burgess had been exploring austere models of sin and redemption at least since his dystopian vision *A Clockwork Orange* in 1962.

Waugh's study *Harvest of the Sixties: English Literature and its Background 1960–1990* (1995) deals sympathetically and extensively with religious concerns in writers like Burgess, Golding, Murdoch and Graham Greene. One way of reconceiving the distinction drawn by Tew is to note that these concerns would be less evidently relevant to a critical treatment of the next generation. Religion can never be relied upon to disappear, and the relative eclipse of Christianity would be matched by the growing prominence of other creeds in British life. But Waugh's discussion of 'sacred impulses in a secular age' makes more intuitive sense in relation to Murdoch and Golding than it would to Jonathan Coe or Irvine Welsh. The 'contemporary' generation of post-1970s writers were more likely to start from a secular position than to spend their careers battling through theological complexities to reach or avoid it. That is one significant and far-reaching historical distinction between Burgess and his successors.

Burgess' historical fiction, however, can be connected to a wider concern with this form in the period. Bradford judges that 'since the 1970s the historical novel has become fiction's most prominent and enduring subgenre and has, moreover, unshackled itself from its earlier image as a somewhat lowbrow cousin to serious writing' (2007: 83–4). Peter Ackroyd was among the major new exponents of the form in the 1980s and 1990s; his *Hawksmoor* (1985) shuttles back and forth between a grisly past and an eerie present, a model echoed in more scholarly and less Gothic tone by A. S. Byatt's *Possession* (1990). That pair of novels won the Whitbread and Booker prizes respectively, another sign of the renewed status of the sophisticated historical novel in this period. Chapter Three of this study will consider at length the turn to what was dubbed 'historiographic metafiction' among contemporary British novelists.

Burgess' late work thus need not be viewed in isolation from literary currents, but can be seen as influencing them – though it must also, above all, be seen as the expression of his extraordinary ego and writerly energy, probably the most boundless in post-war British literature. Upon the publication of *Any Old Iron*, Burgess remarked: '"After some 30 novels," people say, "isn't that enough?" But there's nothing else to do.' In Burgess' case, not to keep writing would have been against nature; but he also voices the stoicism with which other veterans kept going, even when their works were not likely to define their careers or the current era. I shall next consider in turn two of the decade's most celebrated novels, written not by young hopefuls but by veterans nearing the end.

Floating Society

Burgess' most prominent contest in the 1980s was with his near-contemporary, William Golding, when *Earthy Powers* emerged as a favourite for the Booker Prize in 1980 along with Golding's *Rites of Passage*. The televised contest was a signal event in the history of the prize. *Rites of Passage* won. It is worth considering this novel more closely as one instance of the post-war generation's enduring capacities. *Rites of Passage* was only the first of Golding's 'Sea Trilogy', comprising also *Close Quarters* (1987) and *Fire Down Below* (1989). Golding's hero Edmund Talbot is a passenger on a naval vessel bound for Australia in the early nineteenth century. The book is a seafaring yarn that recalls a world popularised by C. S. Forester and Patrick O'Brian's popular novel sequences. Yet *Rites of Passage* features no naval battles or derring-do: as Talbot declares on the final page: 'Why – it has become, perhaps, some kind of sea-story but a sea-story with never a tempest, no shipwreck, no sinking, no rescue at sea, no sight nor sound of an enemy, no thundering broadsides, heroism, prizes, gallant defences and heroic attacks!' (1980: 277–8). Golding here tacitly admits that this naval novel, while conscientiously introducing us to the '*Tarpaulin*' language of the sea, has been as much an investigation of other matters: notably social class and cohesion. The ship is referred to as a 'floating society' in which the captain is 'king or emperor' (144); a warship is 'a tyranny in little' (139). Seeing a parson beside the captain, Edmund Talbot finds a spectacle of Church and State personified, a 'picture in little' of 'English – and dare I say British – society' (78). Throughout the novel, class distinctions are insistent, with different orders of crew and passengers consigned to particular sections of the vessel. As one character bitterly reflects: 'In our country for all her greatness there is one thing she cannot do and that is translate a person wholly out of one class into another. Perfect translation from one language into another is impossible. Class is the British language' (125). We will shortly see that class remained a central concern in major works describing contemporary Britain. Whether genuine class mobility was making 'translation' possible in the 1980s, let alone the nineteenth century, was a matter of debate.

Language in a more direct sense is an equally insistent concern in *Rites of Passage*. The novel's text purports to be Talbot's journal, written for his godfather to read. This format allows it to make regular reference to the act of writing. On its first page Talbot announces:

> (1)
> Honoured godfather,
> With those words I begin the journal I engaged myself to keep for you – no words could be more suitable!
> Very well then. The place: on board the ship at last. The year: you know it. The date? Surely what matters is that it is the first day of my passage to the other side of the world; in token whereof I have this moment inscribed the number 'one' at the top of this page. (Golding 1980: 3)

The '(1)' that commences the reading experience (immediately beneath the page number and the novel's title which heads every page) thus turns out to be Talbot's own work: and in referring to it he immediately instals a reflexivity in his discourse. His narrative is soon interrupted by the word 'LATER' (8), and the numbered headings for his journal are routinely the occasion of discussion in the writing that follows them: 'I have placed the number "2" at the beginning of this entry though I do not know how much I shall set down today' (11). An entry headed '(X)' commences with Talbot admitting: 'I *think* it is the seventh – or the fifth – or the eighth perhaps – let "X" do its algebraic duty and represent the unknown quantity' (46). The textual apparatus will become stranger still, with one entry headed '(?)' (72), another '(Z)' – 'Zed, you see, zed, I do not know what the day is' (95) – and then the whole sequence recommencing with 'ALPHA' (122), 'BETA' (148) and so on. Before the middle of the book Talbot also dubs a section with the symbol '(Ω)': 'Omega, omega, omega. The last scene surely! Nothing more can happen – unless it be fire, shipwreck, the violence of the enemy or a miracle!' (104). Talbot's own discourse and his system of ordering it is undermined by the reader's unavoidable sense that we are not yet near 'the last scene'. Talbot is, or wants to be, in control of the narrative, but his ongoing sense of its shape and length is founded on ignorance of what is to come, and thus different from the ironising knowledge of the author. He concludes the book with the heading '(&)': 'the ampersand gives a touch of eccentricity, does it not?' (264).

In this fashion *Rites of Passage* teases the reader with the production of its narrative. Talbot seems to write the tale as he goes along, recording the conditions in which he does so – which often include those (sickness at sea, lethargy, distraction) that prevent him doing it effectively. Meanwhile the headings and organisation of the journal mutate as Talbot seeks a way to cope with those challenges. Talbot's own discourse also frequently meditates upon issues of writing, genre and representation, reflecting on the procedures it has just employed. 'Your lordship may detect in the fore-going a tendency to *fine writing*', Talbot suggests after concluding a long paragraph: 'a not unsuccessful attempt, I flatter myself' (67). We are regularly reminded that the mode of narration is variable, the product of one man's unpredictable pen; when he rhapsodises over the one young woman on board, he admits that 'The danger here is to invent', warning the reader (as well as the intended reader, Talbot's godfather) that his account is forged by unreliable passions (55). Heightening the sense of literariness, Talbot refers to actual eighteenth-century novels: *Moll Flanders* is in his library (86), and when he conceals a name as 'Lord L---', he remarks to his reader: 'this is perfect Richardson, is it not?' (267). But most telling is the self-admonition that 'My entries are becoming short as some of Mr Sterne's chapters!' (72). Golding thus slyly compares his own rambling narrative to Sterne's *Tristram Shandy*, among the most digressively metafictional works in the English canon, and a significant influence on the self-conscious fictions of the 1970s and 1980s. Theatre – 'our floating theatre' (145) – is another recurring image. Talbot sees his temporary amour Miss Brocklebank as an actress whose words and gestures are made for an imaginary stage (93, 99), and says of his journey that 'It is a play. Is it a farce or a tragedy?' (104).

The journal is the format in which we read *Rites of Passage*; but it is also an object *within* the world of the novel, in which Talbot on the final page will finish writing, then 'lock it, wrap it and sew it unhandily in sailcloth and thrust it away in the locked drawer' (278). The textual character of Golding's novel becomes more emphatic still when Talbot informs the ship's captain that he is writing a journal: 'It is my ambition to out-Gibbon Mr Gibbon' (143). Here the foregrounding of text is also a strategy within the book itself: in informing the captain of the journal's existence, Talbot intends to 'force him to look back over the whole length of the voyage and consider what sort of figure he might cut in an account of it', ultimately provoking guilt (145). The journal is not only the frame through which we read of events; it is also an object that might influence characters' behaviour. In Talbot's own words, 'I must keep all locked away. This journal has become deadly as a loaded gun' (184). This is one way in which Golding's reflexivity does not ultimately obscure his plot and concerns, which are not simply hermeneutic but involve social and ethical issues.

The point becomes clearer when Talbot discovers a long letter from the Reverend Robert James Colley, whom Talbot has represented contemptuously and who has finally been persecuted to death by the crew. Talbot's journal now comes to include Colley's letter itself: 'I will get glue and fix the letter in here. It shall become another part of the *Talbot Manuscript*' (184). The opening pages of Colley's letter are gone; it starts mid-sentence, and Golding's reader is to experience the newly fractured character of Talbot's journal, which is now taken over by another voice. For fully sixty pages we read the events of the novel from the alternative perspective of the devout, hapless Colley. Golding's deployment of a visibly constructed narrative format has already offered a kind of epistemological insight, pointing up the tale's uncertain status. Now it also gains an ethical dimension. For Colley's account of many of the same characters, events and scenes as Talbot produces a second version of the novel that effectively shadows the first, or offers it a distorted mirror in which we can see shipboard life from another point of view. Colley turns out to be an earnest, self-deprecating figure, abused by others but not malicious in return; instead of vengeance he seeks the blame for each situation himself. In particular, Talbot himself, who has scorned and abused Colley throughout, figures in Colley's own narrative as an admirable figure, and is even compared to Christ (212). The clash of points of view is extreme. It exposes Talbot's callow cruelty, and though he seeks to persuade himself not to '[brood] on what is past' (259), he ends the book still piecing together Colley's fate and planning to write a letter to the late parson's sister. 'It will be lies from beginning to end. I shall describe my growing friendship with her brother. I shall describe my admiration for him [. . .] A letter that contains everything but a shred of truth! How is that for a start to a career in the service of my King and Country?' (277). Talbot's intention echoes another writer of naval stories, an evident precursor to Golding's late work: Joseph Conrad, at the end of whose *Heart of Darkness* (1899) the truth about the disgraced Mr Kurtz is to be dissembled for the good of his innocent fiancée. Golding's ending picks up from Conrad's an ambiguity over the ethics of truth-telling. At the end of this overtly written narrative, as with Conrad's ostensibly spoken yarn, the value of delivering a truthful narrative is dismissed in favour of the gentler consolations of fiction.

As a lavish historical yarn that is also cannily, quietly knowing about textual transmission, *Rites of Passage* does not closely correspond to Buford's dominant 'postwar, premodern variety of the middle class monologue'. Other contemporaries of Golding also clearly break that mould. Doris Lessing's post-humanist science fiction is a major example. So is John Fowles' extraordinary blend of speculative, detective and historical fiction in *A Maggot* (1985), a novel that mixes third-person narration with such 'found' texts as (fictional) letters, interrogation transcripts and news reports from the early eighteenth century. Adventurous in form, Fowles' novel is also capaciously imaginative in theme, as its initial eighteenth-century scenario opens on to science fiction and an alternate history of religious dissidence. Fowles' wild inventiveness, like that of Burgess and like Golding's subtle requisitioning of the sea story, it is a reminder of how adventurous the older generation could be. These writers support Dominic Head's case that the novel in the 1980s did not simply see a resurgence after the post-war generation had led it into a sleepy suburban cul-de-sac (2008: 11). There are continuities between the generations – from J. G. Ballard to Martin Amis, for instance, or J. G. Farrell to Salman Rushdie – and the more experienced writers were in several cases producing works of high ambition. But writers of the post-war generation were also producing work on contemporary life that corresponded more closely to Buford's model.

Some of this might fall into the territory of the 'Hampstead novel', though that form itself – Buford's 'middle class monologue' – could be more outward-looking than the labels suggest. Margaret Drabble, identified by Buford as part of a familiar tradition, had been writing contemporary condition-of-England works in the late 1970s and would continue through the 1980s, as we shall see in Chapter Four. Other novelists, more chary of Drabble's metropolitan dinner parties, still belonged to the tradition that Head has identified and promoted as 'provincial realism'. Head champions Stanley Middleton as a central exponent of the form, above all because 'his oeuvre [. . .] charts the subtle ways in which being "middle class" in Britain has shifted' (2008: 72).

Middleton indeed published novels almost every year of the 1980s, and Head is correct to draw our attention to the steady continuity of realist fiction and its quiet rendition of British life, even as more controversial writers blazed across the literary sky. But the most celebrated exponent of such realism in the period is a considerable controversialist himself, and was a dominant presence across the post-war period.

That Next Drink

In literary history, Kingsley Amis is more evidently central to the 1950s than to the 1980s. It was in the post-war years that his early work was seen to embody a generation's attitudes and manners, above all in *Lucky Jim* (1954). By the 1980s Amis was an angry old, rather than young, man, unmatched in the roles of professional drinker and curmudgeon. Yet the decade saw one of his major literary triumphs when, in 1986, he won the Booker Prize for *The Old Devils*. As with Golding six years before, the achievement may have looked merely valedictory, but the work itself was highly acclaimed and a late landmark in the author's career. *The Old Devils* is a good place to consider the fate of a different post-war strain from Golding's: provincial comic realism.

The novel commences as a celebrity author and his wife return to Wales, and goes on to examine the impact of their arrival on their old acquaintances. It is narrated through an omniscient third person, a voice that takes the burden of describing the innumerable small actions and events that compose the story. As an embittered couple return home, Amis' description could not be more mundane:

> These thoughts occupied him while he went and got a couple of cold fish-fingers out of the refrigerator for his lunch, so that he failed to consider whether he agreed with the content of what she had said or not. Muriel pulled on her wellies and tramped off into the garden. (1986: 38)

Much of the novel's largely sedate action is of a kind in which Amis had long been expert: drinking. Excessive amounts of alcohol flow past almost too matter-of-factly for the reader to notice. A character drinks 'a weakish whisky-and-water, having held off till then because he made a point of avoiding early drinking whenever he could': we then learn that it is not yet 11a.m. (77). There is no such thing as a single drink, rather an ongoing process: 'The fresh drinks arrived, whisky and gin to make up for the relative thinness of the wine' (63). After a lunchtime session at their local pub, the main characters 'decided to leave after the next drink, or rather Peter, whose car was outside, decided that and the other two went along. They had that next drink, and then another quick one which Malcolm declined, and then they left' (25).

That last sentence is uncannily reminiscent of the one that Kingsley Amis presented as his model for fictional prose: 'He finished his drink and left.' Amis' point was that such prose should not be an end or delight in itself, but should serve the story and the process of furnishing a reader with information. The sentences just quoted from *The Old Devils* are accordingly unspectacular. Thus, in the first example quoted, the phrase 'he went and got' is succinct, but could not be further from the heightening that is often thought to distinguish literary language: it is wilfully undistinguished, even without the hint of bathos from the cold fish-fingers that are the object of the phrase. The subsequent reflection 'he failed to consider whether he agreed with the content of what she had said or not' is likewise fully informative while pedantically dull. Amis, throughout the novel, is unwilling to write anything ostentatious, and unafraid to write an average, undistinguished sentence. It is not that he lacks linguistic capacity – as a keen scholar of the English language and devotee of the *Oxford English Dictionary* – but that his literary aesthetic positively insists on plain speaking. Prose should be efficient and serviceable, transporting characters from one location to the next and informing the reader of their actions, thoughts and feelings where appropriate.

Characters are not thereby without nuance. The detail of a character 'failing to consider' a small matter because he is thinking about something else also indicates an interest in the minutiae of the mind. Eschewing any hint of modernism, Amis renders thoughts without leaving the third person: a character's impressions are unobtrusively summoned into the unfolding narration. Thus one character reflects as an unknown young woman leaves the saloon bar:

> Malcolm made no sound. He thought the girl's eye had caught his for an instant, not of course out of anything but habit or even politeness, and yet it set him thinking. How many years was it since he had noticed a girl? And what exactly had he seen in this one? – she was not all that attractive. She was young, yes indeed, not that he could have said what age, but not so much young either as fresh, new, scarcely out of the wrapping-paper with no time for anything to have got at her and started using her up. (22)

Amis is able to share any character's interior life with the reader as the narrative focus moves around a scene, but there is little sense that we are moving into a character's private zone of language and expression. Malcolm's words here all belong to the most basic diction ('she was not all that attractive'), and the colloquialisms ('got at her', 'using her up') are much like the ones we observed a moment ago. They do not so much express the stylistic contours of a particular mind as belong to the overall idiom of the book, into which all these minds are translated. In that sense, though *The Old Devils* does contain characters with eccentric traits, appearances and bugbears, it does not trouble to render that human diversity as a formal diversity. Instead Amis' style, moving fluidly between characters, finds common ground as each mind turns out to talk in the same tongue. The novel's low-key realism effects a sort of consensus. The effect is appropriate, as whatever the characters' differences they belong to a close-knit community of acquaintances, reaching back from the 1980s through several decades.

People are often circumspect in speech but unrestrained in thought. But in *The Old Devils* the reverse applies. Reported thoughts, like Malcolm's above, are apt to be tentative and exploratory if not resigned. Out loud, on the other hand, the old folk voice strong opinions. Most of them concern new developments and apparently modern trends. Peter Thomas is relentless in his hostility to any display of Welshness, including the revival of the Welsh language (27, 61). When the group discovers that an Indian restaurant is owned by Arabs, there is 'a united cry of rage and disgust', and a 'glaring' Alun Weaver declaims that it 'makes you sweat' (98). Malcolm issues a jeremiad arguing that Wales is being killed by Anglicisation:

> That's what they're doing everywhere. Everywhere new here is the same as new things in England, whether it's the university or the restaurants or the supermarkets or what you buy there. What about this place we're in? Is there anything in here to tell you you're in Wales? (112)

The pub landlord Tarquin Jones views a couple of young customers as 'an orchestrated onslaught on our whole culture and way of life', at which the novel's central characters should 'take note and consider what is to be done' (24). Those characters view the modernisation of pubs as a plague (94–5), and in another scene three of them compete to see 'who could say the most outrageous thing about the national Labour Party, the local Labour Party, the Labour-controlled county council, the trade unions, the education system, the penal system, the Health Service, the BBC, black people and youth' (60). The book's narrative tone is temperate, but its characters are quite often the reverse. Its pages ring with denunciations and angry laments.

It is not hard to see the hand of Kingsley Amis himself here. As an explicitly, determinedly conservative writer, he was an increasingly unusual figure in the Thatcher years: a period in which most of Britain's writers became oppositional to, or at least aloof from, the centre of power. Amis' political positioning was in part a reaction to this reaction. He became opposed not to the government but to its opponents, whom he viewed as a hegemonic herd. To an extent, the verbal assaults of *The Old Devils* are a direct transposition of this combative spirit. Nonetheless, inserting these opinions in a novel alters their status. For one thing, any fictional character's speech becomes provisional and by definition cannot be identified with authorial opinion. For another, the opinions in *The Old Devils* are spread across a set of characters. Rather than adding up to a monologue, they each become part of a dialogue, and subject to qualification, contradiction or mockery by others. Malcolm's drunken lament at Anglicisation is not taken seriously by his friends, and Tarquin's concern at 'an orchestrated onslaught on our whole culture and way of life' is immediately, dismissively parodied by Malcolm himself (24). It is not even clear that the characters' angry opinions add up to a single conservative case. Malcolm's laments for Wales do not square with Peter's contempt for any mention of Welshness – and even the latter quietly admits, at the novel's end, that a love of the place is acceptable if never voiced (284–5). Indeed Malcolm's anger extends to an attack on Thatcherism and mass unemployment, which is in turn gently deflated (108). Malcolm is naive and vulnerable, but sympathetic; as Neil Powell remarks, his taste in jazz marks him as a good sort in Amis's eyes (2008: 224). There is thus a degree of generosity to the novel that transcends some its protagonists' angriest moments, and shows Amis' ability to stand back from a novel – or to disperse himself into it. 'Keep the reader guessing,' he wrote in a note to himself: 'wch the Amis char?' (Powell 2008: 226).

The Old Devils shows one other thing that the form of 'provincial realism' could achieve. It is thoroughly a novel about old age, and it takes pains to detail the trials of this condition. Characters are shown, at considerable length, coping with constipation, impotence, weight gain, unattractiveness, diminished self-esteem and the difficulty of performing everyday acts. For Charlie Norris, simply rising from bed and beginning a day is an action that takes three pages to describe (1987: 74–6), while for Peter 'getting-up procedures' have likewise become 'a major event of his day' (115). Malcolm's spirits lift on the way to the pub, 'as they always did at the prospect of an hour or more spent not thinking about being ill and things to do with being ill' (10). Charlie's first Scotch of the day allows him to 'turn his head without thinking it over first. Soon it might cease to be one of those days that made you sorry to be alive' (13). That note of optimism is so glum that it might be a deadpan borrowing from Samuel Beckett, for whose wandering figures merely to subsist and maintain the scantiest source of entertainment is a considerable

achievement. Time too has changed for Amis' characters. Alun, though
his philandering maintains his sense of youthfulness, reflects that 'the
most noticeable characteristic of the past [. . .] was that there was so
much more of it now than formerly, with bits that were longer ago than
had once seemed possible' (70). The overwhelming example of Beckett
shows that human frailty and decay are by no means the sole preserve of
realism; but Amis' late achievement demonstrates the insights that could
be gradually marshalled across the slow-moving provincial novel.

Sharking out of Lane

As my cab pulled off FDR Drive, somewhere in the early Hundreds, a low-
slung Tomahawk full of black guys came sharking out of lane and sloped in
fast right across our bows. We banked, and hit a deep welt or grapple-ridge in
the road: to the sound of a rifle shot the cab roof ducked down and smacked
me on the core of my head. I didn't really need that, I tell you, with my head
and face and back and heart hurting a lot all the time anyway, and still drunk
and crazed and ghosted from the plane. (Martin Amis 1984: 1)

The first lines of Martin Amis' *Money* (1984) announce the arrival of
something fast and loud. They have been viewed since as a statement
of intent and a bravura performance in their own right. It is apt that
this novel should begin at speed, in action, with the high-velocity duel
between two cars and the ensuing damage to the narrator – all taking
place, it's immediately clear, in a New York City that can be addressed
('the early Hundreds') with colloquial familiarity. In the present context
it is tempting, and not tendentious, to see an immediate contrast with
the work we have just been considering. The kinetic swoop of Amis'
opening sentences makes a change from the workaday business of his
father's, and we are rapidly immersed in a world of invented brands
('Tomahawk': the car only exists in *Money*) and neologisms ('sharking',
'ghosted'). Continuities can be sought: one can imagine one of Kingsley
Amis' characters talking about various parts of him 'hurting a lot all
the time', and certainly being drunk. But it is truer to say that to read
Money is to enter a different world – of characters and settings, but
more crucially of words and voices.

  Money is an exceptionally rich text, which demands attention in
its own right. But in the present context it also suggests a wider generational shift. What new literary establishment was announcing itself?
We may recall the distinction drawn by Tew and Bradford, in which a
new generation emerges from its literary apprenticeship in the 1970s to
become prominent in the 1980s. This is primarily a matter of fiction,

though it has correlates in poetry also. Dates of birth will again suggest a temporal coherence. Martin Amis' (b. 1949) first novel, *The Rachel Papers*, appeared as early as 1973; *Money* was his fifth novel, by far the biggest and most ambitious. Though Amis had published from the start with the prestigious house Jonathan Cape, he could not initially earn a living from fiction. In the early 1970s he was an assistant editor and regular reviewer, under more than one name, for the *Times Literary Supplement*; from 1977 to 1979 he was literary editor of the left-leaning *New Statesman* magazine; and into the 1980s he was a feature writer for the *Observer*, one of Britain's few liberal newspapers. Politically these berths inducted Amis into a tacitly liberal-left position. They were also centres of activity around which other writers clustered and connections were made. The political journalist Christopher Hitchens (b. 1949) met Amis as early as 1973; while Hitchens has never authored a literary work proper, his authoritatively caustic leftism was influential upon the politics and polemical manners of this generation of London literati. The poet James Fenton (b. 1949) was the *New Statesman*'s political correspondent, and like Hitchens had a background on the Trotskyist Left. Julian Barnes (b. 1946) took a path to the 1980s akin to that of Martin Amis. Before publishing his first novel, *Metroland*, in 1980, he was successively reviewer for the *TLS*, contributing editor to Ian Hamilton's literary magazine the *New Review*, then assistant literary editor and television critic at the *New Statesman* (1977–81). He was also deputy literary editor at the *Sunday Times* (1980–2), but more memorably served as television critic for the *Observer* (1982–6). That role had been occupied for ten years previously by the Australian poet, critic and man of parts, Clive James (b. 1939). James too was part of the *New Statesman* circuit, a regular at their Friday lunches in the late 1970s (Powell 2008: 318). His debut novel *Brilliant Creatures* (1983) is a satire of contemporary London literary and media worlds. While James insists that the characters are merely 'the creatures of my mind' (1983: 9), their alcoholic lunches as 'the Dregs' (85) are clearly inspired by the *New Statesman* set, and the fictional novelist Nicholas Crane has been granted Martin Amis' style of 'cumulative verbal effects' (43). A decade older than Amis, James was something of a mentor to the new generation, as was the revered poet Ian Hamilton (b. 1938). Hamilton nurtured not only Amis and Barnes but also Ian McEwan (b. 1948), who became yet another member of the group despite, unusually for this milieu, lacking an Oxbridge background. A relatively classless exception, he had been educated at Sussex before becoming one of the very first to complete a creative writing MA in Britain, under the tutelage of Malcolm Bradbury at East Anglia. The programme's second graduate,

Kazuo Ishiguro (b. 1954), was hardly less notable. McEwan moved only gradually into the novel form, beginning with two volumes of short stories (1975, 1978) and a brace of novellas. But he was imaginatively engaged with the politics of the present, both in his film script *The Ploughman's Lunch* (1983) and in his first full-length novel, *The Child in Time* (1987), to which we shall turn in Chapter Five.

The generation that is coming into focus here is evidently more socially coherent and connected than the long span of 'post-war' writers evoked earlier. It is more like the loose grouping of the Movement in the 1950s. Like that network, this one appears overwhelmingly male, having bonded over liquid lunches and frames of snooker as well as Oxford connections. A freshet of writers had coalesced through the 1970s who were now, in their early thirties, gaining publicity and success. In the Amises' case, the generational shift was unusually direct, prompting Kingsley's private resentment at his son's earnings as well as his gathering reputation (Powell 2008: 320). The Amises also conveniently suggest a transition from the older generation's conservatism to the more leftist sympathies of the young. This makes Martin Amis' views sound deceptively coherent and committed, where McEwan remembers him as in fact 'brilliantly detached from politics' (Powell 2008: 318); but it is true that the younger writers, first linked by the *New Statesman* and now grouped around the *Guardian* or *Observer*, were likely to be intuitively suspicious of authority in the Thatcher years. In literary terms, though, there is no ready-made label or formula for the Amis-Barnes-McEwan generation. One journalist (Farndale 2005) asserts that the *Statesman*'s tyros were known as 'Howard's Boys', after the magazine's editor Anthony Howard, but the term has made scant impact on literary history. In truth, these writers had by the 1980s already grown into heterogeneity; they were not about to issue a manifesto. The closest they came to that was perhaps in the *New Review*'s symposium on the state of British fiction in 1978. Amis and McEwan offered brief contributions that would henceforth be cited as early mission statements by English fiction's new stars. Both remain telling. McEwan abjured '[the] formal experimentation of the late sixties and early seventies' as a dead end, and called for an end to 'self-enclosed' demonstrations 'that reality is words and words are lies', for 'the artifice of fiction can be taken for granted'. Experiment, McEwan instead averred, could come from subject matter: 'the representation of states of mind and the society that forms them' (1978: 51). Amis, meanwhile, artfully mused that with great effort, he could imagine a fiction 'as tricksy, as alienated and as writerly as those of, say, Robbe-Grillet while also providing the staid satisfactions of pace, plot and humour with which we associate, say, Jane Austen' (1978: 18). Both writers thus acknowledged the recent potency of experiment or 'tricksiness' like the French *nouveau roman* or American metafiction, while aspiring to something different. Though retaining an intellectual and erudite air, they clear the ground for reader-friendliness and even popularity. These aspirations remain relevant to both writers' subsequent development. McEwan, for instance, from *The Comfort of Strangers* (1981) to *Saturday* (2005) and especially in his 1940s thriller *The Innocent* (1990), would try to tap the resources not only of the realist novel, but of action, suspense and genre fiction. In Andrzej Gasiorek's terms, both writers bid to move 'beyond realism and experimentalism' (1995: 179). They were major avatars, therefore, of the shift that Richard Bradford posits, in which a subsequent generation that he calls 'domesticated postmodernists' would craft intellectually playful novels for a mass Waterstone's public (2007: 47–78). 'Postmodernism' – though a significant and influential term in the 1980s, as we shall see in Chapter Three – is too globally capacious to capture the specificity of Amis or McEwan's location and moment. An exhibition of period photographs at the National Portrait Gallery in 2009 was simply called 'Martin Amis and Friends', signalling cultural history's uncharacteristic inability to name this moment.

Turks, Nutters, Martians

The one label that did stick derived from another genre. Craig Raine (b. 1944), in a now familiar pattern, had graduated from Oxford (where he had even taught Amis at Exeter College) before working on Hamilton's *New Review*, then as poetry editor at the *New Statesman*. In 1977 Raine published the poem 'A Martian Sends a Postcard Home', which two years later appeared as the title poem of a whole volume. James Fenton meanwhile secured the idea of a new poetic, in October 1978 reprinting Raine's poem alongside his review, 'Of the Martian School', in – again – the *New Statesman*. The idea was that everyday objects and sights should be described as though encountered by a visitor from Mars: viewed without preconceptions, they could be seen again. Thus the benignly attentive extra-terrestrial reports on the telephone:

In homes, a haunted apparatus sleeps,
that snores when you pick it up.

If the ghost cries, they carry it
to their lips and soothe it to sleep

with sounds. And yet, they wake it up
deliberately, by tickling with a finger. (Morrison and Motion 1982: 169)

The new method is clearly traditional. The Russian Formalist Viktor Shklovsky in 1917 had theorised the 'defamiliarisation' of well-known items as a central property of literary language as such (Shklovsky 1965). The Martian is a device to heighten and ensure this effect. Its lack of human co-ordinates gives the poet a rule to cleave to, making defamiliarisation more constant and thoroughgoing. Raine's method introduces science fiction to poetry: through the narrating presence of a Martian, of course, but also through the imposition of laws (here the Martian's innocence of earthly ways) that the text must uphold. Darko Suvin's notion (1979) of science fiction as a literature of cognitive estrangement is given a verse inflection by Raine's unworldly visitor.

Martianism gathered attention and granted fresh glamour to metaphor, but it was not about to indoctrinate a decade of poets with a new dogma. Michael Hofman (2000) disdainfully looks back on it as 'a movement of one', though Christopher Reid was also thus labelled. By the time Faber published Raine's collection *Rich* (1984: its title harmonising with *Money* the same year) Raine himself was not exhibiting the extra-terrestrial conceit. The volume does luxuriate in metaphor, as in the poem 'City Gent', which commences:

> On my desk, a set of labels
> or a synopsis of leeks,
> blanched by the sun
> and trailing their roots
>
> like a watering can.
> Beyond and below,
> diminished by distance,
> a taxi shivers at the lights:
>
> a shining moorhen
> with an orange nodule
> set over the beak,
> taking a passenger
>
> under its wing. (Raine 1984: 23)

The poem shows its method as it goes along, requiring the reader to pick up the abiding convention. Urban items (labels, a taxi, 'the Chairman's Mercedes') are simultaneously rural ones, images of vegetable and animal life or of a more contemplative existence (a 'four-tier file', 'spotted with rust', is 'a study of plaice / by a Japanese master'). The second set of imagery perhaps gives a solace amid and against the first – or on a more positive view of modern existence, grants it an extra dimension of imaginative enchantment. The taxi as moorhen becomes alive as it 'shivers at the lights', and the image gives it also a benevolent cast as it takes a passenger 'under its wing'. Raine's diction in the stanzas quoted is not recondite: he frequently makes do with very ordinary English words, though as the poem ends he does turn to Ovidian allusion.

That compound of simplicity, metaphor and historical parallel is also visible in the poems of domestic life that *Rich* offers in its first section, also called 'Rich'. In its opening and title poem Raine describes a matriarch whose domestic blessings are the relevant 'riches': 'Her cattle are children, / each with a streaming cold, / and this is her bull / drooling over his dummy' (16). 'In Modern Dress' likewise encodes the life of children at play through allusions. When a child climbs 'the family tree / to queen it over us', the parents look up at 'her face, / its pale prerogative / to rule our hearts'. If this girl has become Elizabeth I, an adjacent boy is cast as a contemporary: 'Sir Walter Raleigh / trails his comforter / about the muddy garden', and in a neat conceit he discovers 'the potato / in its natural state / for the very first time', not to mention another apt discovery, a cigarette end (18–19).

Raine's 'Rich' world is thus apt to be an ordinary one (English, middle-class) in which 'richness' (like the joys of family life) is already owned, and also discovered afresh through an enriching poetry. The book's latter part, 'Poor', returns us to Raine's childhood before the materially enriching translations of class and education, though its central prose piece, 'A Silver Plate', makes it clear that other kinds of riches (of language or of manual skills, or even the pleasures of popular culture like the cinema or *Eagle* comic) were also available to 'my working-class existence' (57). The book's architecture is careful, but its poems are lucid, cast for the most part in steady tercets or quatrains, often with the slender three-stress line of the trimeter. In 'Gaugin' Raine's language suddenly becomes newly challenging: 'They going upstair / take longtime lookit shedownstair. // They going upstair / so hedownstair go plenty upstair' (30). But he also writes in tones which, unlike those in that poem, might have been Philip Larkin's: 'So how is life with your new bloke?', 'An Attempt at Jealousy' chattily commences, wondering 'How is life with an oarsman? Better? / More in-out? Athletic? Wetter?' (28). Raine's epigraphic references to *Ulysses*, Picasso and Dante are erudite, but the poetry retains a desire to communicate, whether through flamboyant metaphor or this display of prurience. It also retains a sense of the personal. This is not exactly 'confessional' poetry, and far more tightly controlled than Robert Lowell's adventures in that direction twenty years earlier, but – as with Raine's Irish contemporary Paul Muldoon – the domestic world, of coupling, childrearing or growing up, is frequently the primary sphere of operations. It would be another decade before Raine produced his most ambitiously public book of poetry, and even *History: The Home Movie* (1994) attends to the twentieth century through the entwined family genealogies of Raine and his wife.

Meanwhile Raine had secured a significant post in the poetry world, as editor at Faber & Faber from 1981. Andrew Motion (b. 1952: another Oxford graduate, who had edited *Poetry Review* rather than working for the *New Statesman*) held the equivalent role at Chatto & Windus (1982–9). Mainstream poetry in Britain was thus to a significant degree in the hands of poets in their thirties, though Raine and Motion would not win the approval of those – like Bob Cobbing, Iain Sinclair or Tony Lopez – who flew the standard of underground and neo-modernist poetry. Indeed Motion ruffled more feathers when with Blake Morrison (b. 1950) he co-edited the *Penguin Book of Contemporary British Poetry* in 1982. We shall return in Chapter Three to this enduringly controversial collection, which presented Martian poems as a significant feature of the contemporary scene.

But Martianism's most notable literary achievement after Raine's keynote poem was arguably in the novel. Martin Amis' fourth novel *Other People* (1981) centres on a woman who wakes from a coma bereft of memory, the ordinary world around her turned unfamiliar. She is thus a book-length version of Raine's alien, who rediscovers everyday objects through conjecture and misunderstandings. That Amis should be the most dedicated Martian after Raine is apt enough, given that 'Martianism' is an anagram of his name. In *Money* the project of estrangement continues. The narrator's local pub is 'full of turks, nutters, martians': 'The foreigners round here. I know they don't speak English – okay, but do they even speak Earthling? They speak stereo, radio crackle, interference. They speak sonar, bat-chirrup, pterodactylese, fish purr' (1984: 87). The complaint starts out looking ignorant, even bigoted; but it slips into a fluency that puts the speaker out ahead of us, on his own high linguistic frequency. The description is prose, but its unfolding lists of transfiguring metaphor might easily be rendered into a richly auditory poem. The speaker complains that foreign drinkers are 'martians', but he is the one who voices the perceptions of the Martian poet. As the novel ends, in a late metaphorical flourish, he is even viewing the sky as an eggtray, seasoned with 'the sunset's streaky bacon': 'the night clouds are gaunt and equine, like doorkeys at an angle or Spanish locomotives' (393). Not only the line's audacious imagery but even its rhythm, finally promising to transfigure itself into a tetrameter, shows the hand of a writer who can treat prose as poetry by other means.

This brings us to a crux in Amis' novel. Its narrator, John Self, is a veteran of resolutely lowbrow television commercials who has been enticed into making a film, to be called *Bad Money* or perhaps *Good Money*, which entails regular flights to New York. *Money*'s plot describes Self's rise and fall: he gains spectacularly in wealth and power, yet they prove illusory and transient, the products of a hoax, and at the end he is once again scraping by in unlovely London. The 400–page book consists entirely of Self's massive monologue. Working-class in origin, he presents himself as 'the new kind' of social actor: 'the kind that has money but can never use it for anything but ugliness. To which I say: you never let us in, not really. You might have thought you let us in, but you never did. You just gave us some money' (58). As a conscious spokesman for the *nouveau riche*, Self represents a significant social development and cultural unease of the period. His combination of wads of cash with coarseness, violence and misogyny make him – even more than Amis may have guessed when he began writing the book – a characteristic period figure. The working-class lad who has struck it rich without bothering to acquire the educational and cultural capital hitherto associated with wealth would be repeatedly echoed later, in the prevalent image of the barrow-boy become successful city trader, or satirically in Harry Enfield's comic creation Loadsamoney, an obnoxious plasterer who waved his 'wad' of cash at the audience. Self is in some respects more sympathetic, despite his wanton, violent and reactionary tendencies. James Diedrick judges him 'so fully, triumphantly realized that most readers will warm to him in spite of themselves' (2004: 77). What he is not is eloquent. His actual speech in the novel is apt to be stumbling and monosyllabic. Yet the book he narrates is among the most flamboyantly written in the history of the English novel: a roller-coaster of registers and an almost unbelievably dense texture of jokes, allusions, repetitions, 'Martian' descriptions and lyrical excursions. Some critics have soberly complained about the inconsistency (Powell 2008: 330), while Amis himself has vaguely called the book 'the novel that John Self, the narrator, had in him but would never write' (Amis 2000: 6), gesturing at the capacity of Saul Bellow and John Updike to produce poetry from an ordinary man's inchoate thoughts. But *Money*'s impossible voice – a yob who thinks the way Martin Amis writes – is better understood simply as a vast conceit, an authorial convenience and the biggest joke in the book.

Money thus yokes two very different tendencies, both of which it performs to an unusual degree. On one hand social reference, an engagement with the changing patterns of the real world; on the other sheer artifice, a delight in literariness and language as ends in themselves. We may hear an echo of Amis' dual aspiration to be as tricksy as Robbe-Grillet and as readable as Austen, though the terms of *Money*'s combination are different: instead of the 'staid satisfactions' of plot (which is among the novel's weaknesses) it bids to bring us news. The duality can also be read as marrying the aesthetics of Amis' avowed literary masters: Saul Bellow's urban vistas and social prophecies, and Vladimir Nabokov's sense of literature as ludic and autotelic, a language game with special rules. In a novel just as pickled with alcohol as *The Old Devils*, we are a long way from reading 'he finished his drink and left'.

If, as Amis later declared, 'the project is to become an American novelist' (Leader 2002: 3), *Money* was the project's most important step. Its narrator, though given to such recognisably English locutions as 'On your bike' (56) and 'Come on, darling, you know you love it' (62), spent half his childhood in New Jersey and 'pitched my voice somewhere in the mid-Atlantic' (206). Something similar can be said of Amis himself, at least in his diction (Powell 2008: 265), and the aspiration to Americana is central to his career. That he has a 'project' at all is striking; the self-consciousness and ambition mark him out in English letters. To be distinct from that world is precisely the point: in his youth, he explains, it had felt 'hopelessly inert and inbred', while 'American fiction was assuming its manifest destiny' (Amis 2004). Amis' attempt to be less English is powered by his own considerable self-confidence, but is also part of a pattern of internationalism among his generation. Amis writes of English writing needing its 'crucial infusion from the "colonials"' (2004), and the great internationalising gesture to match his was Salman Rushdie's arrival with *Midnight's Children* (1981), a book we will consider in detail in Chapter Three. England, it seemed, could be reinvigorated by an Indian 'reverse colonisation'. Meanwhile Ishiguro's first novels *A Pale View of Hills* (1982) and *An Artist of the Floating World* (1986) both returned to the legacy of Japan after the detonation of the first atom bombs in 1945; the author's understated manner as well as his traumatic subject matter suggested an Anglo-Japanese fusion. And Julian Barnes, from *Metroland*'s memories of Paris in the late 1960s to the literary investigations of *Flaubert's Parrot* (1984), was seeking a rapprochement between English and French literature as Henry James, an earlier promoter of Flaubert, had done a century earlier. Michèle Roberts (b. 1949), of Anglo-French dual heritage, explored similar connections, though from her background in feminist writing and activism she took longer to reach the mainstream than the well-connected Barnes. There is thus a diversely centrifugal aspect to the generation of novelists who were around thirty at the start of the decade; in various ways English literature was being renewed or rethought via another national tradition. A new enthusiasm for (largely non-fictional) travel writing added to this outward gaze. It was encouraged by a special issue of

Granta in 1984, and exemplified by Bruce Chatwin in his exploration
of Australian aborigine culture *The Songlines* (1986), not to mention
Rushdie's journey to revolutionary Nicaragua in *The Jaguar Smile*
(1987).

In this respect Amis' transatlantic ambition was historically representative. But he remains a distinctive figure in his single-handed bid to
make literature moody, exciting, fashionable; to give it some of the cool
and swagger of rock & roll. Amis' public persona – drawling, pouting,
chain-smoking, his pronouncements momentous yet laconic – was part
of this. If any major writer in the 1980s was essaying the role of 'celebrity author', it was he. *Money* carefully distinguishes John Self's impos-
sibly excessive lifestyle of drink, drugs and fast food from that of Martin
Amis, through the latter's disconcerting appearance as a character in the
book. But the novel's streetwise ease in London boozer or Manhattan
bar was of a piece with the Amis effect: he did not make his reputation
by writing polite pastoral or middle-class family saga. Neil Powell has
justly pointed to the narrowness of Amis' fictional world (2008: 341,
349). By the pre-millennial apocalypse *London Fields* (1989), let alone
its metropolitan sequels in subsequent decades, Amis' scarred urban
environment, peopled by depthless caricatures and grotesques, seems a
mannerism that he is powerless to escape. In *Money*, though, the hard-
boiled monologue of late modernity is new-minted and endlessly inventive. However weary the battered narrator grows, the puppeteer behind
him is wide awake. He renders the cityscape in subtly rhythmic cadences
and constantly renewed junctures of adjective and noun: 'So now I stand
here with my case, in smiting light and island rain. Behind me massed
water looms, and the industrial corsetry of FDR Drive' (1984: 3). At the
other end of the scale Amis stoops to daft gags that a stand-up comic
might pay to use. A sign in a cab thanks Self for not smoking: 'I hate
that. I mean, it's a bit previous, isn't it, don't you think? I haven't not
smoked yet. As it turned out, I never did not smoke in the end. I lit a
cigarette and kept them coming' (105). *Money* has gone down as one
of the books of the decade because its subject matter is so presciently
close to the image that Thatcherism would leave in the public mind. But
like *Ulysses* and *Lolita* it endures not merely as reportage of a time and
place, but as an astonishing, unrepeatable feat of writing.

Unrepeatable, even for Amis: but could anyone else learn from
Money? Ian Sansom (2004) has joked that everyone on the Left in
Britain used to read *The Ragged-Trousered Philanthropists*: 'Then in
1984 everyone put it down and picked up *Money*.' We shall see in the
next chapter that industry, unemployment and poverty by no means
dropped out of British writing in the 1980s; but some young writers

explored aspects of the territory Amis had broached. Michael Bracewell (b. 1958) supplemented his living by writing for the style press, and remained more interested than any other novelist in the cultural changes overtaking Britain since the 1970s: marketing, shopping malls, exotic sandwiches and 'death by Capuccino' (Bracewell 2001: 37). In *The Crypto-Amnesia Club*, published in 1988 by the adventurous new press Serpent's Tail, Bracewell conjures a stark, stylised London of dark streets and nightclubs, like The Beach:

> Although the marbling on a roll is looking a little tired these days, some kind of corporate identity has evolved that keeps a constant stream of youngsters in there, reciting lists to one another and going to the toilet in between sips of mutant aperitifs and filtered drafts of lukewarm gossip. (1988: 39)

The mutant aperitifs might appeal to John Self, but Bracewell's style is more languid. Eschewing Amis' hyperactive riffing, he aspires to be a Scott Fitzgerald for the late Thatcher years, already nostalgic by his late twenties. Finance, as Peter York has indicated (York and Jennings 1995: 106–8), had become central to Britain's picture of its present by the late 1980s, and Bracewell accordingly meditates on it as his narrator Merril paces the City of London:

> To have that power, the power of obscurity at a dizzy height, the high on the lonely horizon – to not even know what industries one is captain of anymore; to cease caring altogether about the visible and simply play with new sculptures that plate-tectonically reunite the constantly shifting values of abstract currencies – maybe that's a life. (1988: 44)

The invisible motions of money, already discreetly central to the plot of *Money* itself (Amis 1984: 376), were gaining in fascination for writers.

Bracewell would continue to pursue the connections between money and style as the 1980s ended; *Divine Concepts of Physical Beauty* (1989) and *The Conclave* (1992) are significant fictional portraits of London after the Lawson Boom. Geoff Dyer (b. 1959) presents a matching obverse. Where Bracewell's characters are often as slickly wealthy as yuppies in a TV advert or Bryan Ferry video, Dyer's debut *The Colour of Memory* (1989) depicts a batch of unemployed twenty-somethings in Brixton who live largely from the dole and housing benefit in 1986–7. Yet far from showing the desolation of unemployment as other writers were doing, Dyer's dole-agers form an almost utopian community in which work is displaced by the more desirable activities as reading, drinking, music and sport. Amis' trace is visible in the young Dyer's style: in both the continually vivid imagery (in a pub, 'someone with a double barrel gut sucked at his pint like a dinosaur cooling its head in a mug of mud' [39]) and the cheeky inversions of normal sense, akin to Self's declaration that 'Really living is what I'm doing, and it's killing me' (Amis 1984: 270). When Dyer's narrator's useless car (an echo of Self's Fiasco, which 'doesn't *like* driving' [Amis 1984: 261]) is stolen, he wishes he could have been on the street a few minutes earlier, in time to thank the thieves (26). Amis – as Dyer himself would later insist (1999: 237) – is remarkably unconvincing when plotting a long novel; but Dyer has even less affinity for plot, and *The Colour of Memory* proceeds not as a purposeful storyline but simply as sixty numbered sections counting chronologically down to zero through the year. Dyer is interested in the insignificant, or – in the imagery favoured by the novel – in the random details that enter the margins of a photograph (1989: 181–2). When his narrator finds himself alone at a friend's house, the result is emblematic:

> I circled the phone and played the start of some records, looked out of the window at the nothing-happening grey of the sky, turned a tap on and off, read one and a half lines of the paper and then put it down again. I turned on the TV and found horse-racing on both sides. I watched for about twenty minutes, ignoring the horses and concentrating instead on the suburban hinterland in the background: a place where it always drizzled, a place that didn't look like anywhere. I turned the TV off, picked up one of Freddie's books and studied the Olympic coffee rings on the cover. (22)

Dyer's novel effectively switches off narrative, and records the detail and contingency that remain. In eschewing the demands of plot, *The Colour of Memory* leaves itself open to the texture of a time, and becomes one of the finest fictional records of its era.

Coining It

Novelists like Bracewell and Dyer followed Amis as chroniclers of the metropolis, while also depicting the experience of a generation that was already, by decade's end, beyond his ken. But *Money*'s major rival as a literary analysis of contemporary capital arose in another genre. Caryl Churchill's play *Serious Money* was staged at the Royal Court in the spring of 1987, with the consumer boom still at its height. The play depicts traders in international finance, notably on the floor of the London International Financial Futures Exchange (LIFFE). The plot is powered by two developments: the attempted takeover of a large company, Albion Products, by the rapacious businessman Bill Corman, and the mysterious death of the young trader Jake Todd. Jake's sister Scilla decides to investigate, discomfiting a series of high rollers in the process. Drama arises equally from the fluctuating fortunes of Corman's takeover, which is finally abandoned after a quiet word from a Conservative MP anxious to avoid a politically damaging scandal.

Churchill researched the play on the suggestion of Max Stafford-Clark of Joint Stock Theatre Company, a co-operative that had contributed to the blossoming of radical British theatre in the 1970s. *Serious Money* grew from a two-week workshop in 1986 in which Churchill and the company investigated the City of London. The City was preparing for the 'Big Bang' of financial deregulation, a flagship policy of Thatcher's second term. The theatrical collective contrasted deeply with the individualism encouraged by government policy and exemplified by the ambitious trader. But Churchill also found in the City a network of interrelated characters with which to make an ensemble. She produced a play centring not just on individuals but on an institution.

The dramatic material was novel. In the first major speech in the play Jake and Scilla's father, Greville Todd, is describing a chain of hotels that a company has acquired: '70 per cent business, 3 and 4 star. They acquired them for sixteen million, the assets are in fact valued at eleven million but that's historic and they're quite happy about that. The key to the deal is there's considerable earnings enhancement.' It emerges that shares are

> 63 to 4 in the market, I can let you have them for 62½ net. At the moment the profits are fourteen million pretax which is eleven million, the shares pay 4.14 with a multiple of 13.3. With the new hotels we expect to see a profit of twenty million next year paying 5.03 with the multiple falling to 12, so it's very attractive. (Churchill 1990: 197–8)

What does an audience make of this? In truth, most spectators will have to let it wash past them, accepting that this is a discourse that they cannot keep up with in a live performance (and is hard enough to follow on the page). The barrage of numbers may seem lacking in poetry, but continues to crowd Churchill's script. Greville's telephone call is followed by a scene in which a dealing room is juxtaposed with Scilla on the LIFFE floor, each character wielding two telephones:

GRIMES *(on phone)*
Scilla? Sell at 3.
SCILLA *(On two phones. To floor)*
10 at 3. 10 at 3.
(On phone 2)
That's March is it?
MATE *(Phone)*
6 Bid.

GRIMES *(Phone)*
What you doing tonight?
SCILLA *(To floor)*
4 for 10. 4 for 10. Are you looking at me?
4 for 10. (1990: 198)

In a scene like this, the numbers with which the characters constantly work become Churchill's primary material, relegating words themselves to an interloper's role amid the exchange of figures. The new linguistic texture indicates the novelty of the material. But *Serious Money* also opens by indicating that its material is not so new, with a brief scene excerpted from Thomas Shadwell's *The Volunteers* or *The Stockjobbers*. Already in the late seventeenth century two 'Jobbers' are offering 'Patents' to their customers the Hackwells, which promise 'walking under Water, a share twenty pound', to 'kill all fleas in all the families in England', or 'to outfly any post horse'. The offers sound preposterous; the point of the scene is that their substance is unimportant. '[B]etween us,' Hackwell declares, 'it's no matter whether it turns to use or not; the main end verily is to turn the penny in the way of stock jobbing, that's all' (Churchill 1990: 196–7). The principle finds its echo in the main body of *Serious Money*, where Scilla explains the concept of 'futures' in products: '[Y]ou don't have to take delivery of anything at all. / You can buy and sell futures contracts without any danger of ending up with ten tons of pork bellies in the hall' (244). '[O]ptions and futures,' proposes another character, 'are more important than physicals' (267). The Marxist geographer David Harvey would soon argue that such virtuality, trading goods that need never exist, was not only typical but actually formative of the pervading culture of ephemerality and indeterminacy, in an age when the world had 'come to rely, for the first time in its history, upon immaterial forms of money' (1990: 297). *Serious Money* is in this sense a fiction about fictions.

The use of Shadwell's *Stockjobbers* as prologue opens an utterly topical play onto history, prompting the audience to reflect on continuities underlying well-publicised changes in the City. This small gesture is just one instance of the formal diversity and ingenuity of Churchill's play. Another is her decision, arrived at late in the writing process, to cast most of the play in rhyme. Verse drama, though not necessarily rhymed, had been the great theatrical cause of T. S. Eliot and Christopher Fry in mid-century, and is often associated with an unusable past. Churchill reverses this perception, making verse the vehicle of modernity. One of its effects is to make us marvel at the skill of the author who can keep the rhymes coming and the narrative flowing simultaneously – and here form and content also rhyme, for Churchill's feat in keeping the plates spinning is aptly analogous to the dealers' skill in juggling futures. Much of the verse produces bathos:

DUCKETT
I'm Duckett. I enjoy the *Financial Times*.
It's fun reading about other people's crimes.
My company Albion's price is looking perky.
I think I'll buy that villa in the south of Turkey. (226)

The bathos is part of the atmosphere: in its 'consciously graceless doggerel verse' (Shepherd and Womack 1996: 336), the play shuns any pretensions to high lyricism, instead following the characters' low cunning and material interests. Rhyme also lends the whole play an air of artifice, elevating it from documentary detail to stylised cabaret, and ensures that however devious or impenetrable the characters' machinations, the play remains buoyant. The effect is heightened by songs closing the plays' two acts, and by the sheer speed with which the script is to be played. Churchill reprises the series of extra notations, previously introduced in *Top Girls* (1982), that indicate where dialogue should overlap and characters interrupt and speak over each other. A whole page of authorial notes is needed to explain these conventions (195), such is Churchill's dedication to maintaining garrulous speed on stage.

   In another sense also speed is dramatised here. David Harvey observes

Figure 3   Listen To Money Singing: the cast of Caryl Churchill's *Serious Money*, 1987

that twentieth-century technology and finance have induced a process of 'time-space compression', in which distances are effectively abolished through instantaneous communication (1990: 293–5). In *Serious Money* too, space has become fluid, as scenes melt into one another, characters walk on and off for brief cameos from different parts of the globe, and we witness telephone calls between continents. Rather than the drawing-room with its fourth wall removed, a shifting series of locations passes before the audience, talking to each other regardless of their physical separation. Act Two even commences (254–5) with a monologue from an aeroplane. Churchill's open conception of stage space makes the play a significant moment in British theatre's depiction of an ever more interconnected globe.

Serious Money is a critical view of the City, though Peter Womack justly argues that the play 'cannot help, theatrically, warming to the collapse of inhibitions, the sexual rush of energy' associated with its subject (Shepherd and Womack 1996: 336). Three specific strands of political insight should also be noted, all relating to the relation between finance and culture. One is the alternating conflict and complicity of old and new money: the bankers who impress Americans by fox-hunting in the English countryside (211–16), or the stand-off between the traditionalist Frosby ('My lovely city's sadly changed') and the financial 'vandal' Grimes:

> You've all been coining it for years.
> All you fuckwits in the City.
> It just don't look quite so pretty,
> All the cunning little jobs,
> When you see them done by yobs. (282–3)

Grimes insists that class manners should not obscure the continuity: the 'yobs' are no more exploitative than the supposed gentlemen of yesteryear. Churchill echoes this in a second strand, concerning Corman's takeover of Albion. The 'white knight' Biddulph tells Duckett, Albion's chairman, to improve his image – 'Think of it from the PR angle. You're an old-fashioned firm. A good old English firm that has the loyalty of its employees and the support of the local community' – even as Duckett comically continues to insist on his adherence to 'hardhitting' neoliberal doctrine (235). Churchill's uncompromising socialist view is that it is naive to see one company as more ethically acceptable than another: our suspicion of capital should not be assuaged by friendly public relations. These are also involved in a final theme: corporate use of the arts. Biddulph advises Duckett to commission 'a mural called Urban and Rural' (274); Corman's PR advisor responds by recommending 'the National / Theatre for power, opera for decadence, / String quartets bearing your name for sensitivity and elegance, / And a fringe show with bad language for a thrill' (286). It is thus significant that Corman's encounter with the MP Gleason takes place at the National Theatre, during the interval of a production of *King Lear*. Neither of them is really watching the play; Gleason, mixing two tragedies with geopolitics, thinks it involves 'Goneril and Reagan and Ophelia' (297). But the National – mirroring Patrick Mills' view of celebrity publishing – lends them cultural capital to stack atop mere wealth, and will do no harm to Gleason's pursuit of 'Five more glorious years of free enterprise' at the 1987 election (299). The Royal Court audience watch a scene in which theatre's use as political ornament is acknowledged.

Given this canny awareness of theatre's status, it would be wrong to tax Churchill over the widely-reported spectacle of nightly parties of City traders enjoying her play. If it had folded quickly or only been attended by students and CND members, there would be more cause to doubt her acuity in penetrating the financial world. That a feminist working in the theatrical tradition of Bertolt Brecht could seize the attention of a champagne-bar audience, while not stinting in the stringency of her vision of the City, is in fact an impressive achievement. It is also a reminder that the most acute literary accounts of the present did not only come from the newest generations, or those who remained 'brilliantly detached'. Churchill was forty-eight when *Serious Money* appeared, a veteran of socialist and feminist cultural politics. In the next chapter we shall consider the potency of other voices from the political Left, whose characters could do with even some unserious money.

Chapter Two

Disaffections

In *Culture and Society 1780–1950* (1958), Raymond Williams identified the Industrial Novel as a subgenre in its own right: a place where social conditions, indeed the condition of England, were discussed.

> Our understanding of the response to industrialism would be incomplete without reference to an interesting group of novels, written at the middle of the [nineteenth] century, which not only provide some of the most vivid descriptions of life in an unsettled industrial society, but also illustrate certain common assumptions within which the direct response was undertaken. There are the facts of the new society, and there is this structure of feeling [. . .]. (1963: 99)

Williams' last phrase remains a useful way of describing imaginative responses to social change. But where Williams identified a literature of industrialisation, in reviewing the Britain of the 1980s we can more plausibly seek a literature of *de*-industrialisation; and of the landscape, social conditions and identities associated with that process. In the Introduction we considered the culture of public relations and consumption as central to the experience of the decade. But the process of deindustrialisation and mass unemployment was as central to many people's lives. The two processes stood as contrary aspects of contemporary Britain. To an extent they could be distributed geographically. Finance, service industries and increased disposable income were centred primarily in London and the South-East. The industries of coal, steel and shipbuilding were concentrated in the North of England, Wales and Scotland. The North-South divide, already confronted by the Victorian industrial novelists grouped by Williams, became once again a predominant image of national life. Landscape reflected economic activity. The rusting pit-head or abandoned shipyard, as much as the wine bar or renovated high street, were prevailing images. They presented a nation of contrasts, in which economic inequality was verifiably growing.

The historian Eric Hopkins has argued that the comparative standard of living of the British working class reached its high point in the 1960s. Through the 1970s and 1980s, the traditional manufacturing base of the British economy was in decline. In the mid-1980s, foreign imported goods exceeded British exports for the first time: a sign that Britain was becoming less a land of production, more a site of consumption and services. With recession in 1979–81, Hopkins notes, unemployment figures came to match and even exceed the levels of the 1930s, even while government was seen to be massaging the dole figures to keep the official totals down (1991: 195, 215). As the number of unemployed reached 3 million, the bargaining power of those in work was diminished. Unemployment became an additional weapon in the hands of government and employers, to the detriment of trades unions which were being steadily challenged and weakened by government legislation. With pay increases and progress limited, Hopkins avers, the 1980s saw a 'slowing up in the standard of living' for the British working class (1991: 198), and most strikingly a widening of the gulf between employed and unemployed. Hopkins repeatedly draws a parallel between the Depression years of the 1930s and the 1980s with their processes of recession and deindustrialisation. Yet, he proposes, there was no literature of the new dole age to match that of the earlier decade. To be sure, the 1930s remain associated with Orwell, the Left Book Club, documentary and reportage, and even the leftist poets of the Spanish Civil War. But we are about to see that the Thatcher years did produce their own literature of dissidence, specifically in relation to the changing industrial climate and the condition of the working class, not to mention those for whom work itself was a memory. This chapter will pursue the contemporary structure of feeling through a sequence of writers: the screenwriter Alan Bleasdale; the novelist Pat Barker; the poets Tony Harrison and Sean O'Brien; and finally a more formally extreme case, the fiction of James Kelman.

Dominic Head plausibly assesses the long-term effects of Thatcherism on class identity:

> In contemporary Britain, poverty is no longer the province of wage-laborers, whose toil is defended by an effective union, and ameliorated by factory clubs and socials. Changes that have taken place since the rise of Thatcherism – the curbing of union powers, the imposition of strict productivity regimes, and the disappearance of traditional working-class communities – have meant that there is no longer a collective working-class experience with which to identify (as there still was in the 1960s and 1970s). (2006: 229–30)

The texts we are about to consider register the early stages of this process. Unlike later works, they still seek to identify with that 'collective working-class experience'; but they often find that it is already vanishing.

We're Not Winnin' Anymore

The television series *Boys from the Blackstuff* (1982) was among the first cultural works of the 1980s to register these circumstances. In doing so it swiftly became iconic, in an era when television, only just moving from three to four channels, was a major source of shared national experience. The programme followed Alan Bleasdale's earlier, longer film, *The Blackstuff* (1980), in which the main characters were introduced: a group of tarmac layers and builders from Liverpool who travel to undertake a job in Middlesbrough, and wind up losing their life savings as well as their jobs. This pilot set the conditions for the five-part series that followed, which commences with all five main characters queueing to claim benefits in the DHSS office and offering emblematic vignettes of their distinct personalities.

Formally speaking, *Blackstuff* was essentially a piece of television realism, with a conventional use of *mise en scène*, camerawork and editing, spiced and heightened with handheld camera, location shooting and point-of-view shots. It represents the legacy of a particular age of realistic, socially engaged television drama: from the BBC's *Wednesday Play* (1964–70) through to drama about labour activism like *The Big Flame* (1969) and *Days of Hope* (1975). *Blackstuff* was the late-flowering fruit of a particular conjuncture: the admission of artists from the political Left to the channels of public service broadcasting, in the 1960s and 1970s. Bleasdale stated his intentions in November 1978, in a letter proposing the series:

> I think it very important right now to write about the Dole as seen from the point of view of those who are on it, and to side with them against the people and papers who would like us to believe, despite the million and a half out of work and mass redundancies at every opportunity, that the majority of the unemployed are malingerers and rogues. (Millington 1993: 121)

As Bob Millington has pointed out (122), there was a kind of grim fortune in the delay between this proposal and the production and broadcast. The programme would come to seem far more topical in autumn 1982, when unemployment had passed not 1.5 million but 3 million – a figure widely considered to be politically unsustainable.

Some of *Blackstuff*'s impact derives from its mimetic power, particularly in portraying the physicality of poverty. The series repeatedly stages the sheer intransigence of the material world in conditions of extreme poverty. Thus Angie, Chrissie's wife, wonders whether the young children are going to be 'wearing hand-me-downs at eighteen and twenty': 'What are we bringing them up for – and what is the point of livin' our lives when . . . when ye' get up in the mornin' and it's all downhill from then on . . . two ounces of spam and a quarter of brawn.' She shows Chrissie her shoe in which a hole has been filled with cardboard. 'Walk on one leg, you'll be alright,' he drily responds (1983: 143). This sense of the body itself as the centre of suffering or frustration is also visible in the world of would-be work, where Yosser utters Bleasdale's most famous lines as he follows a groundsman marking the touchline for a football pitch: 'Gizza job, go on, gizzit . . . gizza go, go on. I could do that. You only have to walk straight' (152) The work, which is unreachable mana to Yosser, requires the simplest bodily qualification, yet remains tantalisingly unavailable. He says the same to the rent collector's minder – 'I could do that. I can carry things. I've had practice' (161) – and even repeats the motif to the men who repossess his house near the end of his episode.

There is special pathos in this, in that the central male characters have all been men whose living came from working upon and transforming matter. Chrissie's speech to Angie at the climax of episode three voices this explicitly, even sentimentally: 'It wasn't a bad job, and I was good at it. I laid the roads, girl. *I laid the roads.* Motorways, laybys, country lanes [. . .] I could tamper and grit like nobody you ever saw. Nobody put the black stuff down quite like me' (141). Such wistful talk has replaced the action Chrissie describes. Angie thinks that talk, specifically comedy, has taken over from action. Chrissie's wry one-liners draw her ire: 'It's not funny, it's not friggin' funny. I've had enough of that – if you don't laugh, you'll cry – I've heard it for years – this stupid soddin' city's full of it – well, why don't you cry – why don't you scream – why don't you fight back, you bastard?' (143). Angie accuses Liverpool as a whole of taking refuge from oppression in humour, sublimating pain into laughter. She alerts us to the way in which talk can replace action, eloquence displace energy.

The one character in *Blackstuff* who unites eloquence and action is Snowy, the revolutionary who features in the first episode. He is given not only to diatribes about police brutality and the threat of an English fascism – statements that the other characters mock and thus somewhat undermine – but also to perorations about the pride of work, the value of traditional craft in building. He would plaster for nothing if his political principles allowed, he says: 'Y'know, doin' something' y' good at

– there's nothin' like it. Standin' there in the mornin' facin' four empty walls – an' then goin' home at night with the plaster all dry and smooth – an' the bit y've just done all wet an' shinin' . . .' (34). We finally see Snowy etching his own name into the corner of a wall he has plastered, on the model of an old master. He is the one character in the series who manages to engage with the world's matter in what he might call an instance of unalienated labour. But this character, having been allowed to set a utopian example, immediately perishes while fleeing the officers of the Fraud Department.

Blackstuff is not only a slice of dour naturalism. It also marshals black comedy and absurdity. These gather especially in the fourth episode, 'Yosser's Story'. Yosser has undergone a mental deterioration after the pilot film, in which it is his money-making scheme that goes wrong. On the building site in episode one, the contractor, Malloy, tells him 'son, the last time you laid bricks was when you had a Lego set' (43), and is headbutted for his trouble. Yosser is the only character who fulfils Angie's desire to 'fight back'. But fighting in this way cannot ultimately win the day. Yosser's episode traces a downward spiral from an already low point. He loses job, wife and children, and his final suicide attempt in a lake is foiled by police rescue. The episode opens at the same lake, with a dream sequence in which Yosser sees himself and his children drowning. Other characters float by in punts – dressed, the script tells us, for the Henley Regatta. The episode thus starts in the realm of the surreal, though this is diegetically explained as we see Yosser waking in panic. But in a sense Yosser brings his own air of unreality to proceedings, whenever he appears in the series. Other characters have been affected by unemployment – Chrissie driven to shoot his animals, George Malone rising from his sick bed to arrive at the dole queue in pyjamas – but Yosser has been the most deeply warped on the inside. We increasingly hear this in his speech. His discourse is driven to repetition – sometimes of the deadpan refrain 'Gizza job, I could do that', which became the series' call-sign; still more often a paranoiac reiteration of his own name – 'I'm Yosser Hughes' – as though this too is about to be taken away from him. By the end of episode four, he himself has removed it. Sitting in heavy rain in Williamson Square, he again encounters a Glaswegian wino whom he met earlier. 'Don't I know you from somewhere?' asks the vagrant. Yosser has punctuated the entire episode with the phrase 'I'm Yosser Hughes': now he only mumbles 'I'm . . . I'm . . . I'm wet' (183).

Along with this manic assertion of identity, Yosser also brings a fantastic brand of wordplay. In episode three he is called into the Fraud Office, and makes his case:

Figure 4   I'm Yosser Hughes: Bernard Hill in Alan Bleasdale's *Boys from the Blackstuff*, 1982

YOSSER
And – on Malloy's site that particular day, the day in question, in fact, no money parted company to or from anyone. Who was there. When I was there. No money came my way. Not to my knowledge. Not when I was there. And I should know. Being there. And being me. (*He laughs, and stops dead*) Malloy on no occasion never said to me, 'Here y'are, touch for that.' (*Makes a movement with his hand indicating money being passed*)
ASSISTANT
That's a double negative.
YOSSER
Yeah well there's two of you isn't there? And, as a matter of fact, I was there on a trial basis, but left after one wobbly wall and a short exchange of words, or words to that effect. (112–13)

Some of Yosser's speech here is a pastiche of bureaucracy, or of the constable with his notebook – 'on Malloy's site that particular day, the day in question, in fact' – though it is also marked by oddities, like money 'parting company' rather than, more idiomatically, 'changing hands'. His speech becomes staccato as he jerkily gropes after qualifications and relevant additions – 'Who was there. When I was there. No money came my way. Not to my knowledge. Not when I was there.' He also plays on words, with a nervous comedy: 'a short exchange of words, or words to that effect', and the terrific illogic of a double negative to serve two listeners. But we do not read this as the detached wit of a man in control of the discursive situation; rather as the involuntary incoherence of a man discovering accidental comedy in the ruins of his reason.

Yosser's plight implies a connection between social ills and psychic illness. It makes an interesting comparison to statements in this period by the government and the prime minister herself, in which illness and health were crucial ways of describing the state of the country and the policy course appropriate to it. 'Which is the better nurse?', she asked in a 1980 interview:

> The one who smothers the patient with sympathy and says 'Never mind, dear, there, there, you just lie back and I'll bring you all your meals . . . I'll look after you.' Or the nurse who says 'Now, come on, shake out of it . . . It's time you put your feet on the ground and took a few steps . . .' Which do you think is the better nurse? The one who says come on, you can do it. That's me. (Campbell 2003: 87)

This is a recurring Thatcherite trope of its time. One cannot too simply read individual degradation off from public policy. But the image of damaged mental health, in the socio-economic conditions of the early 1980s, is in part a rhetorical, symbolic refusal of the claim that monetarism is the road to health. James Kelman will follow Bleasdale in presenting alienated men who, far from being able to 'shake out of it', have been shaken into their fractured state.

Among the most poignant scenes in Bleasdale's series is a moment not so much of personal trauma, but of broad historical analysis – when the Marxist Snowy passionately explains to his fellows:

> SNOWY
> [. . .] I mean, it was easy to be a socialist when I was growin' up in the sixties, an' even f'most of the seventies. Everyone was a friggin' socialist then. It was fashionable. But it's not now . . . Everythin's gone sour, everyone's lockin' the door, turnin' the other cheek, lookin' after number one. *But now's the time when we should all be together.* Now's the time when we *need* to be together, 'cos . . . 'cos well we're not winnin' anymore. *Don't you see that? (He pauses)* Like, that's all I'm sayin'.
> CHRISSIE *(Gently)*
> Of course we see it.
> JIMMY
> And the last thing we need is t'be told about it, f'Christ's sake.
> CHRISSIE
> 'Cos deep down, most of us know it. But y'don't look that far, not these days. Not when y' scared Snowy. (1983: 29)

The replies from the other characters are neither a ringing endorsement of Snowy's politics, nor a rejection of them. It is moving to see their grudging, reflexive political solidarity with Snowy, despite their mockery of him. But by the same token they identify themselves as victims who are unable to act on his call. Part of the uncompromising achievement of *Blackstuff* was to give such melancholy a place in the national conversation.

Extinguished Fires

Pat Barker would become best known in the 1990s for her *Regeneration* trilogy of novels about the First World War. Those novels offer a revisionist view of the war, treating it through unexpected accounts of gender and psychology. But this approach to history was in fact already prefigured in Barker's earlier fiction. From the early 1980s, she explored the deindustrialising of the North of England with a persistently gendered perspective. While writing about communities that had revolved around male-dominated industries and places of work, she frequently represented the experience of women, and the construction of masculinity and femininity. Numerous critics present Barker as the recorder of historical margins, chronicling 'the lives that history ignores' (Newman 2005: 101). Appropriately, the feminist publisher Virago – committed to republishing out-of-print texts, as well as new fiction, by women, and thus altering the shape of the literary canon – published Barker's first novel, which the feminist writer Angela Carter had encouraged her to write. *Union Street* (1982) details seven different, but linked stories of female working-class experience, in an unnamed north-eastern community dominated by the matriarchal figure of Iris King. The town historically centres around the steelworks, but this industry is shown – already, in the early 1970s when the novel is set – to be running down; much of the male workforce is unemployed. In juxtaposing seven distinct women's stories, *Union Street* suggests the woven interrelations of a local community that seems relatively autonomous of the rest of the world. Barker has spoken of her interest in representing a 'communal voice', true to the intersubjective resemblances of speech (Newman 2005: 107). John Brannigan (2005: 28–31) has shown how the narrative voice of Barker's first novel seeks to avoid the status of an 'omniscient observer' from outside, and to find collective and 'communal' status at the level of form.

Yet Barker's community is fragile. Repeatedly in her early fiction, social dysfunction is manifested in the extreme form of violence against women. In the opening chapter of *Union Street*, a thirteen-year-old girl is raped. Barker's second novel, *Blow Your House Down* (1984), again set in a northern city, describes the life of prostitutes who are menaced by a serial killer; the book was published after the arrest of the real-world Yorkshire Ripper in 1981. The novel largely eschews a focus on the killer himself; one section from his point of view aside, its four sections concentrate on different women's experiences of work, domesticity and violence, and the degree of community they are able to forge. Peter Childs (2006) proposes that the novel makes the Ripper's crimes part of a broader, gendered oppression. At one point a character cynically observes that marriage is virtually another form of prostitution: 'when you got right down to it, past the white weddings and the romance and all that. What they *really* thought was: if you're getting on your back for a fella, he ought to pay' (Barker 1984: 30). But like *Union Street*, the novel seeks to summon a degree of collectivity in resistance to the dismal conditions it evokes.

Features of these first two novels recur in Barker's third. *The Century's Daughter* was published in 1986 but reissued under the new title, Barker's preference, of *Liza's England* a decade later. Liza Garrett's birth coincides precisely with the dawn of the twentieth century, offering her representative status as a witness to history. Barker's second title for the novel shifts the emphasis from time to space, but retains the implication of representativeness. Like another child of midnight, Salman Rushdie's hero Saleem Sinai (whom we will encounter at greater length in Chapter Three), Liza is given a privileged relation to the nation; indeed, where the novel's first title made her the product of a time, the new one offers her ownership of a place. It might thus be read as a rewriting of 'Elizabethan England': in an egalitarian gesture, the queen's centrality to national narrative is transferred to this tale of a working-class woman in the North-East.

Again women's experience is central; notably, here, the experience of childbirth and motherhood, undergone by Liza as well as her own mother, daughter and neighbours. And again the already harsh conditions of the story's milieu are pierced by a violent crime, as a gang of youths breaks into Liza's house and, in a panic, deal her the blow that leads to her death at the age of eighty-four. Like the other novels, too, this one's narrative is internally variegated – but in *Liza's England* this results from an ambitious attempt to narrate a long historical period through Liza's life. As Sarah Brophy remarks (2005: 24), the synchronic snapshot of *Union Street* here becomes a diachronic journey through time. The novel tends to follow a pattern in which alternate chapters are set in the present (1984) and in scenes from the past which gradually move forward, to the point where the two narrative times promise to be united. The 1980s are thus contextualised alongside earlier moments in the century.

The book's vision of the present is bleak. Teesside's urban environment is fraying. Stephen, a gay social worker who befriends Liza, is the protagonist through whom most of the present-day action is experienced. When he seeks a public telephone he finds a box in which 'the phone had been ripped out altogether'; a functioning box 'stank of urine' (107). The physical landscape is being torn up: Stephen's official task is to persuade Liza to vacate the house where she has lived for decades, and the novel closes with a crowd watching a wrecking ball knocking down local buildings (282–3). The slum clearances might ultimately be a positive move, but Barker's depiction of the scene is regretful: 'Most of the crowds were young, excited by the machine's power to destroy, with no memories of the area to make them grieve for these few remaining streets' (282). The longest memories have just vanished, with Liza's death. The urban scene, decaying and being torn up, is repeatedly described as a 'wasteland', marked by the 'black scars' of extinguished bonfires and the '[l]ong scars' running 'through the grass where a vanished street had stood' (281, 284).

The battered physical landscape supports a social world shaped by mass unemployment. Stephen runs a youth club at which the unruly children of the dole age gather. Here as elsewhere, unemployment is the major motif. Visiting his aged parents, Stephen detects a 'Sunday-morning feeling' in the area: 'It was Thursday, but very few people on this estate worked' (104). In a pub Stephen watches young men and considers their generational place in the story of industrial decline: 'Dole-queue wallahs built like their steel-making and ship-building fathers, resembling them in this, if in nothing else' (71). When he asks a young man who is involved in casual labour, 'Are you still claiming?' (73), the phrase needs no further gloss. Seeing two youths asleep at the club, Stephen reflects that 'this turning of day into night was a conscious and deliberate decision, a way of filling in the endless hours when other people were at work' (12–13). The boys go for their fortnightly carousal on 'Benefit day' (15). One of them, Brian Jackson, wryly tells Stephen that

> 'I get pissed off with people helping the unemployed and getting paid for it. It's the only growth industry there is [. . .] Time we had our cut.'
> 'Get paid for being helped?'
> 'Why not? It's bloody hard work sometimes.' (14)

In an era of deindustrialisation, Brian suggests, benefits and social work have become a kind of parasitical industry in themselves, rather as factories and mills were being made over into the secondary industry of museums and industrial heritage. Later Brian shows Stephen the bomb shelter where he used to play as a child, and his voice is 'raw with the kind of nostalgia you expect to hear only in old men' (194). As the pair look out to sea, Brian announces:

'It needs a war [. . .] That's the only way they'll ever sort this lot out. That's how they did last time, isn't it? [. . .] You lot think, because of the Bomb, it can't happen, but it can. Look at the Falklands. The lads round here lapped it up. Why else do you think they voted for Thatcher? They loved every minute. It was the only *real* thing that'd ever happened to them.'

Stephen protests that it wasn't that real: 'They watched it on the telly!' (196). But he finds it '[u]seless to argue' with Brian's bread-and-circuses logic, in which war seems the best way out of the lethargy of the dole.

The bored and violent young are ominous signs of the effects of unemployment in this novel, but the most extensive and bitter reflection on redundancy comes from Stephen's dying father Walter, who talks with rare openness to his son after many years of stilted silence. 'They never give us any warning,' he recalls of his employers at the steelworks, 'and they must've known, mustn't they? It stands to reason they knew. You don't close a place that size down and not know.' He has been unable to adapt to the loss of his job, initially persisting with his daily routine ('Be halfway downstairs sometimes before I remembered there was nowhere to go'), then paralysed with fear at the knowledge that he would 'never work again' (115). Time has taken on a different texture for him: 'You don't kill time, it kills you. [. . .] Some afternoons I used to look at the clock, and I swear it didn't move' (117). The ailing patriarch has been stricken by the loss of his role. '[I]t isn't his death that hurts,' Stephen decides, 'It's the way he was made to feel *useless* for so long before he died. I don't forgive this country for that' (168). The main characters' view of the government of the day is a given, summed up when Liz scornfully remembers a doctor who came to test her mental faculties: 'He asked such bloody stupid questions: who was the prime minister. I told him I was trying to forget' (19).

Yet Barker allows no easy contrast between the failing present and a wholesome past. In the 1910s Liza's mother, Louise, cleans the house of the Wynyards, the rich local family who own the steelworks. Liza is puzzled and troubled by her mother's extreme deference toward her high-handed employers, manifested in 'a timid, apologetic smile, that seemed to get onto her face without her knowledge or consent'. Following her mother home, unable to ask, 'Why did you smile?', Liza hears the flap of her mother's torn boot sole as 'the *b-b-b-b-b* of a blocked tongue' (34). The image connects the humiliating scene of class deference with the motif of silence that runs through the book. Others are enduringly afflicted. Stephen sees his dying father's mouth as 'tight, blackish-looking, as if even in life it had never spoken': 'the strongest impression was of silence, as if he were bonded into silence, welded to it, and this final speechlessness revealed a truth about his life that Stephen had never recognized till now' (122). The proletarian past, at least as represented by Walter, has been one of denial and constriction. When Stephen tells him why he left his previous post, Walter responds with scornful mimicry:

> '*Started to question what I was doing* [. . .] Bloody hell, man, where do you think I'd've been if I'd *started to question what I was doing*? Turning the same bloody crank handle forty, fifty, sixty thousand times a day for thirty bloody years. Where do you think I'd've been if I'd questioned that?' (40)

Walter's avowal that even to contemplate alternatives would have been pointless may be founded in the truth. But it does not cancel Stephen's doubts about the ethics of his own career: it only shows that Walter's horizons and material prospects were more limited. Past decades of working-class life are not necessarily to be envied.

This is truer still for those who have lived through and died in the two world wars: women drafted in to test munitions in the First World War, with a 'yellow tinge in every skin' in a factory 'full of powder and dust' (51–2); or Liza's husband Frank, traumatised by the same conflict and seeing death around him on his return to peacetime life (84). The Second World War is suffered on the home front, as houses are destroyed by German rockets. Liza sees a local home torn open like a doll's house (187). The image is picked up at the book's end, as Stephen watches a house hit by the wrecking ball (282–3): what the Luftwaffe could not destroy, slum clearance in 1984 will (170). But what we have witnessed of the century does not make demolition seem a great loss.

With its landscape of scarred ground, wastelands, abandoned steel-works and houses facing demolition, *Liza's England* partakes of a vision of the modern nation as a melancholy place of social and physical ruin. The vision was shared by texts like *New Socialist*'s polemical survey *Thatcher's Britain: A Guide to the Ruins* (Allen 1983), or later by Patrick Wright's idiosyncratic inquiry *A Journey through Ruins* (1991). Raphael Samuel observed that the 'journey through ruins' had become the major genre of northern travel writing in the 1980s (1998: 160). A similar vista can be seen in the other texts examined in this chapter, or in the passage late in Barker's novel where Stephen takes Liza for a last day out.

> High, barbed-wire fences enclosed work yards that would never work again. The wires throbbed and hummed as the wind blew through them. Bits of cloth and polythene clung to the barbs and snapped. [. . .]
> 'There's nothing left,' she said, and, although she'd known that it must be so, her voice was raw with loss.

Tansy, dog-daisies, rose bay willow herb grew and flourished where the houses had been. Here and there, half-hidden in the grass, was the kerb of a forgotten road.

The wind keened across the brown land, and it seemed to Liza that it lamented vanished communities, scattered families, extinguished fires. [. . .]

Silence. Silence from hearth and road, from pub and church, from foundry and factory yard. (216)

The scene is uncannily close to – perhaps even partly derived from – the sequence in the final episode of *Boys from the Blackstuff*, 'George's Last Ride', in which Chrissie wheels George Malone along what the script calls '*the dead docks*'. The two scenes demonstrate the importance of elegy in the representation of working-class life in the period. Ian Jack (1996) has claimed that the 'literature of farewell' was a significant element in the last decades of the twentieth century, and both Bleasdale and Barker partake of it in these scenes. In *Blackstuff*, a series of extended shots follows the pair across the landscape; in Bleasdale's stage directions, '*Each phase of George's speech is shot in a different area of wasteland and indiscriminate destruction*' (1983: 211). As elegiac music plays on the soundtrack, George recalls the docks themselves as a centre of activity; like Liza, he declares his disbelief at their present silence, before dying himself. *Liza's England* offers, if anything, an even starker vision: the blankness of the scene is not repopulated with memories, met only with Liza's statement that 'There's nothing left'. George's talk, while prompted by disbelief, seeks to establish some kind of framework for confronting the post-industrial landscape, gathering the emotional resources to surge to his final, plaintive declaration: '[T]hose dreams of long ago, they still give me some kind of hope and faith in my class . . . *I can't believe there is no hope. I can't*' (1983: 214).

Barker's characters do not seek to match such political directness. But they do debate the relation between history and hope. Stephen tells Liza he cannot imagine any of the youths at his club joining the Labour Party, as she did as a young woman. Liza is reminded of a day in the 1960s when she met a friend who had become a Labour activist. Looking around a new shopping centre, she recalls, 'it was like a different world':

It was all *money*. You'd have thought we had nowt else to offer. But we *did*. We had a way of life, a way of treating people. You didn't just go to church one day a week and jabber on about loving your neighbour. You got stuck in seven days a week and bloody did, because you knew if you didn't you wouldn't survive and neither would she. We had all that. We had pride. We were poor, but we were *proud*. (218–19)

Liza disagrees with Stephen's lament that this working-class ethic has vanished entirely; for his part, the estate-dwellers and jobless teens with whom he works give him the sense of 'witnessing the creation of a people without hope' (219). In both Bleasdale and Barker, a dying pensioner has more hope and conviction than an able-bodied younger man. *Blackstuff* as a whole ends with Chrissie and Loggo reflecting after George's wake:

> CHRISSIE
> George is dead [. . .] you know what he stood for, don't y'?
> LOGGO
> What do you mean?
> *Chrissie shakes his head.*
> CHRISSIE
> Yeah. Well that's dead an' all isn't it? [. . .] What is going wrong, Loggo? What is going wrong?
> LOGGO
> Everything, lah, everything. (Bleasdale 1983: 230)

In a televisual *coup de théâtre*, as the characters walk away, the wreckers move in to destroy the Tate & Lyle factory. *Liza's England* likewise ends amid physical destruction and a sense that most things are going wrong. Yet the length of its historical vision makes it impossible to see a mere decline into entropy and anarchy. Its story of the century is one in which some values – old community bonds and 'pride' – have been jeopardised, but as Liza insists: 'You're bound to think them days were better, aren't you? But I try not to slip into that, I try to remember what it was really like. Women wore out by the time they were thirty. Because they were, you know. You were old at forty' (218). Barker's novel shows Britain in decline, while registering scepticism about that very analysis.

An Accident of Meaning

Founded in 1978 by Neil Astley, Bloodaxe Books was named after the last king of Northumbria. The Viking Eric Bloodaxe had been brought to poetic attention by Basil Bunting's *Briggflatts* (1968), a long poetic exploration of the North-East of England. The poem would become recognised as a major late modernist work in the tradition of Ezra Pound, and an inspiration to subsequent experimental poetry in Britain. The publisher's redeployment of Bloodaxe's name signals regional pride, to an almost parodic degree. Bloodaxe was a publishing success story of the 1980s. It became a home for poetry more formally 'mainstream' than Bunting's, but its motivations and choices have also been politically dissident. The publisher boasts of more women poets than any other imprint, and its commitment to regional writing has been accompanied by the publication of poets on the political Left. We shall now consider in sequence two of those poets: Tony Harrison, in his celebrated and controversial *v.* (1985), and Sean O'Brien, in work from his collections *The Indoor Park* (1983) and *The Frighteners* (1987).

If elegy was a significant mode for representing the North in the 1980s, *v.* uses it with particular self-consciousness. Intertextually linked with Thomas Gray's 'Elegy Written in a Country Churchyard' (1751), the poem is set primarily in a graveyard on Beeston Hill, above Leeds in Yorkshire, where Harrison visits his parents' graves. He finds their stones, like others in the cemetery, defaced by graffiti; some of it obscene, some inspired by the local football team Leeds United. It is a hurrying football fan, the narrator thinks, who has ended up spraying a series of 'v's on 'every space he finds' through the graveyard. Harrison's poetic persona ponders the meaning and motives of the graffiti, and seeks a benign reinterpretation of it. His meditation leads him to imagine a dialogue with a foulmouthed skinhead vandal, whom he sees as his alter ego, before he walks away and voices his hopes of domestic and global harmony.

In 1987, the poem was broadcast by Channel Four, with its remit to transmit innovative programmes and cater for minorities. The presence in the poem of four-letter obscenities ignited a furore among right-wing politicians and tabloids, increasing the poem's public profile and audience. The *Independent* newspaper published the poem in full. Introducing it for the paper's readers, Blake Morrison called *v.* 'a real state-of-the-nation poem' (Harrison 1989: 57). The poem indeed claims such scope, discussing Britain's experience in and since the war. But the state of the nation is to be considered in a place of death, decay and obsolescence. The graveyard 'stands above a worked-out pit': 'Subsidence makes the obelisks all list' (9). Mortality thus leaks into deindustrialisation: the graves' stances are themselves distorted by the remains of a primary industry no longer in operation. With the collapse of old industry has apparently come a weakening of value. The poet imagines that the vandals resent the jobs that were held by the dead and have now disappeared. '*This lot worked at one job all life through*' (19), complains the phantom skinhead; '*When dole-wallahs fuck off to the void / what'll t'mason carve up for their jobs?*' (18). The poem offers this as a possible reason for the desecration of the graves, but laments that Britain's public space has reached this degraded level. Where Philip Larkin's 'Church Going' (1954) conveyed the gentle de-enchantment of the world (his church retaining a 'serious' aura even as religious belief fades), Harrison's records the violent vandalisation of places of mourning: and *v.* seeks to place this activity in historical perspective.

The narrator contrasts the sprayed V-signs with the letter's meaning earlier in the century: in wartime he 'helped whitewash a V on a brick wall', and the victory sign was welcome to the rest of the community (11). Now, intended as 'versus', it brings an inherent divisiveness: in sport ('LEEDS v. / the opponent of last week, this week, or next' [10]), or more ambitiously in the whole of society. In a climactic passage, Harrison reflects:

> These Vs are all the versuses of life
> from LEEDS v. DERBY, Black/White
> and (as I've known to my cost) man v. wife,
> Communist v. Fascist, Left v. Right,
>
> class v. class as bitter as before,
> the unending violence of US and THEM,
> personified in 1984
> by Coal Board MacGregor and the NUM. (11)

The graffiti on the graves testifies to the death of respect between generations; it also becomes a figure for national disunity. Britain has come from wartime collectivism to the fissiparous state of the miners' strike (during which the veteran industrialist Ian MacGregor headed the National Coal Board and led fractious negotiations with the miners' union). The conflict is not between Britain and an external enemy but between government and labour movement; we have come from mid-century solidarity to the cracking of the post-war settlement. If this is among the great motifs of the 1980s, Harrison's poem stages it as starkly as any text of the period.

Much of Harrison's literary vocation has been to extend the poetic franchise: a fight for the rights of dialect against Standard English, or of working-class speech against the exclusions of the canon. This was the burden of his earlier work *The School of Eloquence* (1978). The poem 'Them and [uz]' recalls a schoolteacher's admonition of Harrison for his South Yorkshire pronunciation, which is seen as violating the grandeur of Keats' 'Ode to a Nightingale'. The imposition of Received Pronunciation or (in the title of another of Harrison's poems) 'The Queen's English' is an act that Harrison repeatedly presents as oppressive. His work takes a stand for the value of regional dialect and the speech of the working class. It also laments the distance that a classical education established between Harrison and his own parents. In a familiar narrative of post-war Britain, already told by Richard Hoggart in *The Uses of Literacy* (1957), education for the working-class child on a scholarship may be a liberation, but it amounts also to a separation from roots. But Harrison does not renounce the resulting erudition.

He has repeatedly returned to Greek tragedy, producing translations for production at the National Theatre. In 1985 he likewise revived the medieval York mystery plays as *The Mysteries* on the National's Cottesloe stage. In a gesture of geographical and class reclamation, Harrison insisted that they be played in northern accents.

But the obscenity of *v.* is not part of this noble extension. *v.* does not revel in obscenity but seeks its roots: it wants to read the four-letter words as historical symptoms. It does so in page after page of steady quatrains in iambic pentameter. In an insightful close reading, Sean O'Brien has drawn attention to the way that *v.*'s first stanza (as in the third line 'butcher, publican, and baker, now me, bard') strains at the metrical frame taken by the poem, and shown how Harrison's description of the collapsed mine climaxes in the 'spondaic piledriver-blows' of 'shored slack, crushed shale, smashed prop' (O'Brien 1998: 60–2). Yet despite such canny local effects, the poem's larger impression is of regularity. The metrical framework, rhyming quatrains and identifiable speaking voice create a place of steadiness from which the polarised world of the mid-1980s is viewed. Despite the claims of the poem's assailants, it does not match the vandals by committing poetic vandalism; on the contrary, it seeks a form to contain the aggression and anger it describes. Indeed, when Harrison finally turns his gaze to the *longue durée* of geological development, the pace of change involved seems suited to the dignified, reflective manner of his poem.

v. provoked a contest of interpretations, while also staging its own struggle over interpretation. Harrison's narrator wants to read the signs of the graffiti against their authors' intent:

Though I don't believe in afterlife at all
and know it's cheating it's hard *not* to make
a sort of furtive prayer from this skin's scrawl,
his UNITED mean 'in Heaven' for their sake,

an accident of meaning to redeem
an act intended as mere desecration
and make the thoughtless spraying of his team
apply to higher things, and to the nation. (1989: 15)

In playing on the 'accidents of meaning', Harrison shows how much can reside in a word or a single letter. V is versus but also victory; it resembles a teacher's marginal tick; and 'versus' rhymes with the 'verses' the poet produces, and on whose capacity or impotence the poem explicitly reflects. The writer is also a rereader of the world, who seeks to remake it through creative construal, and perform an imaginative healing with the 'magic wand' (15) of his pen.

In doing so, he risks making his own generous imagination over-compensate for the state of the world around him. In imagining the vandals' motivation as envy for the jobs of the dead, he may be falsely imputing his own subtlety of imagination to them. His penitent reflection on the graffiti – 'It isn't all his fault though. Much is ours' (13) – looks implausible. The poem is an ambitious and anguished political statement, but not an incontestable one. Luke Spencer points out (1994: 95–6) that while the vandals support the neo-fascist National Front, when the phantom skinhead speaks he offers a rhetoric of 'class war' and articulates Harrison's own characteristic anxiety about the fraught relation between working-class roots and classically-educated culture: *'Don't talk to me of fucking representing / the class yer were born into any more'* (1989: 22). Harrison's view of the vandal is split, between outrage at his actions and sympathy for his class position and his entrapment by an age of mass unemployment. The political vision of the poem is likewise divided. Harrison's poetry is used to taking sides, speaking for his people. But the poem more insistently wants not to take sides, aspiring not to the victory of a class but to a nation at one with itself. The poem is prefaced by a quotation from NUM president Arthur Scargill, but it speaks of 'Coal Board MacGregor and the NUM' as another antagonism to be overcome, and 'police v. pickets at a coke-plant gate' (30) do not appear to represent a conflict in which one side has more virtue than the other. O'Brien (1998: 63) perceptively sees that the sheer scale of the poem, along with its tendency toward formal regularity, reinforces the text's yen for unity. This ambitious state-of-England poem confronts social fracture, but strongly yearns to overcome it. It finds continuity in the dead generations of the graveyard whom Harrison expects to join; in the 'diurnal courses' of the Earth (32); and in the persistence through its pages of English poetic tradition.

A Summer that Never Began

Sean O'Brien, like Harrison, is a poet with roots on the political Left and in the North of England. Both poets were raised in one major northern city (Harrison's Leeds, O'Brien's Hull) before moving to another (Newcastle). There are some evident continuities in their preoccupations. Yet the two also belong to successive poetic generations, producing suggestive differences. Harrison, born in 1937, lived through the war and, as we have seen, can still refer to it as a memory of national solidarity. O'Brien, born in 1952, was only in his late twenties as the 1980s commenced. The younger poet thus has a different relation to consensus and the post-war period.

A theme that unites them is the relation between social class and language. If Harrison has agonised repeatedly over the rift with his origins produced by education, O'Brien also meditates on the lasting traces and obligations of class. In 'The Allotment' he pictures himself standing as a child amid his grandfather's contemporaries, out of place as 'the future, a gaberdined dwarf / In the cap of the privileged school', whose honoured names 'had employed the men / I stood among' (2002: 35). Education advantages the child but also sets him apart from the elders of his class who 'did not mention this / Or speak to me at all'. O'Brien approaches class identity more directly in 'Cousin Coat' (2002: 44–5). The poem would remain sufficiently central to O'Brien's sense of his work to give its name to his selected poems in 2002. A coat becomes the emblem of O'Brien's roots, a reminder of what he must not or cannot leave behind. The coat bespeaks (and O'Brien plays on the term 'bespoke' for fabric) a class history that precedes the poet, but to which he wishes to swear allegiance; or which, alternatively, he could never really escape.

> You must be worn, as intimate as skin,
> And though I never lived what you invoke,
> At birth I was already buttoned in,
> Your clammy itch became my atmosphere,
> An air made half of anger, half of fear.

O'Brien replays the opposition between working-class origin and high-cultural escape so insistently worried at by Harrison: 'And what you are is what I tried to shed / In libraries with Donne and Henry James'. In recording a responsibility to class, the poem lines up with an old school of proletarian solidarity, against the erosion of the labour movement and working-class culture.

Yet the defiance of 'Cousin Coat' is born partly from its slight anachronism. O'Brien describes working-class experience not as a personal memory but as something he has learned about an earlier era. The truths that the coat holds – 'the weight and stink of black canals', history enduring like old labour's sweat – are not about contemporary housing estates or people buying their council houses, but the residue of past decades:

> You're here to bear a message from the dead
> Whose history's dishonoured with their names.
> You mean the North, the poor, and troopers sent
> To shoot down those who showed their discontent.

'The North, the poor' are large, sketchy ideas. To need a reminder of 'the North' may suggest less a complex historical responsibility, more the one-upmanship of the 'professional northerner' for whom a compass-point is a badge of authenticity. Yet the poem becomes more precise, and insists that old wrongs persist into new forms:

> No comfort when the poor the state enlists
> Parade before their fathers' cenotaphs.
> No comfort when the strikers all go back
> To see which twenty thousand get the sack.

'Cousin Coat' sets the poet a riskily high political standard. It insists on 'facts' which officialdom has 'cauterized'; the coat is asked to keep the poet 'cold and honest'. The poet knows that this standard will not always be met: in the last line he imagines that he may 'lie' and need the coat to remind him of his purpose. In 'The Allotment', recalling his grandfather's war-veteran contemporaries who are 'tending their plots and choking to death', he feels 'guilt' – at their suffering, or at his generation's escape from it – turn into 'anger, to stiffen my hand / While I write' (36). O'Brien's political line is harder than Harrison's; the older poet remains more conciliatory even while insisting on the historical wounds of class. It is a difference between the poet of the post-war consensus lamented in *v.*, and the poet who bitterly surveys the breaking of that settlement.

O'Brien's other work in this period can be directly polemical in the manner authorised by 'Cousin Coat'. In his first collection *The Indoor Park* (1983), 'The Police' sketches its subject in mock Gothic as pitiable villains:

> It rains in their yards and their kids
> Dress in black and are sullen and pasty.
> Their wives would like going to hangings:
> They knit and they think about crime.

The poem makes the forces of authority the prisoners of their own suspicion and brooding. The police here are not a valued force of order but an unwanted source of surveillance, enemies of the people:

> We are all called *Sunshine*,
> Or else we are liars, or both.
> [. . .]
> The world is guilty of itself,
> Except the police, that is. (O'Brien 2002: 19–20)

Characteristically O'Brien turns to the trimeter for atmosphere, though he also characteristically breaks and varies the metre. The beat of 'The Police' makes for an ironic harassment, a tongue-in-cheek spookiness. In 'London Road' in the next collection (39–41), he again reflects on the police force in black-comic mood; but here the steady tetrameter produces a folksy sing-song. 'As I walked out on London Road / Towards the close of day', he begins, echoing W. H. Auden's poem of 1937:

As I walked out one evening,
  Walking down Bristol Street,
The crowds upon the pavement
  Were fields of harvest wheat. (Auden 1979: 60–2)

O'Brien's tale, though, becomes politically sinister. He encounters a blockade of policemen who accost him with suspicious questions:

'You wouldn't be a picket
Or a dike from CND?
We've orders from Her Majesty
To round them up, you see.'

The police are mobilised against minorities and perceived subversives: trade-union activists, peace campaigners, lesbians. The policeman who addresses the narrator talks of 'rehearsing / For insurgencies ahead', and warns of the brutal consequences of insubordination. The police are seen as happy to beat confessions out of suspects and to lock prisoners away indefinitely:

'Take our advice: get off the street.
Stay in and watch TV.
Unless the law is absolute
The people can't be free.'

Repressive policies are presented as the guarantor of freedom: the policeman's apparent paradox reprises a duality that is characteristic of Thatcherism as a whole. Private pleasures ('stay in and watch TV') are the compensations that replace even walking the street, let alone the collective gathering that the authorities fear it portends.

The poem's vision of the police is very historically specific. Its police force features neither the community bobbies of the post-war television series *Dixon of Dock Green*, nor the service placed under public scrutiny and charged to police its own 'institutional racism' since the 1990s. It is a brutal, cynical tool of government, the uniformed wing of the Conservative Party. O'Brien thus plays upon the colour blue, as in the opening of the poem:

For when I stopped and looked around
The hills of Housman's blue
Had ceased to be a colour
And become a point of view.

It matched the spanking outfits
Of the cops who blocked the road.
The only things they seemed to lack
Were bucketfuls of woad. (2002: 39)

The colour blue was associated, in A. E. Housman's verse, with rural, southern England; that landscape is now part of the base, in electoral terms and in the ideological imaginary, of contemporary Conservatism; and Tory blue is also the colour of the police who act as governmental muscle on the home front. Woad would make them bluer still, and image them as a fierce, tribal army. 'Spanking' suggests not just the state of the police uniforms but punitive violence. The 'point of view' which blue has become is not just a matter of voting intention, but of reactionary suspicion and exclusiveness. The response is a fifth kind of blue, alongside the colours of memory, the police, the Conservative Party and tribal decoration: the *blues* which the poet, in a 'land of lost content / Where facts are redefined' is finally condemned to sing.

O'Brien's view of the police is undoubtedly informed by their role in the miners' strike. He addresses the event in other poems. In 'Unregistered' an uneven metre – four stresses to a line, five, then three, and the pattern varying through the poem's four stanzas – sets up the uneasy atmosphere of a secret dock where 'Baltic vessels come / With

Figure 5   Gizza Job: life imitates art at a miners' demonstration, March 1984

coal to break the strike' (2002: 38). The content of the poem is entirely occluded until the last stanza, in which the italicised voice of, we may guess, a Baltic seaman, sardonically asks, '*Does Mr Scargill think we think / The revolution starts like this?*' There is a mocking brutality to this conclusion, especially as the poem appeared after the strike's failure. This effect emerges all the more sharply out of the blank, inscrutable surfaces of the first stanzas, in which the unregistered ships dock at a place 'for which nowhere / Is far too precise', and in which the only tattered detail in the unpeopled landscape is 'the pub / And the poster of Showaddywaddy'.

'Summertime', in the same collection, echoes the epigraph from Scargill that Tony Harrison gave *v.*, misconstrued as a 'dedication' by some tabloids, with an actual dedication to 'Richard Richardson, Kent NUM'. The poem plainly takes off from the summer of 1984. June that year saw the bitter and violent struggle between police and pickets at Orgreave's coke plant, and the poem begins:

> The news is old. A picket line is charged and clubbed by mounted police.
> *Regrettable. Necessity.*
> *You have to take a balanced view.*
> *That kind of thing can't happen here*
> *And when it does it isn't true.*

In this poem the roman type announces weary truth, while italics speak a different voice – the voice of the news, perhaps, ostensibly committed to 'balance' between different political perspectives, or of a government spokesman who moves from 'regretting' the action to declaring it impossible and erasing it altogether. The poem will end with a reprise of these lines; before that, it develops an obscure vision in contrast to the opening image of state violence. In italics again, the voice goes on:

> *Adore yourself and in the body's*
> *Shrivelled province bask and breed.*
> *Indulge your fudged affairs and lust*
> *For what your terror says you need.*
> *It's hot. Lie down and vegetate.*
> *There are no politics, no state.* (32)

The voice of authority instructs Britain to go to sleep – to 'lie down and vegetate' in the summer sun. The heat of 'Summertime' induces a trance in the nation: life is reduced to the '*shrivelled province*' of the monadic, individual and ('*Adore yourself*') narcissistic body. To '*lust / For what your terror says you need*' is to embrace one's own oppression, to submit willingly to the control of the state. In his paradoxical linkage of lust and terror, which the context clearly makes into a political issue,

O'Brien here articulates the inquiry of the Left into the population's enthusiasm for a politics founded on pain and suspicion, the appeal of firm authority at which Denis Healey's coinage 'sado-monetarism' had gestured (Campbell 2003: 83).

Several of O'Brien's poems at this time reflect on his time working in Brighton, but his most vivid landscapes are northern. 'The Park by the Railway' (2002: 3–4) depicts a world of industrial decline, tinted with late-summer light. Its main note is of loss and last things:

> Industrial pastoral, our circuit
> Of grass under ash, long-standing water
> And unimportant sunsets flaring up
> Above the half-dismantled fair. Our place
> Of in-betweens, abandoned viaducts
> And modern flowers, dock and willowherb,
> Lost mongrels, birdsong scratching at the soot
> Of the last century. Where should we be
> But here, my industrial girl?

'Industrial pastoral' sounds a paradox. Pastoral is the poetry of the rural, often signifying a return to an arcadia lost to industry. Yet for O'Brien, the landscape of romance itself has been shaped by industry. The physical world is thoroughly marked by this encounter. But the encounter seems to be over: the pastoral bespeaks a crumbling, arrested land of loss and longing. The railings are missing; grass is buried 'under ash'. Water – in canals, docks, reservoirs – is 'long-standing', going nowhere and lifting no boats. The viaducts – the routes of the railway – are 'abandoned'. Birdsong is 'scratching at the soot / of the last century': the last hundred years, prior to the 1980s, or perhaps the last full century, the nineteenth, an epoch in which the railway that so fascinates O'Brien led mechanisation across the landscape.

Nature and artifice have found an improvised accommodation in an era of 'in-betweens'. The viaducts are overgrown with 'dock and willowherb' and with 'modern flowers', which like 'unimportant sunsets' is a neat, estranging phrase. Randall Stevenson observes that rosebay willow-herb had already become a frequent symbol in English poetry 'both of urban dereliction and of nature's resilient capacity to profit from it' (2004: 250). At the end of *Liza's England* the torn townscape offers one compensation: 'tall spires of rose bay willow', each hung with 'cottony seeds', which offer a faint promise of renewal (Barker 1996: 284). O'Brien's verbal hybrids of the natural and the industrial look odd, but his poem's deindustrialised landscape, where hardy weeds are emblems of endurance, is quite recognisable. It also pushes further back into history. The poem's wispy protagonists are

Not quite convinced there will be no more trains,
At the end of a summer that never began
Till we lost it, we cannot believe
We are going. We speak, and we've gone.
You strike a match to show the china map
Of where the railways ran before us.
Coal and politics, invisible decades
Of rain, domestic love and failing mills
That ended in a war and then a war
Are fading into what we are [. . .]

The list of terms from the past – coal, politics, rain, failing mills – gives atmosphere, but this cannot quite be taken at face value. These words are tags for a second-hand past. O'Brien immerses us in a historical imagination, but with a sense that history is being viewed at a remove, just as in 'Cousin Coat' the poet must admit to having never lived what the coat invokes. In the tumbling abstractions of 'The Park by the Railway' O'Brien makes what will become a characteristic move: he gives us not history but a history of representations. O'Brien's 'polite incapables' feel ghostly next to the substance of history that precedes them, which 'faded into what we are'. Their belatedness is so great it has made them spectral. The mood is of lingering after, 'not quite convinced there will be no more trains'. O'Brien's tone is poised between the northern elegy we have already observed, and a wry sense that such elegy must be framed by irony.

Nae Breath at Aw

Merseyside, Teeside, South Yorkshire, Humberside. But much of the most vital dissident writing came from still further north. In a 1979 referendum Scotland voted on political devolution. While a small majority of voters favoured the transfer of powers from London to Edinburgh, the conditions of the referendum required the assent of 40 per cent of the electorate for the measure to proceed. Even on a 60 per cent turnout, devolution was thus denied. A subsequent campaign protesting that Scotland had in fact said 'Yes' would be echoed by the narrator of Alasdair Gray's novel *1982 Janine*, who complains that 'the usual sporting rules for electing a new government had been changed' to forestall even a modicum of Scottish legislative independence (1984a: 66).

Through the 1980s the refusal of political autonomy was gradually compensated for by an ersatz republic of arts and letters. Writers, academics, artists and politicians hammered together a new discourse on national identity, which laid the ground for a Constitutional Convention in 1989 (Harvie 1994: 204), and ultimately thereby for devolution at the century's end. Thatcherism's more bellicose assertions of Britishness ironically saw the ties of union fray. Politically, Scotland was gradually ceded to Labour, Nationalists and Liberals, increasing the impression of a distinct, more egalitarian nation whose governance from Westminster made decreasing sense. Scotland, like Liverpool (capital of Labour's entryist Militant Tendency) or South Yorkshire (drolly calling itself a socialist republic), was thus a significant source of opposition to the main flow of politics. In Scotland this political atmosphere accompanied a wave of writing that had built since the 1970s, and that was increasingly seen as a Caledonian Renaissance.

Numerous writers and institutions contributed. In publishing, the establishment of Canongate and Polygon in Edinburgh meant that a Scottish writer need not necessarily aspire to be published in London. The revived *Edinburgh Review* and the annual anthology *New Writing Scotland* were significant outlets for poetry, stories and work in progress. The poet and academic Philip Hobsbaum had moved to the University of Glasgow in 1966; in 1971 he founded a fortnightly writers' group that would prove important. Hobsbaum's record as an organiser of such salons was already considerable. His 'Belfast Group' in the mid-1960s had nurtured the first poetry of Seamus Heaney, Michael Longley and Derek Mahon. In Glasgow the group's emphasis was on prose. James Kelman has often referred back to the supportive network of fellow artists he encountered in this period (1992: 82). They included Tom Leonard, Liz Lochhead and Alasdair Gray. Kelman and Gray encouraged Agnes Owens, who produced a large body of short stories while working as a cleaner and factory worker, and shared the volume *Lean Tales* with them in 1985. From 1978 to 1980, the Glasgow Print Studio Cooperative was also a centre of collaborative activity, distributing booklets containing the latest work of those who had met through Hobsbaum's group. Kelman himself organised poetry readings and writing groups in the early 1980s, in his temporary role as Writer in Residence for Renfrewshire District Libraries. Thus he met and nurtured the former factory worker and shop steward Jeff Torrington, whose hefty novel *Swing Hammer Swing* would appear in 1992 after many years in the making.

Gray issued the epic of this era in *Lanark* (1981), a vast, multifaceted novel which frames a realistic history of Glasgow with the darkly fantastic story of its alter ego, Unthank. We will consider the novel more extensively in Chapter Three, but can note here its importance to the Scottish scene. In a speech that would become emblematic, Gray's protagonist proposes that Glasgow has suffered from a dearth of artistic representations: '[I]f a city hasn't been used by an artist not even the inhabitants live there imaginatively [. . .] Imaginatively Glasgow exists as a music hall song and a few bad novels. That's all we've given to the world outside. It's all we've given to ourselves' (Gray 1985: 243). This posits artistic expression as a necessary condition of civic pride. Several younger writers have talked of Gray as a pioneer who revealed that it was possible to write imaginatively about Scotland. 'Scottish writing needed a *Lanark*', recalls Kevin Williamson; 'Scotland needed a *Lanark*' (2002: 171). Yet if Scotland was freshly available to writers, it was not simply to be feted. The revival was no tartan gala. Realist writing exposed poverty and destitution in a Clydeside whose shipyards, once the heart of socialist radicalism in Britain, were stilled; or, as in the stories of William McIlvanney, it presented isolated, emotionally frosted lives. Gray's own *1982 Janine* (1984), the extraordinary follow-up to *Lanark*, is the interior monologue of a Scottish analyst of security systems over one night in a Greenock hotel. His life, since an abandoned early relationship, has gradually become a solitary routine of whisky and masturbation. Gray does not stint in linking personal and political life. His protagonist's retreat into alcoholism and sadistic fantasies explicitly parallels Scotland's trajectory from post-war optimism to the contemporary moment when it is 'wired for war' (Gray 1984: 134). Yet the novel, in a reflection of Gray's political temperament, finally affirms the possibility of starting anew.

Other strains existed. Scottish Gothic was revived by the poet and dramatist Liz Lochhead. Her volume *Dreaming Frankenstein* (1984) featured a verse account of Mary Shelley's conception of her modern myth. The story arrives spontaneously but also with a troubling conjunction of sexuality and violence associated with Gothic tradition, as Shelley wakes 'with him in / her head, in her bed': 'he came with a name / that was none of her making' (Lochhead 1984: 11). Lochhead's work for the stage also revisited the Gothic canon with versions of *Dracula* as well as *Frankenstein*. But her play *Mary Queen of Scots Got Her Head Chopped Off* (1987) deals with gender and violence in a historical rather than supernatural setting. The play dramatises the relation between Queen Elizabeth I and her Scottish counterpart Mary, who never meet on stage but vie for control of the royal line of descent. The duo are echoed by a series of other characters, of varying social ranks, to be played by the same actors. These figures duplicate the queens' stand-off and bear versions of their names: Marian, Mairn, Marie; Bessie, Leezie, Betty. The play explores the strategies available for women in the otherwise male world of sixteenth-century high politics, and the roles into which women from other social classes are cast. But the play is not only an exploration of gender politics but a reconsideration of the matter of Britain. Mary's Catholicism and Elizabeth's Protestantism are implicitly shown to be enduring forces in the sectarianism of modern Scotland, in the encounter between the twentieth-century schoolgirls Marie and Betty. Lochhead creates suggestive historical parallels through a dramatic blend of repetition and difference.

A younger generation of writers emerging in the 1980s was visibly indebted to pioneers like Gray and Lochhead. Iain Banks, like many of his literary compatriots an avowed leftist, divided his work between utopian science fiction and imaginative contemporary narratives. These ranged from the teenage Gothic of *The Wasp Factory* (1984) to the fantasy of *The Bridge* (1985), where – in an echo of *Lanark*'s parallel worlds – an immense, lonely realm is hallucinated out of a national landmark, the Forth Rail Bridge. Janice Galloway would be inspired by the veterans of Hobsbaum's group in producing her debut novel. *The Trick is to Keep Breathing* (1989) is the first-person interior monologue of a traumatised young woman schoolteacher, Joy Stone. Galloway's prose drifts through a series of darkly playful techniques representing Joy's fractured, circling state of mind. The novel manages to combine a dogged, council-flat mimesis with the flair for typological experiment licensed by *Lanark*.

In poetry, Tom Leonard's work from the late 1960s on upheld the value of Scottish speech in a way comparable to Tony Harrison's defence of Yorkshire dialect. Leonard likewise viewed Standard English as a political imposition. His volume *Intimate Voices* (1984) gathered material from the previous two decades, including work from his collection *Ghostie Men* (1980). *Intimate Voices* is irreverent as well as sometimes belligerent. It juxtaposes Leonard's brief dialect poems with essays on Scottish culture or the American modernist William Carlos Williams, alongside stick-man sketches and speech bubbles. Leonard's most influential earlier poems, reprinted here, had attacked the implication of the English language in the maintenance of class authority. 'The Six o' Clock News' expresses cool indignation at the presumed arrogance of a BBC newsreader, whose delivery seems to exclude voices bearing the traces of other classes and regions. The 'trooth' would not be accepted if it arrived in the accent of 'wanna yoo scruff': one of the ordinary people around Britain who do not share the newsreader's accent (Leonard 1984: 88). The poem runs down the left-hand margin of its page, a thin trickle of uncapitalised words, many spelled out phonetically. The more recent poems of *Ghostie Men* pursue similar strategies. Several are grim parodies of nursery rhymes:

baa baa black sheep
have you any wool
yes sir yes sir
three bags full

one for thi master
n anuthir wan fur thi master
n wan fur thi fuckin church (112)

A serious political position is implied: material resources are inequitably distributed to those with power, secular or ecclesiastical. But such a poem derives power from its brazen simplicity and apparent casualness. The collapse of rhyme and metre in the second stanza is darkly comic. It is as though, confronted with the familiar structure of injustice, the poet cannot be bothered to follow poetic etiquette. In other poems Leonard explicitly focuses on language and literature. A prisoner is arraigned

fur this aforesaid crime
uv writn anuthir poem
awarded thi certificate of safety
by the scottish education department

He has failed to break the rules, his work 'huvn no bad language / sex subversion or antireligion'. The bland versifier is accordingly sentenced

tay six munths hard labour
doon nthi poetry section
uv yir local library
coontin thi fuckin metaphors (110)

Poetry is the crime, but also the punishment. Traditional literary culture, apparently, is a tiresome business, a fitting penance for the writer who fails to challenge the status quo. Leonard's own writing seeks to steer clear of this milieu rather than enter it. In another poem he reports that 'ma language is disgraceful', then proffers a list of those who have told him so, from his landlady to the Scottish National Dictionary. The self-dramatization latent in Leonard is evident here. There is never any danger that he will give credence to the supposed complaint. His critics are thoroughly straw targets. It is no surprise when Leonard concludes 'all livin language is sacred / fuck thi lohta thim' (120). Work like this is the weaker for neglecting to seek any real challenge to its own indignant premises. The closest we come to such doubt is Leonard's claim that his wife has scolded his language 'jist-tay-get-inty-this-poem'. This hints that the poem's sense of controversy is somewhat factitious, and that Leonard's characterisation as 'disgraceful' is in part a performance which has benefited rather than hindered his career. Yet Leonard's reclamation of dialect is historically important. It is polemically emblematic of an opening of language beyond Standard English in the post-war period. Among the richest instances of that stylistic challenge has been offered by Leonard's friend and contemporary James Kelman. His work offers us a final, powerful instance of the writing of working-class experience in the 1980s.

Kelman learned his trade through the 1970s as a writer of short stories. He was initially published primarily in Scottish magazines and the annual *Scottish Short Stories*, though his first volume *An Old Pub Near the Angel* was issued by Puckerbrush Press in the United States as early as 1973. Kelman's fiction of the 1980s – the novels *The Busconductor Hines* (1984), *A Chancer* (1985) and *A Disaffection* (1989), and numerous short stories and vignettes – centres on ordinary people: mainly working-class and frequently unemployed; predominantly Glaswegian and male. He has claimed that when he began to write, few useful models existed:

> Whenever I did find somebody from my own sort of background in English Literature there they were confined to the margins, kept in their place, stuck in the dialogue. You only ever saw or heard them. You never got into their mind. You did find them in the narrative but from without, seldom from within. And when you did see them or hear them they never rang true, they were never like anybody I ever met in real life.

The analysis implies a manifesto. Kelman's work systematically seeks to overcome this scenario: people from 'his own sort of background' are released from the margins, seen from within, allowed to do more than speak dialogue. This last point Kelman explains further. Glaswegians in English literature, he says, talk in 'a strange hotchpotch of bad phonetics and horrendous spelling', while English characters are allowed to speak in a normative idiom that is, crucially, continuous with the narrative voice: 'the narrative belonged to them and them alone. They owned it' (1992: 82). Kelman's mission is thus not only to write about the people with whom he identifies, but to seize control of the means of narrative production on their behalf. The Gorbals bus driver or Maryhill barfly must not be framed by a storytelling voice that is set apart from and above him. Narrative voice should be in solidarity with the people it describes; in any case it must never exoticise them or present their speech as deviant from its own norm. Kelman's writing thus politicises the use of language with rare intensity.

The formal outcome is not entirely self-evident. Given his attack on the 'bad phonetics' that English literature uses to convey Scotland, one might expect Kelman to render every Glaswegian's words in Standard

English spelling, insisting that Glaswegian speech is a valid oral rendition of it. In fact, like Tom Leonard, he regularly turns to phonetic spelling and unorthodox vocabulary and syntax. This is at its most emphatic in the story 'Nice to be Nice', told by the veteran Stan who, in an exemplification of Kelman's ethics, tries to help his impoverished neighbours in their dealings with the oppressive 'coarpiration'.

> A hid tae stoap 2 flerrs up tae git ma breath back. A'm no as bad as A wis bit A'm still no right; that bronchitis – Jesus Christ, A hid it bad. Hid tae stoap work cause iv it. Good joab A hid tae, the lorry drivin. Hid tae chuck it bit. Landid up in the Western Infirmary. Nae breath at aw. Couldny fuckin breathe. Murder it wis. Still, A made it tae the toap okay. (Kelman 1983: 31)

For the reader – English or otherwise – used to reading Standard English, Stan's monologue is a technical challenge. Its physical appearance on the page is initially startling. The reader adapts to Stan's voice, directed to hear its tones by Kelman's careful rendition of these socially specific sounds – though to do this successfully probably requires some pre-existing, extra-literary acquaintance with accents like Stan's. The implicit claim of the narration is not only that everyday stories like Stan's deserve to be told, but that voices like his can, even should, be written out in these often new words and spellings, uncompromisingly distinguished from other kinds of English speech.

Kelman's mastery of dialect has been immensely influential on younger writers like Irvine Welsh and Alan Warner. But little of his work is quite like 'Nice to be Nice'. More commonly he establishes a fluid voice which moves from occasional phonetic spellings and local diction to unadorned English, and all the way to technical jargon. While it might seem logical for Kelman to hand full narrative authority to his characters by writing in the first person (as he does in 'Nice to be Nice' and several short stories), his full-length novels of this period instead maintain a third-person perspective which closely follows the protagonist and readily shades into his own stream of thought. Even its borders with speech appear porous, as Kelman increasingly eschews punctuation to separate dialogue from the rest of the text. Speech comes to seem less a discrete action, more an additional by-product of the discourse that is always flowing through and around a character's consciousness.

By *A Disaffection* Kelman's mobile, improvisatory narrative mode is in full flow. Kelman can write a plain external description of events: 'He smiled and stood up, walked across to the bar and ordered a tomato juice' (1989: 2). But such seemingly neutral narrative never lasts long without becoming admixed with the protagonist's perceptions:

He glanced at the temporary English teacher who smiled but looked away immediately. He was not at his ease with Patrick. That was for definite. It was as if he was just – as if he was maybe thinking he was not really able to say what might happen in the next couple of minutes. As if he was worried Patrick might break down or something maybe and end up

not well perhaps. As if Patrick would end up not well.

Fucking not well! He was fucking not well right now. Right fucking now. He was christ almighty in fucking bad trouble. Bad trouble. What did it take! What did it fucking take! (39)

By the third sentence here, narrative is picking up Patrick's colloquial judgement. As it then breaks up, stopping and restarting its thought, it has effectively become his own veering, backfiring vehicle. Kelman is unafraid to fragment the page by ending a paragraph in mid-flow, then starting the next without a capital letter, as though the movement of thought has hit a momentary lacuna and jolted over it. By the final paragraph the sentences – 'Fucking not well!' – are effectively direct renditions of Patrick's concerns, though they never resort to the word 'I'. The heavy repetition is typical; the entire novel circles around a limited set of problems and options, and in Kelman a character's conversation with himself is extensively constituted of words and phrases that are replayed time and again.

Trapped in his alienation, Doyle seeks a margin of freedom in thought, constructing conspiratorial theories about the machinations of the state and diverting himself with eccentric ponderings:

If prostitutes' feet are not warm should the client accede to the moral imperative vis-à-vis the bearing of hot water bottles as the universal male obligation? And the corollary:
    what is the nature of a contract?
    And:
    was Kant a frosty auld shite?
    Who knows. Who cares. Nowadays people don't even consider such idle controversy. (216)

The mind's pained, futile diversion into such intellectual trails is among Kelman's motifs. His characters often expand into a wonky formality as they construct their internal inquiries. Thus *The Busconductor Hines'* protagonist reflects:

His goal was twofold: to obtain a PSV licence, to acquire a sum of money – a sum of money which while of unknown extension was nevertheless taken for granted as settled in some unshadowy region as for example consider the striving to a goal where the goal lies in between the lines while the lines themselves are the striving and can produce the goal seemingly in themselves but not really in themselves for the goal lies in between and though some daft cunts have no knowledge of this they assume its existence in accordance with the existence of the lines. (1984: 97–8)

Hines becomes lost in an apparently technical idiom which becomes absurdly distended as its meaning slips away. Like Yosser Hughes, his mind is capable of forming what looks like official discourse, but becomes instead an empty parody of it. Kelman's narrators are plagued by this fruitless inner fluency, and are apt to break it off in frustration and contempt. Thus Hines tries to start again – 'Now: let us take it slowly, slowly and calmly' – but almost immediately interrupts again into a bitter recognition of his own precarious, impoverished situation:

> One might start off by too late it is too late, too fucking late, it is too fucking late for the shite, for this imbecilic carry on; it is too late. The problem is that it is too late. 5 years is not 10 minutes. This is the problem. Hines really does know it now, at long last, he is in full realization of it, as he has been before right enough it has to be admitted at this stage of the game that eh he has known it before. (98)

Kelman grants Hines, like Doyle, a complexity of consciousness and language, and this is a polemical gesture against a literary tradition that Kelman believes has excluded working people or made them figures of fun. But this is a mixed blessing. The men's inner complexity yields not a capacity for serene contemplation, but an endless mental struggle. To be revealed as richly human is not such an advance, if the conditions in which one lives make it painful to occupy that humanity. Kelman's writing stands as one of the decade's most dedicated and demanding fictional projects. More than the other writers considered in this chapter, he makes his own rules and takes literary language to extremes – of repetition, monotony, fragmentation and intensity. Yet his writing does not experiment for innovation's sake. Its extremities, Kelman implies, are no more extreme than the lives they depict.

Chapter Three

Modes

If one cultural label held sway in the late twentieth century anglophone world, it was postmodernism. And if any one decade must be named as postmodernism's temporal heartland, it is arguably the 1980s. Major theoretical formulations of the term were in place by the start of the decade. The single most cited work on the subject, Fredric Jameson's essay 'Postmodernism, or, the Cultural Logic of Late Capitalism', also became one of the most cited works on any subject in the humanities, following its initial appearance in *New Left Review* in 1984. By 1990 the British theorist Kobena Mercer, in an essay subtitled 'A Postscript to the 1980s', could declare that the term, as the 'prevalent name' for the decade's 'vertigo of displacement', had 'already been and gone as a best seller ideology' (2000: 285). That was premature: Jameson's book-length *Postmodernism*, for instance, would not appear until the following year, and he would still be reflecting on the term two decades on. If there was any truth in this entire body of theory and analysis, as an account of an epoch, then it could not disappear as swiftly as that. Yet Mercer at least demonstrates that, among intellectuals and writers, the term had thoroughly entered regular parlance by this point; so thoroughly that it already risked expiring from its own buzzing fashionability. The term had years of life left, whether among those who had not yet heard it or those who, like Jameson, considered it not merely a glib tag but a way of naming an important truth about the present. But it can be said that the major features of the idea, or even the constellation of different ideas, of postmodernism were in place by the end of the 1980s, whatever further exemplification they would receive from subsequent cultural developments.

To name those features was a task undertaken by many around this time: from Jameson's magisterial monologues to the more immediately user-friendly forms of the academic introduction and even the journalistic enquiry or television documentary. The academic Steven Connor recalls (2007) that in 1987, an editor at Blackwell publishers remarked to me how much he would love it if he could persuade someone to write a book with the words 'theory', 'introduction' and 'postmodernism' in the title. In 1989, my *Postmodernist Culture: An Introduction to Theories of the Contemporary* was published.

The anecdote suggests not a unique event but a general climate.

But to summarise postmodernism was a considerable challenge. Postmodernism was unusual in advancing across many fields and disciplines at once. This gave the impression of intellectual omnipresence, even hegemony. It also threatened to diminish the term's coherence, as its meanings in two distinct fields might be quite different, deriving from different internal histories. For instance, 'Depending on the artistic discipline,' Hans Bertens observes, 'postmodernism is either a radicalization of the self-reflexive moment within modernism, a turning away from narrative and representation, or an explicit return to narrative and representation' (1995: 5). Rather than seeking coherence across its conceptual continent, it is better to accept postmodernism as a federation of different, roughly simultaneous developments with a common name and numerous family resemblances. Accepting that caution, we can still identify major motifs.

Versions of Postmodernism

The term implies a relation to modernism: of break or extension, in different accounts. Jameson notes that one of its causes was the postwar institutionalisation of modernism, in art galleries and university syllabi, while the poetics of T. S. Eliot in particular became a critical orthodoxy. Hence 'the younger generation of the 1960s will now confront the formerly oppositional modern movement as a set of dead classics' (1991: 4). In this belatedly institutionalised form, leaving aside the myriad complications of its actual development, modernism was equated with solemnity, heroically embattled individualism, and a commitment to art's splendid autonomy. All this invited an irreverent response. American fiction of the 1960s provided one. The work of Kurt Vonnegut, Donald Barthelme, John Barth and Robert Coover was arguably the first sustained wave of writing that can cogently be labelled postmodern. It was adventurous, often fragmented, sometimes challenging the conventions of reading and demanding a struggle for sense from the reader. But it also typically struck a new tone: brash, quirky, suffused in everyday American idiom and imagery. Hollywood iconography had become as much a shared reference point and ready source of allusion as classical myth was to the modernists just a few decades earlier.

What is distinctive about the emergent postmodernism, then, is its combination of sophistication with the demotic: an avant-gardism for the age of *The Brady Bunch*. This would remain as plausible a formula as any for the postmodern. At the end of the 1960s it received polemical codification from the maverick critic Leslie Fiedler, who approvingly saw a movement 'to turn High Art into vaudeville and burlesque at the same moment that Mass Art is being irreverently introduced into museums and libraries' (1972: 78), and encouraged contemporary writers to try their hand at genre fiction. Jameson would confirm postmodernism's fascination with 'this whole "degraded" landscape of schlock and kitsch' (1991: 2). Not all work identified as postmodernism would demand such lurid terms of description. But a certain populism, or desire for accessibility and public address, would remain consistently prominent. At its broadest this is reflected in the renewed emphasis on narrative, which will be a recurring theme in this chapter.

The 1970s saw the discourse of postmodernism proliferate. In architecture it was again associated with populism, as the authors of *Learning from Las Vegas* (1972) recommended the fullest embrace of commerce; and with eclecticism, as Charles Jencks led the call for the functional modernist block to be embellished and leavened with the borrowed traces of architectural history. But a stronger influence on literary and critical discourse came from philosophy. What had been in part a response to contemporary American conditions was now joined by advanced intellectual work from France. Numerous thinkers retrospectively grouped as poststructuralists – centrally, at this point, Roland Barthes, Jacques Lacan, Michel Foucault and Jacques Derrida – became the focus of intellectual excitement in Britain by the start of the 1980s. Their impact on academic literary criticism was extensive. Readers' guides, introductions, handbooks and anthologies proliferated to serve a population of students, as well as academics, for whom French theory offered fresh models of reading. In some respects the poststructuralists' reception (celebrated for Parisian sophistication or decried for foreign obfuscation) replayed the relation of the British establishment to modernism decades earlier (Brooker 2004: 151–8). Indeed, in its experimental form and labyrinthine rhetoric this generation of French theory was closer to a rerun of modernism than to the demotic engagements of American metafiction or pop art. Such disjunctures and uneven developments across national cultures are a major source of postmodernism's apparent inconsistency. The above-named Parisians' ideas, and their reworking within the anglophone academy, were vital components of the intellectual atmosphere, and contributed, whether explicitly or indirectly, to literature itself, as we shall see later in this chapter. But they were not primarily labelled postmodern. Two other thinkers took that honour.

Jean-François Lyotard's *The Postmodern Condition* (1979), translated into English in 1984, provided an impressively succinct new formula: 'I define *postmodern* as incredulity toward metanarratives' (1984: xxiv). In modern times, Lyotard proposed, people had told overarching stories to legitimate their activities and ground their beliefs. Such narratives included Christianity, Enlightenment or the pursuit of scientific truth, but for the disillusioned militant Lyotard, Marxism was central among them (Anderson 1998: 29). These metanarratives, he asserted, had lost their credibility. Society's forms of belief and legitimation were becoming more localised and provisional. The *petits récits* or little stories could flower in the ruins of modernity's guiding myths.

Lyotard thus sponsored an extensive scepticism. 'Totalising' claims to knowledge were suspect. He was repeatedly attacked from the political Left, for his potentially demoralising rejection of ambitious projects of emancipation. Postmodernism, it was alleged, in dissolving epistemological certainties, disabled radical critique of the state of things and ultimately supported the status quo. Contrarily, such scepticism could be celebrated as anti-authoritarian. Postmodernism's demolition of what were sometimes translated as 'master narratives' might clear ground for the claims of so-called 'new social movements': notably feminism. In a world more open to plurality, minorities and hitherto silenced voices might be heard. These political ambiguities fuelled much discussion. Dina Sherzer could assert that '[f]eminism is an essential part of postmodernism', sharing its 'decanonization of all master codes, all conventions, institutions, authorities', to the point where 'a feminist text, but also any ethnic, minority, or Third World text, can be nothing but postmodern' (1991: 156). Others registered reservations, arguing for instance that feminism had long preceded postmodernism and was, if anything, a product of Enlightenment, even a metanarrative. In general, such political debate ranged between the poles of euphoria – from critics keen to make common cause with the most celebrated contemporary term, at the risk of being merely *à la mode* – and puritanical disdain, in which (as on much of the Marxist Left) the refusal of postmodernism became a self-confirming pleasure in its own right.

The latter camp sought corroboration in the writing of Jean Baudrillard. The Parisian sociologist had spent the 1970s outflanking his contemporaries, dwarfing their already flamboyant claims by taking ever wilder rhetorical positions. In his signature work of the 1980s, *Simulacra and Simulations* (1981), from which an English selection appeared in 1983, Baudrillard effectively denied the existence of reality. The contemporary image, he postulated, had slipped the moorings of reference. It had moved from being 'the reflection of a basic reality', far beyond the ideological role in which it 'masks and perverts a basic reality', all the way to autonomy: 'it bears no relation to any reality whatever: it is its own pure simulacrum' (Baudrillard 1983: 11). In Baudrillard's vision, the modern media had bleached the world of its reality. Contemporary Western life was so thoroughly mediated that one should no longer seek authenticity in it. To pursue the machinations of power, as Foucault had influentially done, was 'useless', as power was 'there only to hide the fact that it no longer exists' (Baudrillard 1987: 51). Baudrillard gave the most extreme twist to long-standing anxieties about the media's effects on social life. His writing was declamatory, but could be also viewed as a kind of science fiction, generating experimental, even satirical hypotheses about the present.

Sold in attractively slim volumes or (in the case of his travelogue *America*) illustrated coffee-table format, Baudrillard was able to enter the intellectual conversation of the 1980s. Perhaps the finest literary response to his vision was Don DeLillo's *White Noise* (1984), in which tourists gather to photograph a barn in homage purely to its status as the Most Photographed Barn in America (1984: 12–13). Few British writers matched the New Yorker DeLillo's deadpan verve. But Baudrillard's work joined Lyotard's in suggesting an atmosphere of epistemological scepticism. Doubt flourished in their wake. If few could espouse literally Baudrillard's rhetoric of the death of the real, a much more widespread current suggested that the real was not given but constructed: a matter of narrative and perception, shaped by particular interests. A more homespun version of this case was available in the 1980s, in the neopragmatism of the American philosopher Richard Rorty. He proposed that truth was made, not found, and that the self was a matter of the stories people told about themselves. His ideas were in tune with much contemporary fiction, and might have been cited more often if he had delivered them in a gnomically Gallic idiom rather than in his own blend of analytics and fireside folksiness. Rorty's work, though evidence of its direct impact on British writing is scant, is further circumstantial evidence of an intellectual mood in which truth, knowledge, selfhood and value were considered sceptically, as local human fabrications rather than divinely, or even scientifically, sanctioned. This mood found extensive expression in the literature of the 1980s.

Live by Satellite

Indeed it informed major theories of postmodernism in literature. Brian McHale's *Postmodernist Fiction* (1987) argued that the break from modernism to postmodernism was a shift from 'epistemological' to 'ontological' fiction. In the former, questions of knowledge and its reliability remain urgent but vexing. The world (let alone the mind), in James, Conrad or Woolf is elusive; the novelist must seek to render it accurately while being aware of the difficulties of doing so. In McHale's postmodernism, this tension has slackened. The business of fiction is no longer to struggle to represent a pre-existing world, but to fabricate interesting fictional ones. All fictional worlds are constructs, but in postmodernism this fact is registered and explored. Characters might reflect on their own textual status, or cross from one textual realm to another. Narrators suddenly interrupt stories to reflect upon their arbitrary activity of world-making, or even enter their own texts as characters.

One of McHale's major rivals as a theorist of postmodern fiction also stressed fiction's actively constructive status, but with a greater emphasis on the world beyond it. In a steady series of books and articles through the decade, Linda Hutcheon identified 'historiographic metafiction' as the most interesting and valuable form of postmodern writing. Metafiction – fiction about fiction – had been recognised as part of the postmodern arsenal since the 1960s, when Barth and Coover published texts that commented on themselves, and Vonnegut strolled into his own narratives. The best-known British contribution was John Fowles' *The French Lieutenant's Woman* (1969), a Victorian romance that is interrupted by an intrusive, reflective authorial voice. That book finally offers the reader a choice of endings, an idea scorned by the narrator of Julian Barnes' *Flaubert's Parrot* (Barnes 1984: 89) – which in turn demonstrates how postmodern fiction could become a developing, reflexive tradition in its own right. In writing of the nineteenth century, Fowles also supplied the other half of Hutcheon's formula: the novel, she writes,

> requires that historical context in order to interrogate the present (as well as the past) through its critical irony. Parodic self-reflexiveness paradoxically leads here to the possibility of a literature which, while asserting its modernist autonomy as art, also manages simultaneously to investigate its intricate and intimate relations with the social world in which it is written and read. (1988: 45)

Hutcheon thus seeks to combine the social referentiality of the nineteenth-century novel with the formal hesitations of the twentieth century, in a mode that is politically virtuous for its work in alerting us to the constructed and partial nature of our accounts of the world. 'History,' Hutcheon explains, 'is not made obsolete: it is, however, being rethought – as a human construct. [. . .] We cannot know the past except through its texts: its documents, its evidence, even its eye-witness accounts are *texts*.' Postmodern novels, she affirms, 'teach us about both this fact and its consequences' (1988: 16). Hutcheon's theory gained great credence from the sheer proliferation of instances in this period. She located them in diverse national literatures, from E. L. Doctorow's *Ragtime* (1975) to Umberto Eco's *The Name of the Rose* (1980) and J. M. Coetzee's *Foe* (1986). Along with McHale she provided a plausible model for theorising the fiction of the 1980s even as it emerged.

The most influential account of postmodernism did not confine itself to fiction. Fredric Jameson's celebrated 1984 essay, and the other elaborations with which he followed it, set all existing discussions in a new political frame. Established as America's leading Marxist critic, Jameson presented postmodernism as 'the cultural logic of late capitalism': the last, apparently optimistic phrase borrowed from the Trotskyist economist Ernest Mandel who had theorised an advanced stage of global capitalist integration. Jameson proceeded by analysing a range of instances: the art of Andy Warhol, the new architecture of Los Angeles, the fiction of E. L. Doctorow and poetry of Bob Perelman, and many more across his subsequent essays. These cases exemplified key tendencies in the art and experience of the present: a privileging of surface and loss of depth; a 'waning of affect' as traditional emotions were replaced by hallucinogenic 'intensities'; the eclipse of the human subject itself; a loss of historical consciousness even as decontextualised images of the past were projected everywhere. Some of Jameson's more flamboyant assertions are unpersuasive. The notion of the 'death of the subject', for instance, was a fashionable motif from poststructuralism but had scant correlative in actual life, where the tendency was in fact toward greater individualism than ever before in history – from Thatcherite privatisation to the aggrandisement of the self in the memoir boom of the 1990s. Yet as a whole, Jameson's analytical project was the most brilliantly capacious formulation of the postmodern, in its unparalleled range of reference and its eagerness to situate the entire field historically. It provided a model of postmodernism that, like Baudrillard's, could feed back into and influence the very cultural production it was describing. It also sealed the association of postmodernism with commerce, apparently licensing the political Left's suspicions of the term or its referent. Jameson himself was at pains to insist that a 'moralistic' refusal of postmodernism was inappropriate: the field must be confronted as a complex reality, not judged good or bad (1991: 46–7). But his own rhetoric could slide into implicit denunciation, and thus give some succour to those viewing postmodernism as a lucrative decadence.

Whatever the prominence of postmodernism, to seek it in British fiction could seem an unpromising project. For one prevailing image of British cultural life is of anti-intellectualism, suspicious or plain ignorant of foreign developments. The parody headline 'Fog in Channel: Continent Cut Off' satirises a British insularity in which London is the complacent centre of significance. In fact the cultural breadth of postmodernism is one argument against this view. If the postmodern was a 'cultural dominant' as Jameson proposed (1991: 4), then it would manifest itself across British life regardless of tradition's blinkers. A spirited mapping of such manifestations came from the cultural critic Dick Hebdige, whose study *Hiding in the Light* (1988) treated contemporary ideas not as a foreign affair but as embedded in the changing Britain of Live Aid, *The Face* magazine and *Biff* cartoons. '[L]ook down any British high street', urged Helen Carr, 'at mock-mock-Tudor shopping centres, Crystal Palaces crossed with Covent Gardens, brick Palladio hotels' (1989: 11). By the end of the decade popular television programmes would commonly be labelled postmodern for their irony, self-consciousness and range of cultural reference, though many of the more celebrated – *Moonlighting* (1985–89) or David Lynch's *Twin Peaks* (1990–1) – were American imports. Even into the apparently ephemeral discourse of pop music criticism the maverick scribe Paul Morley inserted destabilising portions of Derrida or Barthes, while honing his own intensely recursive, ironic style. When the carefree bohemians of Geoff Dyer's *The Colour of Memory* (1989) visit a country fair in a South London park, they see a world music act on stage, picked up also on a giant screen: 'The dancers and musicians looked as if they were playing at the County Fair in Brockwell Park; the pictures on the video screen looked as if they were being broadcast live by satellite from Harare or Lagos' (1989: 218). Here indeed is Brixton's answer to DeLillo. The Baudrillardian experience in which replication outperforms reality is worth remarking, but familiar enough to provoke no ontological apocalypse: just one of those 1980s things.

But if versions of postmodernism could be found in everyday life, what versions was the British novel evolving? The cantankerous experimentalist B. S. Johnson considered in 1973 that if literature was a relay race, then '[t]he vast majority of British novelists has dropped the baton, stood still, turned back, or not even realised that there is a race' (1990: 182). Randall Stevenson picks up the metaphor to concede that 'The baton of innovation [. . .] sometimes has to be carried by another team before the British outfit can continue its own erratic course down the tracks of literary history' (1991: 31). Yet he insists that British fiction, while often viewed as though Kingsley Amis or C. P. Snow were its exemplars, has in fact maintained a productive contact with foreign modes – from the *nouveau roman* to metafiction – which has given it at least a submerged avant-garde tradition. Besides B. S. Johnson himself, a significant instance is Christine Brooke-Rose, a theorist as well as novelist. In *Granta*'s 1980 symposium on the British novel it was Brooke-Rose who took on the legacy of American metafiction and the demanding theoretical formulations of postmodernism that had coalesced in the 1970s. In the 1980s she extended her already voluminous fictional output with the punning, pan-historical *Amalgamemnon* (1984) and *Xorandor's* exploration of computer technology (1986). Writers like Brooke-Rose, as Stevenson maintains, have kept open 'a wide spectrum of possibility, even for authors who may not always wish to go so far in such radical directions themselves' (1991: 31).

Indeed, British postmodernist fiction of the 1980s would centre on this last group of authors. In what follows I wish to focus not on uncompromising experiment, but on those writers who sought a pact between reflexivity and storytelling, the intellectual and the mainstream. These writers did much to define the shape of British fiction in the 1980s, and even to influence theories of postmodernism itself. Their work might plausibly be seen as a typically British compromise with populism, and thus as symptomatic of national culture. Yet that very compromise, as I have already indicated, has been a central strain in postmodernism itself all along, thus making the British novelists exemplary of a far broader trend too.

In the final section of this chapter we will observe another version of these issues in relation to poetry. First, however, let us consider a sequence of central candidates in the making of the British postmodern novel. We will begin with a comparative examination of two pivotal texts of the decade: Salman Rushdie's *Midnight's Children* (1981) and Angela Carter's novel *Nights at the Circus* (1984). Then we will consider a cluster of other novels that show a kinship to these influential works: Julian Barnes' *Flaubert's Parrot* (1984) and *A History of the World in 10½ Chapters* (1989), Graham Swift's *Waterland* (1983) and Jeanette Winterson's *Oranges Are Not the Only Fruit* (1985) and *The Passion* (1987). Each of these texts is keenly interested in the status of truth and fiction, and the forms of representation in which history is cast. Central to these concerns is storytelling: the activity that Lyotard had presented as the model of contemporary knowledge. But storytelling is not only a theme but the inevitable activity of the novels themselves. It is both explicitly, even obsessively, discussed within the novels, and ostentatiously performed by them.

Mythical Bombs

Salman Rushdie and Angela Carter were central figures in the British novel of the 1980s. In *Midnight's Children* an alternative version of India's post-war history is narrated by Saleem Sinai. Independent India came into existence at midnight on 14 August 1947; Saleem was born at the same instant, and comes to experience his life as the 'mirror' of the postcolonial state's trajectory. In *Nights at the Circus*, set in 1899, the American journalist Walser follows the inexplicably winged woman Fevvers on her picaresque journey to Russia with an American travelling circus. Both Rushdie and Carter, in these works and elsewhere, were seen to be finding fictional forms for contemporary concerns; above all, respectively, postcolonial and feminist issues. These issues will be considered in their own right in the next two chapters. Both could qualify the writers for the dissident postmodernism announced by Dina Sherzer among many others. In what follows, we will consider how these novels contribute to the new fictional trend, by tracing four aspects across both texts: narration, commentary, history and the fantastic.

'And there are so many stories to tell,' Rushdie's narrator Saleem Sinai warns on his first page, 'too many, such an excess of intertwined lives events miracles places rumours, so dense a commingling of the improbable and the mundane!' (1981: 9). 'Can any narrative stand so much?' he wonders later: he is referring to the story's sensationalism, but could equally refer to its plenitude. In any case, he immediately resumes, 'Once upon a time . . .' (280). *Nights at the Circus* likewise bulges with stories. It commences with a sustained act of storytelling: Fevvers' oral rendition of her past. But this act includes numerous subsidiary narratives. They detail the brothel in which Fevvers was raised, her prostitute friends and their fates since the establishment's closure (2006: 49–51); the oddities she encounters at a 'museum of woman monsters' (70–7); and the effectively self-contained episode at the house of a homicidal Rosicrucian (84–97). The arrival of Colonel Kearney's circus provides a whole new set of characters whose back-story asks to be told: the Colonel himself (115–16), the taciturn Princess of Abyssina (173) and the extended story of Mignon (149–65), which itself includes sub-plots like her spell with the fin-de-siècle fake Herr M (154–62) – which itself in turn contains a brief digression into the departure of Herr M's previous assistant to Rio (154–5). Even once the circus has been derailed, the book has a compulsion to find narratives, looping back into the formative past of each new character who turns up. Walser, listening to Fevvers and Lizzie early on, feels 'more and more like a kitten tangling up in a ball of wool it had never intended to unravel in the first place; or a sultan faced with not one but two Scheherezades, both intent on impacting a thousand stories into the single night' (43). This is in part the novel's description of its own effect on the reader.

Rushdie's narration extends itself back and forwards in time. It is full of prolepsis, pointing teasingly to future events. It is not surprising, in this novel, to read, 'Years later, in Pakistan, on the very night when the roof was to fall in on her head and squash her flatter than a rice-pancake . . .' (157). The novel also compulsively looks back: large chunks of text are taken up with recapitulation of the story so far (106–7, 213–14, 216–17, 237, 303–4, 382, 405). Both prolepsis and recap are implicated in the novel's compulsive search for patterns (12). Rushdie's world is an echo-chamber, a place where everything resembles or recalls everything else. Though much is vivid, little is truly unique. Saleem theorises the point as an Indian obsession with 'correspondences', a 'national longing for form' (300).

He adumbrates here an inveterate tendency not merely to tell but to explicate and comment on what is told. In Carter commentary becomes especially autonomous: in effect, the one thing that stops her narrating is her urge to expostulate on an idea. Sometimes characters do this for her. Thus the Marxist Lizzie proffers lengthy disquisitions on human nature and 'the anvil of history' (2006: 282–3), while the head clown Buffo's lengthy pontification on the nature of his trade (137–43) is unmistakably an essay in fictional costume. Carter's main narrative voice itself is also given to thematic reflections. Thus Walser's adoption of a clown's face prompts a note on 'the freedom that lies behind the mask, within dissimulation, the freedom to juggle with being, and, indeed, with the language which is vital to our being, that lies at the heart of burlesque' (119). Here the dissimulation of fiction is almost cast aside: it could be the voice of Carter the journalist.

Among the largest ideas in both novels is history. Carter's is a historical novel, but in its revisionism it belongs to a very contemporary trend. She has fun with the fin-de-siècle, claiming that Fevvers has met Toulouse-Lautrec and Jarry and preceded Freud (8). She is also precoccupied with time, from the chimes of Big Ben that sound midnight every hour through the first section, to the arrival of the twentieth century in the book's last moments (348). Carter uses the Siberian tribe's world-picture to enquire into the constructed character of Western time or 'Yanqui history', noting that if the whole world had been allowed to vote on it in 1899, then 'the twentieth century would have forthwith ceased to exist, the entire system of dividing up years by one hundred would have been abandoned and time, by popular consent, would have stood still' (314). The twentieth century thus acquires, for this novel, a somewhat provisional character. Even if, as Carter immediately admits, the tribe are already on the verge of entering Western history, the book is dotted with utopians – like the lesbian escapees from the Siberian prison – who seek a future different from the one that we know has happened.

Then again, Carter's narrator seems aware of how the new century will turn out. When the circus arrives in St Petersburg, Carter observes that the local peasants 'do not know what we know about their city':

> They lived on, without knowledge or surmise, in this city that is on the point of becoming legend but not yet, not quite yet; the city, this Sleeping Beauty of a city, stirs and murmurs, longing yet fearing the rough and bloody kiss that will awaken her, tugging at her moorings in the past, striving, yearning to burst through the present into the violence of that authentic history to which this narrative – as must by now be obvious! – does not belong. (111)

Carter overlays her historical Russia with understated reference to the revolution that is due within two decades. The imminent movement of real history is asserted, even as the novel's membership of that history is emphatically rejected. The implication is that this is only a fabulous tale. But the very reference to this distinction keeps Carter on terms with the real. In a sly return to the theme she finally implies that Lizzie has encountered Lenin in the British Museum, and that her whole journey has helped lay the path to the revolution (346). The mixture here – of history and fantasy, a desire both to refer to political events and to rewrite them – is typical of the fictional trend we are tracing.

Rushdie's narrator bridges private life and public history. A letter from the new nation's prime minister informs him that his life 'will be, in a sense, the mirror of our own' (1981: 122). This point is literalised when a mocking schoolmaster compares Saleem's ugly and stained face to the map of India (231). But it is more deeply fulfilled in the parallel that Saleem discerns between India's history and his own. Almost every major historical event becomes improbably twinned with the latest twist in his own biography. Thus Saleem's father suffers a stroke on 'the first day of the "false peace" which would last a mere thirty-seven days' between India and Pakistan (337), while the arrival of Saleem's warlike nemesis Shiva into his life happens on the same day that India first detonates a nuclear bomb (406–7). The personal and the political proceed in uncanny parallel. But Saleem also claims to have been the reluctant cause of many political events: partition (192), two wars (338, 373) and the mass sterilisation programme ordered by Indira Gandhi (432). Explaining that 'I was linked to history both literally and metaphorically, both actively and passively' (238), he systematically combines these four elements into the potential 'modes of connection' between himself and the nation. The book is never more reflexive than this: Rushdie himself sketches a series of theoretical formulations that it would otherwise have taken a literary critic to produce, and he subsequently uses them to comment on the action (290, 299, 329, 351). Here, as in Carter, the novel temporarily becomes a form of critical theory.

Rushdie is insistently but ambiguously preoccupied with the possibility of historical truth. At times he seems to embrace plurality and uncertainty: 'There are as many versions of India as there are Indians' (269). Saleem declares that '[r]eality is a question of perspective; the further you get from the past, the more concrete and plausible it seems – but as you approach the present, it inevitably seems more and more incredible' (165), and later repeats that 'we are too close to what-is-happening, perspective is impossible [. . .] only subjective judgments are possible' (435). Yet the book is unwilling to leave it at that. In narrating the Indo-Pakistan war, Rushdie veers between insisting on 'good hard facts' and despairing at their indeterminacy: 'But which facts?' (388). He presents a good deal of historical information, but also notes the extreme discrepancies between the two sides' accounts of the fighting, and insists, 'Nothing was real; nothing certain' (339–40). The novel registers an irrepressible desire for historical truth, especially when this has been suppressed by state power: the Emergency had 'a white part – public, visible, documented, a matter for historians – and a black part which, being secret macabre untold, must be a matter for us' (421).

Here the novel allies itself with a hidden counter-history, and can hardly help implying the validity of that hitherto occluded narrative. But it is too dominated by doubts and fictions to present this as authoritative. During the war, 'the story I am going to tell [. . .] is as likely to be true as anything; as anything, that is to say, except what we were officially told' (335). In any case, as a novel, *Midnight's Children* cannot beat historiography on its own ground. 'Aircraft, real or fictional, dropped actual or mythical bombs,' Saleem recalls: 'It is, accordingly, either a matter of fact or a figment of a diseased imagination' that three of them happened to hit buildings containing members of his family (341). The first sentence here – 'actual or mythical bombs' – might appear to anticipate Baudrillard's contention a decade later that the 1991 Gulf War had never taken place; but in context it seems sarcastically to insist that the carnage of war is real, however it might be denied or mythologised. But the second sentence takes us into fiction: those family members never existed, so what Saleem describes is not a 'matter of fact' but, indeed, the figment of someone's imagination. *Midnight's Children* cannot authoritatively rewrite history: instead it uses its fictional licence to work around what is known.

It does so most boldly in its deployment of the fantastic. Saleem's greatest coup is to disclose that all the children born between that first midnight and 1 a.m. were blessed with remarkable powers: from death-dealing beauty and time travel to Saleem's own ability to read minds. His telepathic power leads him to convene the Midnight Children's Conference, in which all thousand-and-one super-children confer and dispute. They thus offer an allegory of the political potential of an independent India – which, the novel implies, is itself a kind of fiction, hardly less fabulous than the children. Saleem's fiancée Padma understandably accuses him of hallucinating, which he denies: 'I am not speaking metaphorically; what I have just written (and read aloud to stunned Padma) is nothing less than the literal, by-the-hairs-of-my-mother's-head truth' (200). There are many such moments: repeatedly Saleem defies the disquiet of the implied reader, insisting simply, 'That's how it was; there can be no retreat from the truth' (195–6); 'believe don't believe but it's true. [. . .] It happened that way because that's how it happened' (460–1).

The tone here is complex. Within the novel, Saleem insists on his plain fidelity to the truth. Outside the novel, Rushdie and we know that these events did not happen. Yet the novel repeatedly suggests that fantasy and history are mutually implicated. Saleem speaks of 'the whole disjointed unreality of the times' (76), and of independent India as a 'mythical land', 'mass fantasy' and 'collective fiction' (112). Anything can happen 'in a country which is itself a sort of dream' (118). While denying that midnight's children are merely metaphorical, he elaborates that

> [r]eality can have metaphorical content; that does not make it less real. [. . .] Midnight's children can be made to represent many things [. . .] they can be seen as the last throw of everything antiquated and retrogressive in our myth-ridden nation, whose defeat was entirely desirable in the context of a modernizing, twentieth-century economy; or as the true hope of freedom, which is now forever extinguished. (200)

In a sense Rushdie gives us the truth about the children here. They really are an elaborate, open-ended metaphor, a way of thinking about India. But this cannot be admitted within the novel itself, where they are all the more vivid for being as real as anyone else. Saleem speaks of '[m]atter of fact descriptions of the outré and bizarre, and their reverse, namely heightened, stylized versions of the everyday' (218): this is another of the novel's self-descriptions. History, *Midnight's Children* intimates, can be experienced as a fantasy or a myth; it can also generate fantastic results which might seem quite realistic from a different perspective.

This desire to entertain the fantastic is among Rushdie's strongest imaginative bonds with Carter. He paid tribute to it upon her death in 1992, calling her 'a very good wizard'. Both writers also paid homage to Gabriel García Márquez, the Colombian exemplar of 'magic realism' in which the fantastic occurs as matter-of-factly as the mundane. In a 1982 review of Márquez Rushdie explicitly described magic realism as 'a development out of Surrealism that expresses a genuinely "Third World" consciousness'. In that 'half-made' world, 'impossible things happen constantly, and quite plausibly, out in the open under the midday sun' (Rushdie 1991: 301–2). In describing Márquez, Rushdie also offers a gloss on his own fiction. Carter noted that both writers' third-world roots allowed them to draw on actual peasant folklore, 'shamans who are actually *real*' (Haffenden 1985: 81). She lacked that background, but *Nights at the Circus* equally haunts the boundary between the real and the unreal – most evidently in the figure of Fevvers herself. 'Is she fact or is she fiction?' asks her official slogan (2006: 3). The status of her wings is contemplated several times by Walser. Suddenly approaching 'the absolute suspension of disbelief', he considers the paradox that 'in order to earn a living, might not a genuine bird-woman [. . .] have to pretend she was an artificial one?' (16).

Carter's novel is drawn to what it dubs 'the radiant shadow of the implausible' (317). It does deploy a discourse of hard-headed material-ism, via the grizzled political activist Lizzie, but it also indulges in flights of fancy that do not answer to such tribunals. One is Fevvers' escape from the predatory Grand Duke in St Petersburg, in which a toy train seems to allow her to leap onto the real circus train (226). Another occurs when bandits blow up the train in Siberia, and the circus tigers vanish into the mirrors with which they have travelled: 'On one broken fragment of mirror, a paw with the claws out; on another, a snarl' (242). Carter's reference to the shaman's world as one of 'magic realism' (308) is tongue in cheek, but these moments give her novel a foothold in the same literary continuum as the fairy tales in which she took a sustained and influential interest.

String Full of Knots

These novels were exemplary for much British fiction that would be called postmodernist. Several major novelists of the period shared aspects of their aesthetic. Jeanette Winterson is an important example. Her first novel, *Oranges are Not the Only Fruit* (1985), is a fictional-ised autobiography in which everyday events are intercut with episodes from fairy-tale and romance. Parallels suggest themselves between the two textual levels: so when the young Jeanette is condemned by her Pentecostal church, we read of Sir Perceval's exile in a wood (Winterson 1991: 132). The narrator's dream of studying at Oxford is figured as the sorcerer Winnet Stonejar (an anagram of Winterson's name) thinks of 'a beautiful city, a long way off, with buildings that ran up to the sky', where '[t]he city dwellers didn't sow or toil, they thought about the world' (149). But where, in Rushdie and Carter, the jostling, mutually modifying coexistence of the realistic and the fabulous is crucial, in this novel Winterson largely keeps the two realms separate. The episodes of Arthurian romance belong to a different plane, separated from 1960s Lancashire by a line of white space. The exception is the feverish Jeanette's encounter with an orange demon (106–7), which blithely gives her advice.

Among the book's most striking features is a brief chapter, 'Deuteronomy', which seems to step outside the fictional frame, as a miniature essay on the nature of history. The piece employs plentiful metaphor and anecdote, but also talks at us very directly:

> Everyone who tells a story tells it differently, just to remind us that everybody sees it differently. Some people say there are true things to be found, some people say all kinds of things can be proved. I don't believe them. The only thing for certain is how complicated it all is, like string full of knots. It's all there but hard to find the beginning and impossible to fathom the end.
> [. . .]
>   People like to separate storytelling which is not fact from history which is fact. They do this so that they know what to believe and what not to believe. This is very curious. (91)

Here are some increasingly familiar concerns: belief and disbelief, the knowability of history, the role of narrative in our knowledge. Here, too, is an extreme form of the discursivity in which these concerns are so often voiced. The novel is a space not only for narrating the doings of fictional characters, but for essayistic reflection; and the reflection is upon the properties of the novel itself. In one sense the text looks inward, becomes self-molesting; in another, its oration on history entertains unusually ambitious designs upon the world.

Winterson's third novel, *The Passion* (1987) is less emphatically essayistic, but highlights many of the themes we have been tracing. The era of Napoleon's European wars is dramatised through the experiences of marginal characters: Henri, Napoleon's cook; and Villanelle, a Venetian casino worker. While major events in the novel's background correspond to the historical record, Winterson's central story is more akin to fable than to historiography. As in Rushdie and Carter, different levels of the implausible and fabulous are at work. Even if we grant the lush descriptions of Venice as a city of mazes in which 'there is no such thing as straight ahead' (Winterson 1987: 49), we enter a different plane when we read of boatmen with webbed feet (129), a lookout with a telescopic eye (21–3) and a woman whose heart is stored in a jar (120–1). This is a historical novel that wants to partake of the possibilities of fairy-tale. The briskness of Winterson's prose contributes to this:

> They talked about the mountain ranges and the opera. They talked about animals with metal coats that can swim the length of the river without coming up for air. They talked about the valuable, fabulous thing that everyone has and keeps a secret. 'Here', said Salvadore, 'look at this', and he took out a box enamelled on the outside and softly lined on the inside and on the inside was his heart.
>   'Give me yours in exchange.'
>   But she couldn't because she was not travelling with her heart, it was beating in another place. (97–8)

Where the sentences of Carter and Rushdie fatten on their own self-referentiality, Winterson seeks an elemental simplicity. Her repetitions ('They talked about') are childlike, or incantatory. But despite the difference in style, Winterson is also fascinated by storytelling. The whole novel is made up of first-person acts of narration (first Henri's, then Villanelle's): some are embedded within others, as when Henri's narrative hosts Villanelle's life-story (89–99). Narrative, Winterson suggests, is a process of persuasion, and the audience's credulity is uncertain. Hence the novel's *leitmotif*, repeated by both main characters after narrating something unlikely: 'I'm telling you stories. Trust me' (5, 13, 160). The phrase summarises a whole strain of literary endeavour in this period: at once emphasising, even delighting in, the act of narration and placing in question its veracity, while leaving us no firm ground on which doubt could end. In interview, Winterson glosses her phrase as representing

> the trustworthiness of the unreliable narrator, in that nobody is going to pretend that this is objectivity. [. . .] And in those hesitations and gestures, I think, we come closer to a truth than in any possible kind of documentary objectivity. So we trust writers because they *are* untrustworthy, because they do not claim to have that certainty and that knowledge. (Reynolds and Noakes 2003: 21)

While epistemological certainty is bracketed, narrative is prized.

This is equally true of other writers in the 1980s whose work did not so favour the fantastic mode. Julian Barnes' novels *Flaubert's Parrot* (1984) and *A History of the World in 10½ Chapters* (1989) exemplify the recurring concerns of narrative and history. *Flaubert's Parrot* comprises the drily melancholy reflections of the retired doctor Geoffrey Braithwaite, who rarely strays from the subject of Gustave Flaubert. The *History of the World* is much less of a continuous narrative than its title grandly promises: its ten chapters are a set of suggestively linked short stories. One chapter title, 'Three Simple Stories', suggests the real status of narrative in Barnes' work: he shuns the overarching story in favour of brief tales, which illustrate or hint at the issues in hand. Like Rushdie and Carter, he oversees a proliferation of narratives, but these are not marshalled by a garrulous speaker with a compulsion to narrate; more often, rather, by an urbane voice using stories to highlight its thoughts. In his distinct way, Barnes presents us yet again with insistent discursivity.

Some of the *History*'s stories have specific implied readers; other narrators invoke us in that capacity, like the woodworm who narrates the first chapter and the heaven-dweller of the last. What is more distinctively Barnesian is the even more direct address, in which facts and thoughts are presented to us with scholarly precision: the extended analysis of Gericault's *Scene of Shipwreck* (125–39), the exegesis on Jonah and the whale (175–81), and most strikingly of all the half-chapter 'Parenthesis'. This is not a story at all but an essay on love and history, which admits that 'when I say "I" you will want to know within a paragraph or two whether I mean Julian Barnes or someone invented' (227). Writing like this has earned Barnes the tag of a novelist who is really an essayist (Childs 2005: 86). But his discursive play with ideas is also historically typical, characteristic of the mode of fiction we are tracing here. Barnes' deployment of the essayistic parallels Carter's allegorical tableaux of the circus clowns.

Like several contemporaries, Barnes is persistently concerned with the status of historical fact. His novels suggest a certain relativism in their sheer multiplicity. *Flaubert's Parrot* splices genres of writing: Geoffrey Braithwaite's discourse co-exists with three differing chronologies of Flaubert's life (themselves arranged to tell three different stories), a dispute with an imagined foe of Flaubert ('The Case Against'), the voice of Flaubert's lover Louise Colet, an A–Z of Flaubert and an examination paper. Numerous ways of seeing are available, each of them rooted in recorded fact. A similar gesture is implicit in *A History of the World*: the book's internal heterogeneity posits human history as itself rangy and varied, though also honeycombed with odd connections and echoes. The overweening title already contains its own touch of Monty Python bathos. The book itself is modest: it offers not an authoritative history but a series of very partial perspectives, of which the first, told by a woodworm, is the lowliest imaginable.

Barnes addresses history as explicitly as any of his contemporaries. For Geoffrey Braithwaite, what did not happen is as interesting as what did: the books Flaubert conceived but didn't write, the lives he didn't lead (115–25). Ascertaining what anyone *did* do proves hazardous enough. Comparing a film of the Normandy landings with the Bayeux Tapestry, Braithwaite ventures a typically Barnesian combination of question and metaphor:

> How do we seize the past? Can we ever do so? When I was a medical student some pranksters at an end-of-term dance released into the hall a piglet which had been smeared with grease. It squirmed between legs, evaded capture, squealed a lot. People fell over trying to grasp it, and were made to look ridiculous in the process. The past often seems to behave like that piglet. (14)

The animal image is characteristic. Braithwaite seeks Flaubert's parrot, the stuffed bird that the writer kept on his desk while writing his late story 'Un Coeur Simple'. His discovery of two contenders is troubling enough; but on the final page he finds three more, the survivors from a vanished battalion of fifty (190). The possible truths are at least that many. Braithwaite multiplies other images for the past. It is a riot-wrecked city in which, 'Lost, disordered, fearful, we follow what signs there remain; we read the street names, but cannot be confident where we are' (60). Like Flaubert studying the Normandy countryside, 'we must look at the past through coloured glass' (94). Or, in keeping with the narrator's cross-channel trajectory:

> The past is a distant, receding coastline, and we are all in the same boat. Along the stern rail there is a line of telescopes; each brings the shore into focus at a given distance. If the boat is becalmed, one of the telescopes will be in continual use; it will seem to tell the whole, the unchanging truth. But this is an illusion; and as the boat sets off again, we return to our normal activity: scurrying from one telescope to another, seeing the sharpness fade in one, waiting for the blur to clear in another. (101)

The piglet represents the slipperiness of the past; the telescopes signal the multiple perspectives from which we look back at it, their clarity changing according to our location. 'We can study files for decades,' Braithwaite admits, 'but every so often we are tempted to throw up our hands and declare that history is merely another literary genre: the past is autobiographical fiction pretending to be a parliamentary report' (90). In 'Parenthesis', seemingly unconcerned by the loud echo of Winterson's half-chapter of direct address in *Oranges*, Barnes is still more direct:

> History isn't what happened. History is just what historians tell us. [. . .] And we, the readers of history, the sufferers from history, we scan the pattern for hopeful conclusions, for the way ahead. [. . .] The history of the world? Just

voices echoing in the dark; images that burn for a few centuries then fade; stories, old stories that sometimes seem to overlap; strange links, impertinent connections. (1989: 242)

It is striking, in this novel and its contemporaries, how directly such historical scepticism is registered. Barnes can always find another elegant metaphor for it, akin to Rushdie's invocation of a cinema screen which becomes less clear the closer we approach it (1981: 165–6). But essentially we are being *told* about our relation to history and truth. It is a paradox, though not necessarily disabling, that these texts speak so authoritatively about the loss of epistemological authority. Indeed they share this position with Lyotard, who was frequently accused of the performative contradiction of recounting a grand narrative of the end of grand narratives.

If any novel of this era is even more obsessed with history, it is Graham Swift's *Waterland* (1983). The novel's narrator Tom Crick is, emblematically, a history teacher in a London school. He tells the history of the English fens, the landscape of his own family background, while also detailing the early-1980s present in which his job is assailed by gloomy pupils and government cuts. Like Barnes' Braithwaite, Crick provides an urbane medium for Swift's narrative, readily swinging into miniature essays on matters of fact. The novel's often short chapters signal these: 'About the Ouse' recounts the natural and social history of the Suffolk river, and 'About the Eel' does the same for the animal (1983: 124–7, 169–77). Much like Barnes, Swift splices facts into his fiction, elegantly allowing them to combine in a continuous, recursive speculation on the nature of knowledge. This takes the form of Crick's wandering address to his class of schoolchildren. He offers them a scattered series of definitions of history: 'this cumbersome but precious bag of clues' (92); 'that impossible thing: the attempt to give an account, with incomplete knowledge, of actions themselves undertaken with incomplete knowledge' (94); 'a lucky dip of meanings' (122); 'a settling for roles' (143). All of these stress the limits of history: the necessary incompleteness of human knowledge, the randomness of meaning, the role of performance. Indeed Crick also notes history's proximity to histrionics, defining it afresh as 'the fabrication, the diversion, the reality-obscuring drama' (34). Human beings, Crick avers, seek causality: man is 'the animal that asks Why' (92). History is thus hard-wired to humanity. But it is less solid than it seems. From the start, Crick emphasises the role of narrative, which is equally native to humanity, 'the story-telling animal' (53). His family told stories to 'outwit reality' (15). Crick repeatedly deploys the fairy-tale opening 'Once upon a time', foregrounding the shaping action of his narration on the family history he recounts. Fairy tale is an explicit analogy: Crick 'grew up in a fairy-tale place' (1) and refers to real lives as 'those most unbelievable yet haunting of fairy tales' (6). We 'can't get away', he avers, from 'our fairy-tales' (155). Seeking explanations in history, he has discovered 'more mysteries, more fantasticalities', and concluded that 'history is a yarn'. The reassuring 'Grand Narrative', he reports in Lyotardian phrase, has proved unavailable (53).

In a world of depleted certainties, Barnes' *History* offers a new key word. '"The technical term is fabulation,"' one character is told by a psychologist. '"You make up a story to cover the facts you don't know or can't accept. You keep a few true facts and spin a new story round them"' (Barnes 1989: 109). The status of these words is itself very uncertain: we cannot decisively tell whether their addressee, Kath Ferris, is hallucinating her medical interlocutor, or whether he represents the real world in which she is unknowingly fabulating her escape to a desert island. Barnes picks up the term in 'Parenthesis': 'Our panic and our pain are only eased by soothing fabulation; we call it history' (242). Here is Barnes' version of Winterson's 'I'm telling you stories': the catchword that points to both the inevitability and the treachery of narrative.

Yet the historiographic novel is not generally ecstatic about its relativisation of history into narrative. The British novelists we are considering do not make radically autotelic fictions. Their scepticism tends to be matched by their enduring desire for knowledge. *Waterland*, for all its talk of fairy tales, still defends historical enquiry. Progress does not exist, Tom Crick declares, but we can aspire to 'the reclamation of land': a fenland metaphor for the slow recovery of historical fact. This 'dull yet valuable business' should retain its modesty, and not be mistaken for 'the building of empires' (291). History, Crick opines, can at least teach mistakes, against those who claim to know 'how to do it' (203). Julian Barnes, too, for all the wry scepticism fostered by his work, maintains a commitment to what he dares to call 'objective truth': 'we must believe that it is 99 per cent obtainable; or if we can't believe this we must believe that 43 per cent objective truth is better than 41 per cent' (245–6). Braithwaite's search for Flaubert's parrot is not necessarily unsuccessful: he may have found the right bird, even if he cannot identify it. 'Perhaps it was one of them,' is his last line. It sounds despairing, but might be more straightforwardly positive: perhaps it *was* one of them, after all. Barnes' novels, like *Waterland*, make truth ironic, elusive and questionable, but they do not dissolve the possibility of happening upon it.

Welcoming to Variety

These novelists are postmodern in one quite literal sense. A major strain of modern fictional aesthetics abjured discursive interventions into the novel, in the name of a purified narrative space. Henry James complained in 1884 about novelists with 'a habit of giving themselves away': Anthony Trollope's confession mid-novel that he is only 'making believe' and that he can 'give his narrative any turn the reader may like best' seems to James 'a terrible crime' against literature (James 1968: 80). James followed Flaubert, for whom the novelist's vocation was famously impersonal: in a formulation quoted by Barnes' Geoffrey Braithwaite and echoed by James Joyce, '[T]he artist must no more appear in his work than God does in nature. Man is nothing, the work of art everything . . .' (Barnes 1984: 87). For this strain of modernist fiction, writing was a profoundly self-conscious activity, but such self-consciousness should not take the form of writerly asides to the distracted reader. This stricture is renounced by the writers considered in this chapter. Their readiness to talk at the reader is in a sense a return to pre-modernist fictional aesthetics, the licence to chatter that was revoked by Flaubert and James. 'Postmodernism' here is among other things a cheerful reclamation of textual possibilities that at least some versions of modernism had denied themselves.

The prominence of narrative in these novels is another aspect of this. Modernist fiction, to be sure, contained narrative. But as Paul Sheehan (2002) has argued, narrative was among the concepts most problematised by modernism. The surges of story in Rushdie and Carter are quite different from Joyce's stylistic efflorescences, or Woolf's desire to render moments of thought and emotion – both of which are instances of modernist writing reaching away from narrative, toward some other value. Some have argued that storytelling, suspended or frozen in modernism, makes a comeback in postmodern writing. Michael Wood, considering contemporary fiction, invokes Walter Benjamin's lament for oral storytelling, which Benjamin thought had been replaced by the novel. Since the Second World War, Wood proposes, there has been 'a crisis in the novel and the beginning of a liberation of the story' (1998: 1). It is not that novels are no longer written, but that many of the most interesting and prominent seem like anthologies of anecdotes. 'Stories come back, more often than not, *inside* novels,' Wood ventures: 'The story is less fussy than the novel in this view, more welcoming to variety, less keen to sift the plausible from the fantastic, memory from history' (2–3). Wood's hypothesis is hospitable to the novels we have considered in this chapter. It suggests a fiction that is not so much dominated by one sequential narrative as studded with many irrepressible smaller ones. It is apt that this aesthetic should historically coincide with Lyotard's vision of a profusion of small stories.

Did real connections exist between novelists and contemporary theory? By the decade's end Rushdie was in hiding, in an episode to be considered in the next chapter. But his 1990 essay 'Is Nothing Sacred?' displayed a keen interest in contemporary ideas and retrospectively aligned his work with postmodernism. He associated Lyotard with 'the acceptance that all that is solid *has* melted into air, that reality and morality are not givens but imperfect human constructs' (Rushdie 1991: 422). Rushdie also associated this view with Foucault and Rorty, who had emphasised the historically constructed character of human values and traditions (423). The Francophile Julian Barnes was naturally acquainted with the work of Roland Barthes, by now a French institution. *Flaubert's Parrot*'s narrator implicitly invokes Barthes' celebrated essay 'The Death of the Author' in talking of '[c]ontemporary critics who pompously reclassify all novels and plays and poems as texts – the author to the guillotine!'. On the same page he registers more generally the linguistic turn in post-war thought: 'We no longer believe that language and reality "match up" so congruently – indeed, we probably think that words give birth to things as much as things give birth to words' (1984: 88).

Angela Carter, who had taught at British and American universities, is a still stronger case of the fictional deployment of theory. Just as her *The Passion of New Eve* (1977) had openly dramatised the varieties of 1970s feminism, *Nights at the Circus* stages the ideas of Foucault and Mikhail Bakhtin. The latter had theorised the idea of carnival as that realm of earthy comedy which could bring high ideals down to size and temporarily invert social hierarchies. Carter's play with the clowns – and indeed with the separate, performative world of the circus as a whole – looks like a reference to this theme. Still more ostentatiously, her portrait of the women's prison in Siberia is clearly inspired by Foucault's account of the panopticon, a penitentiary built around surveillance from a central point. Foucault had outlined the importance of this mode of imprisonment in the formation of modern society and selfhood in *Discipline and Punish* (1975, translated in 1978). By the time of Carter's novel this work was starting to have an impact on literary critics in Britain, such as the cultural materialist accounts of the Renaissance offered by Francis Barker (1984) and Catherine Belsey (1985). Carter's panopticon episode would undoubtedly set off a more specific set of triggers for readers involved in the academic Humanities than for others.

Other writers stood at a greater distance from such ideas. Graham Swift, for instance, told a correspondent that he was 'almost entirely ignorant of the revolutions and counter-revolutions in critical theory': 'and I do not regret this ignorance. I am not very interested in critical theory' (Swift 1989). Creative writers have often been wary of academic criticism, even in an era when more of them have entered the academy in teaching roles. But by the early 1980s a degree of cultural cross-reference was already visible, in which theory – even if only vaguely understood – became part of the intellectual substance of the world in which novelists worked. Meanwhile, academic acclaim could encourage the writing of certain kinds of fiction. Critics like Hutcheon could either inspire writers by identifying a possible mode of writing, or make such works more readily marketed by publishers – if only for study on university courses on contemporary fiction. As Steven Connor has noted, since the Second World War an increasing proportion of the readership of the British novel has gone through higher education (1996: 24–5), and the role of the university in forming readerships for novels was thus greater in the 1980s than ever before.

In a reprise of a central postmodern motif, this also gave writers a better chance of squaring the circle of intellectual acclaim and mainstream success. Rushdie and Barnes explicitly address complex subjects like history, truth and authorship. Hutcheon could read their novels as literary companions to Foucault, Derrida and Hayden White. But they are not ostensibly difficult books. The textual experiments of *Flaubert's Parrot*, for instance, are readily subsumed within the book's gently questioning vision, anchored by its melancholy narrator. Rushdie and Carter's inability to stop spinning yarns might tire some readers, but their tall tales are essentially inviting, in a way that linguistic abstraction or Beckettian minimalism would not be.

This contributes to the commercial prospects that Richard Todd has seen as emerging for the novel in the 1980s. In the mid-1990s he averred that literary novelists now enjoyed commercial possibilities that had hitherto belonged only to writers of genre fiction, and observed that '[t]he serious literary novelists of the 1980s and 1990s tend to have a much higher media profile than their peers of a generation ago' (1996: 59–60). In the era of Waterstone's and the Booker Prize, the relative accessibility of Rushdie, Barnes and Carter could win them a broad readership while their explicitly intellectual content gained them respect among academics. The French sociologist Pierre Bourdieu has argued (1993) that 'cultural capital' is usually won at the expense of worldly success, but these writers secured a measure of both.

Years of Toil

Lanark (1981) won Alasdair Gray more cultural capital than hard cash. In the early 1970s he received £75 from Canongate for first option on the novel, and within a year of the book's publication he had run out of money to support him in writing its successor (Gray 1984b). While *Lanark* is acclaimed as Scotland's modern epic, Gray has been notoriously ineffectual at making money from his own work, often giving away paintings and labour for free. If this reflects absent-mindedness, it can also be a matter of principle. On 10 May 1984 the *Glasgow Herald* recorded that he had been awarded the Frederick Niven award, worth £500. Four days later it noted that he had given the entire sum to the striking miners (Kravitz 1997: xiv). Postmodernism might be the cultural logic of late capitalism, but Gray's commercial logic has been less advanced than others'. To assess his relation to the term requires care.

Lanark fits numerous postmodern bills. Its narrative of life in mid-century Glasgow is framed by lengthy sections describing life in Unthank, a city akin to Glasgow yet condemned to almost perpetual darkness. Characters and places in one zone of the book parallel another; thus when the Glaswegian sections end and we return to Unthank, the protagonists perceive that they have been hearing tales of their alter egos or former selves (Gray 1985: 357). The movement of Gray's characters between worlds realistic and fabulous suggests McHale's image of the postmodern novel as a world-generating artefact, whose narrator asks (in Dick Higgins' words): 'Which world is this? What is to be done in it? Which of my selves is to do it?' (McHale 1987: xx). Gray's shuffle between worlds also produces an ingenious shuffling of the novel's order: with the two Glasgow chapters as the middle of the sandwich, the 'books' are numbered 3, 1, 2, 4 – with a 'Prologue' appearing in the last section for good measure. McHale cites *Lanark* as the only text to exploit this technique, in order to 'foreground the order of reading' (1987: 193). *Lanark* is a peculiarly complex artefact, whose reader needs to be ready to grasp narrative order from a wilfully disarrayed structure.

Gray's book can also be viewed as postmodern in its deployment of genre. The story's fantastical narrative is a kind of science fiction, which performs the critical function often attempted by that genre. *Lanark*, McHale notes, is 'transparently indebted to science fiction' (1987: 65). In McHale's terms this fact is significant, for he argues that science fiction is '*the* ontological genre *par excellence*' – a genre in which world-making is plainly dominant – and hence 'postmodernism's non-canonized or "low art" double' (1987: 65, 59). Lanark travels through

Figure 6   Let Glasgow Flourish: Book One of *Lanark* commences 119 pages into the novel

an 'inter-calendrical zone' between worlds, and journeys in an 'eagle-machine' (Gray 1985: 472) to the town of Provan for an international conference where geopolitical inequalities are discussed. In the dystopia of Unthank, a poor family lives in a car but is soothed by idyllic alternate worlds, which are selected and projected on demand (446–7). The scene suggests a critique of television, in particular, as the balm that has pacified the post-war working class. In its combination of technology, illusion and social control it is reminiscent of the work of the American science fiction writer Philip K. Dick. In a more explicit nod to post-war American fiction, the general assembly is attended by a 'Governor Vonnegut of West Atlantis' (473).

Gray himself has suggested that other genres are also in play. In a belligerent retrospect, his occasional alter ego Sidney Workman has criticised *Lanark* as a novel appealing to academics who were just beginning to work on popular culture. Gray, Workman alleges, assembled a set of fairytale, science fiction, horror and 'fashionable' literary influences, and 'boiled them up into that 560–page Postmodern stew, *Lanark*' (Gray 2007: 306). Workman also cites the influence of Fowles' *French Lieutenant's Woman*, again the prototypical British postmodern novel, on Gray's play with authorial status. This occurs above all in *Lanark*'s wilfully misplaced 'Epilogue'. The protagonist walks through a door and encounters a figure, 'Nastler' (which McHale reads as an echo of 'Alasdair' [1987: 214]), who appears to be writing the entire novel. He shows Lanark a page of the text on which he has just written the sentence that we are still in the midst of reading. '"The critics will accuse me of self-indulgence but I don't care,"' he tells Lanark. The sentence bears a footnote: at the foot of the page Gray adds: '1. To have an objection anticipated is no reason for failing to raise it' (Gray 1985: 481). The manoeuvre is archetypal Alasdair Gray, in disarmingly anticipating criticism but also rounding on itself and self-critically disarming the author's own defensive strategy.

Nastler's declarations lay the writing process almost embarrassingly bare:

> 'Though not essential to the plot it [the Epilogue] provides some comic distraction at a moment when the narrative sorely needs it. And it lets me utter some fine sentiments which I could hardly trust to a mere character. And it contains critical notes which will save research scholars years of toil. In fact my epilogue is so essential that I am working on it with nearly a quarter of the book still unwritten.' (483)

His account of the book's genesis (492–3) is identical to that given elsewhere by Gray himself (2002). The Epilogue is thus tantamount to a piece of text from outside the novel – a post-publication interview with the author – that has been placed on its inside. It bears still another layer of commentary, in the footnotes sparring with Nastler and an extensive list of plagiarisms that seizes a third of the page for a spell. *Lanark*'s Contents page informs us that these annotations are by Sidney Workman, who signs off the Epilogue by delegating responsibility and credit for the book to numerous individuals besides Gray: from James Kelman to the novel's American typesetters. Few British novels have been as radically, dizzyingly devoted to displaying their own workings.

The encounter between Lanark and Nastler is among the richest instances of a major tendency in postmodern fiction. Nastler cites Vonnegut's *Breakfast of Champions* (1973) as a recent precursor (481). In the 1980s themselves Martin Amis' improbably erudite namesake stalks *Money* and converses with his narrator, and Salman Rushdie's *The Satanic Verses* features a self-deprecating apparition from the God-like yet dishevelled author that is perhaps indebted to *Lanark* (Rushdie 1988: 318–19). Such encounters violate the Flaubertian aesthetic noted earlier, instead breaking fiction's frame and making the construction of a text part of its subject matter. In Gray, especially, the authorial surrogate appears as a flawed figure, a God who has failed to retain convincing authority. In this respect Roland Barthes' 1968 declaration of the death of the author – signalling a demotion of writers as the prime determinants of textual meaning – can be dramatically fulfilled even while the authors visibly come to life within their works.

Sidney Workman thus seems plausible in declaring that Gray's materials are 'welded together by techniques that had come to be called Postmodern by the 1980s' (Gray 2007: 306). Randall Stevenson, outlining British postmodernism, proposes local roots for Gray's literary innovations, in Scotland's 'strong feelings of cultural, linguistic and political autonomy' (1991: 34). The importance of such feelings to Gray's work is indubitable. But they actually suggest another turn of the screw. What if Gray's relative 'autonomy' is not only from London, but from postmodernism itself? The question returns us to the enduring ambiguity of the term, which has variously figured as literary period or technique, as banner of emancipation, or as licence to make money. If postmodernism is, as Perry Anderson (1998) and others on the Left suggest, ultimately an advanced aesthetic of Americanisation, the repro wallpaper in the mansion of corporate triumph, then nothing could be further from it than Alasdair Gray. His Clydeside socialist republicanism does not simply inform his work but is extensively stated and argued within it. Yet to define postmodern fiction in this way would slight the other writers we have considered here – all of them, in the 1980s, liberals or leftists – and miss the loose association drawn between postmodernism and the opening up of other voices. Feminism, for instance, is subtly insistent in *Lanark*, in the complaints of the heroine Rima about the lonely masculine heroism of Lanark, whom she ultimately, cheerfully leaves for another partner (1985: 556).

Gray allows no such niceties in his own verdict on postmodernism, in the notes to his 1994 novel *A History Maker*. *Pace* the many critics who had annexed him to the postmodern canon, he framed it as a season of reactionary decadence:

> Postmodernism happened when landlords, businessmen, brokers and bankers who owned the rest of the world had used new technologies to destroy the power of labour unions. Like owners of earlier empires they felt that history had ended because they and their sort could now dominate the world for ever. This indifference to most people's wellbeing and taste appeared in the fashionable art of the wealthy. Critics called their period *postmodern* to separate it from the modern world begun by the Renaissance when most creative thinkers believed they could serve their community. (1994: 202–3)

The service of the community is a motif and motive throughout Gray's work, from the pedagogical tones of the fiction to the public art projects on which he has worked for half a century. It is perhaps this extended span of time that is most significant in placing Gray.

Lanark is a literary monument of the 1980s, and among the decade's most fruitfully influential works. But it responds to the conditions of earlier decades. Its earliest drafts date back to 1954. Gray began with the story of Duncan Thaw: the seed of *Lanark* was an autobiographical tale of Glasgow in and after the Second World War. The world of Unthank came later, when Gray decided to attempt a modern epic. The final *Lanark* is an unwieldy assembly in which Gray 'put the realism inside the fable' (Acker 2002: 46–7). It is easy to overlook how much of the book – 230 pages of its 560 – is taken up with a relentlessly dour linear narrative of mid-century Glasgow. In itself this narrative has little to do with postmodernism; it is its combination with fantasy and metafiction that has prompted this categorisation. The preservation of Thaw's *bildungsroman* within the 'hull' of *Lanark* effectively records the real conditions of the work's origins and Gray's concerns. The latter – equality, the struggle against exploitation and unhappiness – are in principle global and universal, and *Lanark*'s alternate universe gives them such a stage. But as Liam McIlvanney notes, they are rooted in a very local history:

> The motto emblazoned on the boards of Gray's books – 'Work as if you live in the early days of a better nation' – points backwards as well as forwards.

[. . .] it commemorates the 'better nation' of 1950s Britain in the 'early days' of the Welfare State. [. . .] Gray's great theme is the long transition between 'DECENT BRITAIN' and 'INDECENT BRITAIN', between the Britain of full employment and free school milk and the Britain of Thatcher and Polaris. (2002: 199)

Remarkably, *Lanark* was written *during* that transition, not after it. Somewhat like Pound's *Cantos*, it is the epic that its author dragged around with him for decades, making it a record of his own life as well as a series of political arguments. It is in this sense that the book's post-modernism, apparently timely in the 1980s, may be superficial – or, to interpret the case more positively, that *Lanark* shows how diverse and distant the springs of British postmodernism could be. Jonathan Coe catches the sense of Gray's difference, recalling his dissatisfaction with the much recommended works of 'Martin Barnes, Julian McEwan' in the early 1980s: in Gray he found 'the absolute antithesis of metropolitan cool' (2002: 62).

Poetic Bizzarrerie

Whatever Gray's heterodoxy, one can plausibly identify a significant strain in British fiction of the 1980s bearing the label postmodernism. But if we switch genres, the matter is less clear. What was postmodern poetry in Britain?

In fact the term was claimed by one of the most prominent attempts to set the poetic agenda for the decade. Blake Morrison and Andrew Motion were poets themselves but also editors and journalists: 'middle-men' as Sean O'Brien (1998: 219) dubs them. In 1982 they edited *The Penguin Book of Contemporary British Poetry*. The volume includes a generous sample from each of twenty poets. Morrison and Motion's introduction proposed that a new sensibility had coalesced in the decades since Al Alvarez's *The New Poetry* asserted the poetic claims of confession and trauma in 1962. The new poets 'represent a departure, one which may be said to exhibit something of the spirit of post-modernism' (1982: 20). The new poets, from Northern Ireland in the 1960s and then from England through to the early 1980s, 'show greater imaginative freedom and linguistic daring than the previous poetic generation': this last a reference to the post-war 'Movement' that centred on Philip Larkin and Kingsley Amis and was typified by empiricism, caution and formal traditionalism. The more recent poets, reckoned Morrison and Motion, had 'developed a degree of ludic and literary self-consciousness reminiscent of the modernists', exhibiting 'a preference for metaphor and poetic bizzarrerie to metonymy and plain speech'. This was most flamboyantly evident in 'Martian' poetry: Craig Raine and Christopher Reid both appeared with keynote poems near the end of the volume, as though they were the latest development.

The new poetry also demonstrated 'a renewed interest in narrative' which allowed for 'the difficulties and strategies involved in retailing them. It manifests, in other words, a preoccupation with relativism' (12). There is a clear resemblance between this assertion and the claims made for, and in, the British fiction we have surveyed. Narrative that reflects on its own difficulties and strategies – 'contemporary poets write their stories with more reference to what the process involves' (19) – is precisely the business of Rushdie, Barnes and others. The evident echo gives some plausibility to the editors' claim to have discovered a postmodern strain in British poetry, which might be analogous to contemporary metafiction.

The *Penguin Book* is one of the most frequently assaulted anthologies in modern British letters. The attacks have been made on both political and aesthetic grounds. Seamus Heaney's dissent is the best known. He led off the volume with twenty poems and the editors' acclaim, but in a pamphlet published by the Irish cultural group Field Day he published an 'Open Letter' in verse declining this privilege. Heaney objected to travelling under the 'British' banner. Raised as a member of Northern Ireland's Catholic population, his national identification was with Ireland: a fact he had concretised by moving South and taking Irish nationality in the 1970s. He thus warned his Penguin editors that 'My passport's green. / No glass of ours was ever raised / To toast *The Queen*' (1983: 9).

He might just as legitimately have objected to being called a postmodernist. Heaney has written admiringly of the lessons of T. S. Eliot (2002: 26–38), but his own poetry has never approached the fractures of Eliot's most influential work, *The Waste Land* (1922), still less surpassed or built upon its formal novelties. Since his debut in the 1960s he has consistently produced metrically regular stanzas, sometimes working deliberately in particular poetic forms (like the Dantean *terza rima* he adopts in 1984's 'Station Island') and usually implying (unlike *The Waste Land* and many poems since) a consistency of address from the poetic subject. Moreover his work to the 1980s maintained an elemental emphasis on earth, roots and local ground that could not be further from the winkingly ironic, eclectically cosmopolitan atmosphere of the postmodern.

Yet Heaney can be seen to edge toward postmodernism in the 1980s in two respects. One is his self-conscious reference to literary precursors, no longer just quoted but dramatised: notably the modernist James

Joyce who materialises and advises Heaney at the end of his long poem 'Station Island' (Heaney 1990: 192–3). The other is Heaney's turn to parable. In *The Haw Lantern* (1987) a series of poems sketch abstract conditions – 'From the Republic of Conscience', 'From the Frontier of Writing' – which suggest an intellectual space distinct from Heaney's frequent fixation on the local; indeed they were informed by his reading of Eastern European poets. The poems perform a dry distancing of the real, and take this soberly cautious poet further than usual into the precincts of irony.

Nonetheless, for several commentators, Heaney is the latest in a line of poets whose work has been formally conventional and whose prominence has obscured the existence of alternatives. In 1983 Andrew Crozier identified a prevailing mode since the Movement of the 1950s, in which lyric poetry articulated the feelings of an individual speaker with a measure of figurative language (1983: 229–30). Alternatives had existed: Basil Bunting, Charles Tomlinson, Roy Fisher, W. S. Graham. American exemplars were also important. Louis Zukofsky, Charles Olson and Charles Bernstein, among others, had extended the lineage of Ezra Pound, developing the schools of L=A=N=G=U=A=G=E poetry and Open Field poetics through the 1960s and 1970s. The American poet Ed Dorn was one significant go-between, introducing new ideas to Britain in the 1960s through his association with Donald Davie at the University of Essex. Such influences had nourished the 'British Poetry Revival' that Eric Mottram (1993) locates in the 1960s and 1970s. Through and beyond the 1980s, the numerous poets of this revival and its successors would constitute themselves as an 'alternative tradition': rhetorically unified, whatever their differences, by their sense of exclusion from the canon from Larkin and Hughes to Heaney and Raine.

Writing in 1988, Ken Edwards draws the distinctions: 'No longer does the establishment revile modernism in poetry; it simply ignores it. The models to follow once again are Hardy and Larkin, the main axis of the poetry the quiet, singular, individual voice.' The 'extravagance of metaphor and simile' in Martianism, Edwards reasons, is probably what 'led Morrison and Motion to claim the "spirit of postmodernism" for their much criticized *Penguin Book of Contemporary British Poetry*; an interpretation of that abused and hackneyed term which appears to mean a *rejection* of modernism rather than a going beyond it' (1988a: 265). Edwards' own relation to the term is ambiguous: if the term is already so 'hackneyed', why worry about its abuse or try to reclaim it? But his complaint does plausibly suggest that a postmodern poetry ought to be extending modernism, not retreating from it. Perhaps, then, Britain's postmodern poetry could be found in the work favoured by

Edwards: in small-press pamphlets and fervently attended readings, and later in university berths and substantial anthologies of diverse poets. *A Various Art* (1987), co-edited by Andrew Crozier and Tim Longville, was followed by Mottram's and Edwards' selections comprising half of *The New British Poetry* (1988); Iain Sinclair's *Conductors of Chaos* (1996) juxtaposed contemporary poets with their obscure forebears from previous decades.

The alternative tradition is plural, but possesses recurring features. It is often metrically irregular, rarely beholden to conventional metre or rhyme, often indifferent to traditional poetic forms – though these (like the sonnet) may be retained as the site of subversion. Its language is apt to be opaque, challenging, unavailable to instant comprehension. Sinclair declares that '[t]he work I value is that which seems most remote, alienated, fractured. I don't claim to "understand" it but I like having it around. [. . .] If these things are "difficult", they have earned that right.' They reflect, he says, 'the complexity of the climate in which they exist': the reader must be prepared 'to make an effort, to break sweat' (1996: xvii). Registers are mixed: in an influential strategy, J. H. Prynne has juxtaposed the language of science, bureaucracy and government reports with other voices. Closely related to this, the poem is detached from a conventional speaking subject. A poem is to be read less as the coherent voice of a meditating consciousness, more as a field of linguistic possibility. Peter Middleton outlines the avant-garde's 'disrespectful junking of the expressive self that dominates establishment poetries': while it may give 'much play' to subjective expression, it also contests it (1993: 118–20). This severance of poem from secure selfhood may be literature's closest thing to an enactment of the 'death of the subject' entertained by Jameson.

Different poems perform these strategies to greater or lesser extremes. For instance, Douglas Oliver's 'The Infant and the Pearl' (1985) offers a political satire whose reference to Thatcherism is explicit, and which, rather than abolishing the poetic subject, directly mentions the author and his family. The poem makes dense and unmistakable reference to the real, contemporary world. Yet its long sentences produce a troubling strangeness as rhymes are repeated and intoned:

> I glossed over Margaret's giant, *Inflation*:
> wages were hiked when unions pushed
> hardest; this, helped by a hapless nation
> whose purchasing exceeded production, pushed
> up prices; then the pound's depreciation
> pushed up import prices, and that pushed
> up not just prices but the expectation

of price rises to come, which pushed
up purchasing demand – then the wage push would
renew: it was 'who pushed who', if alas
you plumped for the policies the Tories had pushed. (Oliver 1988: 221)

We need not necessarily take the economic assertions here at face value. What is most striking about them is their harsh, monotonous occupation of the poem. The effect is comparable to that we noticed in Churchill's *Serious Money*, where numbers are granted a new status in dramatic dialogue. Although Oliver's language and syntax are clear enough, his tone is harder to place. There is an excess to the rather corny economic rhymes ('nation', 'depreciation') and continual repetitions ('pushed') that detaches him from Edwards' 'quiet, singular, individual voice' and makes the poem an eccentric public challenge.

The political is insistent in many of the innovative poets, most of whom situate themselves between the Left and some form of anarchic, paranoid libertarianism. But politics often emerges in more implicit and diffuse ways than in Oliver's dream poem. Allen Fisher's 'Birdland' (1985) sketches the predominantly black south London area of Brixton, which in 1981 had been the site of riots. 'Endless destruction / makes Brixton', the poem asserts: 'Call it the coexistence of prohibitions and / their transgression / Call it carnival and spell out jouissance and horror' (Fisher 1988: 165).

Fisher's political analysis of the place takes on the language of contemporary cultural theory: Foucault's exploration of power and transgression, Bakhtin's celebration of carnival, Barthes' notion of *jouissance* or transformative bliss are bundled rapidly together. Fisher's language is thus keen to take on abstract concepts, but it also returns to the particular place, where

someone has dragged
a felled lime onto the walkway.
Its leaves make a green path
A pack of dogs surround this, yelp
out of phase. Down the High Road
a new siren on a police weapon
fills the walkway. (166)

Fisher is interested in local details – the felled tree, the dogs, the poster through the letterbox inviting him to 'Paradise in Brixton's Coldharbour' – but he returns to the image of a repressive state ('Beneath helicopters / Brixton abandoned'), concluding that 'The irrational State insists on control' (167). 'Birdland' is typical of its 'alternative' poetic milieu in its eschewal of predictable metrical pattern, its minimal punctuation, its mingling of concrete images and wilfully abstract terms, its relative diminution of the speaking subject, and its suspicion of power.

It also noticeably lays its scene in the city. Cambridge had become a centre for the alternative tradition, grouped especially around Prynne's example. But it is also noticeable how many avant-garde poems engage with the larger and apparently messier world of the capital. Ken Edwards offers his own portrait of South London:

> the city sky almost white
> space.   Children
>
> smelling subways
> lead & rain speckled glass

while the radio chatters: '"LBC, it's 17 minutes past 9"' (1988b: 295–6). Peter Barry (2000) has argued that the emphatically urban settings of such poetry offer a shift from traditional associations of the poetic and the Arcadian in English culture. For all the poems' occasional obscurity, they also bear an element of naturalistic reportage, even if this is presented in disjointed sentences and fragmenting two-line stanzas. In fact there is arguably a homology between the city and the poetic form: the poet's uncompromising way with language is akin to the indifferent world of 'walls of galvanized iron' and 'bills posted crooked' where 'drunks beat dustbin lids' (295–6).

This association is sealed in the work of Iain Sinclair. In the late 1990s Sinclair would become prominent as a chronicler of contemporary London: his immensely dense and inventive prose books have been central to the formation of millennial 'psychogeography'. Sinclair had been a publishing poet as well as sometime bookseller through the previous decades. His poetry takes surreal, sometimes ominous titles – *Flesh Eggs & Scalp Metal*, *Autistic Poses*, 'immaculate corruptions', 'chernobyl priests'. Though Sinclair's prose books have been voluminous, many of his poems are brief, sometimes a mere three or four lines. They seem terse, but also inexhaustible, as though thousands more flashes of semantic challenge could follow this one. Sinclair's 'hurricane drummers: self-aid in haggerston' is a miniature tale of mid-1980s London. The unattributed epigraph reads 'Ronnie Kray is now in Broadmoor and brother Reggie in Parkhurst from where he is trying . . . to get a security firm called Budrill off the ground.' The report is improbable, and conjures a London in which surreal corruption is workaday; in its reference to notorious East End gangsters it also situates Sinclair amid the mean streets and violent pubs of Whitechapel. The poem accordingly sees him at his most hard-boiled: 'there's a mob of rumours from s. of the river / challenging the teak and shattering glass / with dropkicks honed on GLC grant aid'. The abbreviated location and casual reference to the Greater London Council – at the time a politically contentious site of resistance to central government – declare Sinclair's local affiliations, while his poetic voice also sounds coolly indifferent to threat and violence.

> a couple of vehicles are cased
> and a couple elbowed
>
> in reply the locals can offer
> a squadcar of handy lads looking for lefty,
> cruising on new rubbers that
> give the game away, authentic
> as any red-light disco chuck-outs (Sinclair 1996b: 104)

The voice of this poem, and some of Sinclair's others, carries an element of imposture, the scribe unfazed by 'handy lads', gangsters, car thieves and 'wolf importers'. Sinclair wants to be not only erudite ('remote, alienated, fractured') but also fearlessly streetwise. The aspiration to urban swagger as well as lyric brilliance is curiously reminiscent of a writer Sinclair has tended to belittle: Martin Amis (Sinclair 1997: 92, 97). Sinclair's work suggests that the cultivation of poetic persona can survive the avant-garde's cancellation of conventionally 'expressive' poetry.

A still more radical break with conventional expression can be found in the work of Maggie O'Sullivan. In 'Busk, Pierce' from *States of Emergency* (1987), she takes the page to breaking point, setting lines of varying length in sinuous shapes against empty space. The poem starts by mixing invented words with real ones:

> fusen deam stroboscope deam skidder
> ----------------------------
>   TLOKETS
> mourn, leaden
>
>   belenders
> lie & blister----------------
>   (1988: 320)

Just to quote the poem is challenging, not only because O'Sullivan's neologisms must be correctly observed but because it is difficult to replicate the space of her page, in a work that appears as emphatically visual as concrete poetry. The poem does not necessarily become clearer. More familiar English words appear, and even phrases that might tempt the reader to interpretation: '*Keep / Geographies*', 'rebellion / backwards', and even – two years after the miners' strike – 'inadequate coal'. But while a poem like 'Busk, Pierce' offers such shards of meaningful English, it seems illegitimate to provide it with a coherent interpretation.

The poem is more persuasively an adventure in language and across the possibilities of the printed page, even including a page marked only with a sequence of numbers, like an unexplained code. Work like this represents something of a limit point for literary experiment in the 1980s. Whatever its obscurity, it stands as a demonstration of some of the things that conventional writing never entertains.

One a Gazebo

The 'alternative tradition' is an immensely dense field, increasingly catalogued and researched since the 1970s. Whatever the value of its myriad parts, its relation to postmodernism is questionable. As Ken Edwards observes, the term requires some positive engagement with modernism's legacy; but it can be argued that alternative poetics are a direct extension of that legacy, rather than a swerving away from it in the rumbustious, reader-friendly manner of Vonnegut or Carter. In short, this may be more properly dubbed a neo-modernism. If one writer did merit Edwards' unenviably 'abused and hackneyed term', it may have been one from the mainstream. In the matter of postmodernism, the much-abused Morrison and Motion did possess one ace in the hole, or joker in the pack.

Paul Muldoon emerged from Northern Ireland only a few years after Heaney, but the twelve years between them seem to mark a generational distinction. Through the 1970s and 1980s Muldoon persistently appeared as the Ariel to Heaney's Caliban, a teasing master of artifice rather than the earnest chronicler of bog and soil. This may be to say that Muldoon, next to Heaney, looks postmodern: ironic, witty, an arranger of effects and blender of voices. The distinction can be partially deconstructed (by Heaney's attempt to depart the rhetoric of earth, or by the attachment to local commitments that Sean O'Brien detects in Muldoon [1998: 173]), but retains heuristic value for a reader of Muldoon's volumes *Why Brownlee Left* (1980), *Quoof* (1983) and *Meeting the British* (1987). It is no value judgement, only a classification, to say that Muldoon rather than the vigorous pamphlets of Sinclair or O'Sullivan belongs convincingly to the picture of postmodernism that has been limned here. This postmodernism is an art of irony, self-consciousness, play with form in the knowledge of modernism's example; knowledge is inevitably shaped by language and history is partly a matter of storytelling. It also tends toward accessibility. Narrative's centrality may undermine historical certainties, but it also offers the compulsiveness of the yarn; and the panorama of twentieth-century mass culture (Hollywood, pulp, pop) is available for literary redeployment.

Muldoon often foregrounds words simply by rhyming them. 'Immrama' rhymes 'scarlatina' and 'Argentina', 'hazel' and 'Brazil' (2001: 85); 'Yggdrasill' matches 'swell and dandy' to '*Tristram Shandy*' (119). The titles themselves are unfamiliar, and typify a tendency of Muldoon's to confront the reader with the isolated enigmas of foreign or recondite words. Unlike most avant-gardists, though, he relishes not only rhyme (however muted) but regular forms. 'Yggdrasill' itself cleaves to the sequence ABBCA for its eight stanzas. The form not only produces the closure of a stanza's final rhyme mirroring its first; the hanging fourth line ending also seeks its likenesses in other stanzas, so the reader comes to hear 'discern', 'cairn', 'burn' and '*Laurence Sterne*' as a chain of echoes. Muldoon's dedication to this format is wilful, a selection of a set of rules to govern his subsequent choice of words. Such decisions can be seen across his work. In the AABB quatrains of 'Brock', form can be seen to license extravagance. In cleaving to the rule of rhyme, the poet draws attention to it:

> I would find it somewhat *infra dig*
> to dismiss him simply as a pig
> or heed Gerald of Wales'
> tall tales (158)

'Christo's' (164) is more devious. The middle two lines of each of its quatrains rhyme: 'Dingle' and 'angle', 'wraps' and 'landscapes'. Each fourth line rhymes with the first line of the following stanza: 'Brandon' and 'mountain', 'post' and 'Belfast'. The first line, ending 'asbestos', is thus orphaned – until the final line, when a reference to the German artist who covers scenes in polythene issues the title word, which seals the poem's formal unity, even (as this rhymes only with the first line) its circularity.

These are instances of Muldoon's profound formalism. He habitually works with structures that are essentially arbitrary, but which once embraced must be followed to the letter. This paradox is also that of a game, and Muldoon is among the most ludic poets of the age: his shuffling of syllables suggests the fastidious playfulness of Vladimir Nabokov (who is naturally discussed in a 1983 poem [125–6]). Muldoon's ability to work within these self-imposed limits is testimony to his own extraordinary resourcefulness; but it simultaneously points away from the individual poet, toward a history of forms which are a collective product and possession. Muldoon doubtless respects these poetic techniques in which he is so thoroughly schooled. But to master so many forms is also to relativise them, as though Muldoon has jumped through their various hoops and stands at a wry distance from them. In this sense his formalism consorts with a postmodern sensibility of irony, eclecticism and play with the cultural past.

Something similar applies to his treatment of knowledge. In 'History' Muldoon's speaker asks his lover to name the scene of their first sexual encounter. History is evidently fluid, memory problematic, as the poem lists a series of possible sites. It finally lights on 'the room where MacNeice wrote "Snow", / Or the room where they say he wrote "Snow"' (87). History is also hearsay, uncertain report, even if the two lines suggesting fact and doubt end with the non-rhyme or hyper-rhyme of the same word. The conceit is heightened by its literary content: naming a significant Northern Irish precursor introduces the approximations of poetry into the already destabilised sense of fact. The gesture prefigures the extensive literary spree of '7 Middagh Street', in which MacNeice features along with W. H. Auden and others. Muldoon's long poem dazzlingly reworks lines from poetic tradition. The words of W. B. Yeats' 'In Memory of Eva Gore-Booth and Constance Markiewicz' (1933) are ludicrously telescoped into 'Both beautiful, one a gazebo' (189), while Yeats' last line 'Bid me strike a match and blow' is ominously rerouted into the mouth of the Unionist founder of Northern Ireland (192). For all its high spirits, Muldoon's unflappably erudite shuffling of the literary past can be serious, as Yeats' concerns about the political effects of his play *The Countess Cathleen* are taken up and answered: 'For history's a twisted root / with art its small, translucent fruit / and never the other way round' (178). At the poem's end, the speaking 'MacNeice' leaves 'by the back door of Muldoon's' (193). This dizzyingly referential poetry can also be drily self-referential, in something of the spirit of postmodern fiction.

Muldoon indeed issues fictions of his own, in the long narrative poems 'Immram' (1980) and 'The More a Man Has the More a Man Wants' (1983). The latter offers a case for Muldoon as the most prodigious narrative poet of the era, able to spin a yarn taking in Native Americans, Ulster Unionists, Jackson Pollock and *Alice in Wonderland* – across twenty pages in unceasing fourteen-line stanzas. Muldoon's poker-faced formalism is the vehicle for his lavishly signifying tale, which also gradually rewrites its protagonist's name from 'Gallogly' to 'English' (142) and jests with Heaney's solemn poem 'Broagh' (135). If one wanted a poem to prove the existence of postmodernism, in all its neon knowingness, perhaps one could find it here (128):

'Anything to declare?'
He opens the powder-blue attaché-
case. 'A pebble of quartz.'
'You're an Apache?' 'Mescalero.'
He follows the corridor's
arroyo till the signs read *Hertz*.

Chapter Four

Belongings

Cinders in a Riddle

Howard Brenton's *The Romans in Britain* was staged at the National Theatre in Autumn 1980. It became notorious for a scene in which a Roman soldier rapes a young Celtic druid. Reports of the scene raised the ire of Mary Whitehouse, who since the 1960s had become a prominent conservative campaigner against obscenity, sex and violence in the media. Police scrutinised the play, and the director Michael Bogdanov was unsuccessfully pursued through the courts under the Sexual Offences Act. But the controversy distracted from the play's subject. Brenton's play is a vision of British history that swoops from one period to another, juxtaposing and sometimes overlaying different times. In 54 BC, two Irish vagrants happen upon a tribe of Celts in southern England; one vagrant is gleefully killed by the Celtic boys. The Celtic tribe in turn is massacred and ruined by the invading Roman army of Julius Caesar. In AD 515, a century after the Romans have departed, the Celts are in fear of a Saxon army. Another 1,400 years on, at the end of the 1970s, the British Army are on patrol in Northern Ireland, where an undercover British officer, Thomas Chichester, is discovered and shot by Irish Republicans. As the play develops, the gaps between these moments become smaller: different historical moments quickly alternate, cover the same patch of ground, and echo each other.

Brenton has at times written agit-prop, but this play's exact intent is not self-evident. As it jumps between epochs its characters offer various conclusions, which relativise one other. A character who seems set for a major part in the acts to come is often abruptly, brutally dispatched a moment later. In fact this is central to the play's sense: that the history of the British Isles has resounded with brutality, from one age to another; that there are no necessary heroes or happy endings, nor any absolute monopoly on violence. Brenton recalls that the play is drenched in an

'overwhelming *sorrow*, a grief for the nameless dead', to which it tries
to be true; and that this determination 'not [to] sell human suffering
short' was the source of its legal troubles (1989: x). Certainly the greatest source of such suffering here is colonial invasion. The Roman Army
is feared as a 'ship of horror in the water, pushing before it the animals,
men, women and children of the farms' (20). When they depart the play
it is with the policy 'Take their animals. Salt the fields. Kill the prisoners' (51). The young Druid Marban chillingly denies that life can return
to normal after the invasion: '[Y]ou'll never dig out the fear they've
struck in you. [. . .] Generation after generation, cataracts of terror in
the eyes of your children. [. . .] They've struck a spring in the ground
beneath your feet, it will never stop, it will flood everything' (54). This
view colours the present when, in an extraordinary moment of theatrical
shock and suggestion, the actors playing those Romans swiftly return to
the stage in the garb of the contemporary British Army. Their execution
of the pre-Christian Slave as a suspect Irish terrorist ('Kick the shit out
of your fucking country!') echoes the Roman soldiers' casual slaugh-
ter of Celts, whom they view as savages ('A wog is a wog') early in the
play (57, 30). Rome's Caesar is reconfigured as a British general mut-
tering aspirations 'That violence will be reduced to an acceptable level'
(57). The clear implication is that Roman imperial brutality is being
replayed by the British state in present-day Ulster, in another skirmish
with a poorly-understood enemy. The bibulous British agent Chichester,
undermined by his increasing sympathy with the Republican cause, tells
his Irish captors that 'I keep on seeing the dead. A field in Ireland, a
field in England' – a statement true to the rapid juxtaposition of places
and times in this second Act – and articulates an oppressive continuity: '[I]n my hand there's a Roman spear. A Saxon axe. A British Army
machine-gun. / The weapons of Rome, invaders, Empire' (89).

Brenton does suggest repetitive historical patterns. But he also views
the play less as a clear-cut 'anti-imperialist epic' than a drama of 'culture
shock' (xii). Every group and ethnicity in the play is violent, from the
Irish vagrant who rapes a slave to the Republicans who kill Chichester,
via the casually murderous Celts and, above all, the organised violence of the occupying armies (Roman, Saxon, British). 'There are no
"goodies" and "baddies"', Brenton insists (viii). The play ends with a
cook recasting himself as a poet and conjuring the tale of 'a King who
never was' whose utopian reign was 'thought of as a golden age, lost and
yet to come'. Asked for a name for the mythical king, the cook hits on
'Arthur', and the lights go down (94–5). Brenton thus comically stages
the invention of British tradition, in the midst of social collapse; he also
sounds a note of caution about utopias – including the relatively carefree

Figure 7   Culture Shock: *The Romans in Britain*, 1980

age of his own Celts earlier in the play. Freed from the controversy that initially surrounded it, *The Romans in Britain* stands as an extraordinary panorama, epic but jagged, of the centuries of violence and conquest on which the present-day nation stands. At the start of a decade in which many writers would reflect on the legacy of British imperialism, it is also a salutary reminder that Britain itself was once the outpost of another impermanent empire. The rest of this chapter will consider subsequent literary treatments of the matter of Britain.

Ideas of home and belonging have retained deep appeal, even in an age when many global barriers have come down, and when space (as Caryl Churchill dramatises in *Serious Money*) is foreshortened by rapid travel and instant communication. David Harvey observes that the increasingly porous globe, while threatening to undermine national integrity, may actually induce a heightened sense of locality: '[L]ocalism and nationalism have become stronger precisely because of the quest for the security that place always offers in the midst of all the shifting that flexible accumulation implies' (1990: 306). It is possible that late-twentieth-century literature homed in on the nation for similar reasons; that as it became more viable to transcend the nation, the nation became more distinctly visible and interesting as an object of artistic attention. For nation and ethnicity have remained remarkably insistent as the subject of literature and the arts.

At one extreme, writers have taken on a bardic role, presuming to speak for a whole people: officially, in England, with the post of Poet

Laureate. Ted Hughes held this post from 1984 to 1998, and his term produced explicit reflections on the monarchy (collected in 1992's *Rain Charm for the Duchy*) and on the national Bard's relation to a divided national past (in the 1993 critical work *Shakespeare and the Goddess of Complete Being*). Hughes' laureate poems celebrated royal children and senior members of the Royal Family in a grandly symbolic register of lions, unicorns, rivers, floral crowns and even Shakespeare's Falstaff, resurrected as a comic representative of Britain itself. The poetry naturally received a sceptical reaction from those dubious about the monarchy itself. Hughes' commentator Terry Gifford finds the laureate poems diminished by bathos and by a servile attitude to royalty that was unsustainable by the end of the 1980s (2009: 65–6). Unsurprisingly, Hughes' royal poems tended to use natural imagery in celebrating an institution whose status depends upon being 'naturalised', viewed as a permanent part of Britain's landscape rather than as a historical imposition. But Hughes was better able than most to essay this grand style; his own poetry had always been starkly mythic and engaged with the natural world. Even while, as Randall Stevenson observes, the 'consolations of nature [. . .] tended to fade from English poetry' (2004: 243), Hughes' more apocalyptic vision of a harshly uncompromising nature endured. This was visible in his collections *River* (1983) and *Wolfwatching* (1989) and also in the work for children that continued to claim much of Hughes' attention. It could even feed his laureate verse: thus the poem that Hughes dedicated to the christening of Prince Harry in 1984 linked this ritual with the 'drenching' water of the rivers Exe and Dart in Hughes' local area of Devon, and with the water cycle of which they were a part. Watching a storm commence in Exeter, Hughes recalls how 'Thunder gripped and picked up the city. / Rain didn't so much fall as collapse. / The pavements danced, like cinders in a riddle' (Hughes 1995: 285). These brief, vivid lines are enlivened by internal rhyme ('gripped and picked', 'cinders in a riddle'), the figuring of spaces or natural phenomena as subjects (thunder, as though an angry giant, picks up the city; the rainsplashed pavements dance), a hyperbolic reimagination of familiar verbs (we are used to rain falling, so why not collapsing?) and the enigma of the last phrase which seems held together by sound. Hughes' sense of a violent physical world might seem at odds with the stability desired by the royal establishment, but his poetry is all the better for it.

Yet despite the endurance of Hughes' gifts, the bardic bid to speak, or write, for England via the celebration of royalty was increasingly unlikely to convince – not only for sceptical readers on the republican Left, but for everyone else in an increasingly demotic Britain. We observed in the Introduction that market forces and tradition were both central to the ideological programme of the 1980s. Hughes' celebration of Queen Elizabeth II as representative of an eternal principle – notably in the 'masque' he wrote for her 60th birthday in 1986 – is one of the purest literary promotions of tradition in the late twentieth century. But the other side of Thatcherism militated against such conservatism. A telling example is the increasing enthusiasm of the tabloid press and, at the start of the 1990s, deregulated and satellite broadcasting to invade the privacy and expose the shortcomings of the Royal Family itself. It was thus in a less deferential atmosphere that most other writers of the period approached the idea of Britain, let alone its monarch.

Components of the National Conjuncture

Nations stake much of their appeal on the idea of continuity: hence George Orwell's admiration, in the revolutionary pamphlet *The Lion and the Unicorn* (1941), for wartime England as 'an everlasting animal stretching into the future and the past' (1982: 70). But the stakes of nationhood, the pressures upon and assertions of it, are historically variable. In the 1980s, three factors can be observed shaping ideas of Britain's identity and future.

One is the reassertion of Britishness by the Conservative government that presided over the decade. This was a riposte to a powerful 'declinism' that had set in since the Second World War – when the United States definitively displaced a bankrupt Britain as a world and imperial power – and especially through the 1970s, when inflation and fiscal crisis spurred a sense of national malaise, and the relative power of trade unions led commentators on the Right to fear that the democratically elected government no longer governed the country. Margaret Thatcher's reassertion of British pomp, as aspiration and achievement of her government, was virtually constant. But its high tide came with the Falklands conflict of 1982. At the Conservative Party conference in October that year, the prime minister declaimed, to clamorous applause:

> The spirit of the South Atlantic was the spirit of Britain at her best. It has been said that we surprised the world, that British patriotism was rediscovered in those spring days. Mr President, it was never really lost. But it would be no bad thing if the feeling that swept the country then were to continue to inspire us. For if there was any doubt about the determination of the British people it was removed by the men and women who, a few months ago, brought a renewed sense of pride and self-respect to our country. (Thatcher 1982)

British military success in this limited conflict, combined with economic boom by the latter half of the decade on the basis of financial services, offered the conditions for strident reclamations of national pride. The Falklands even allowed Thatcher to summon echoes of earlier, iconic naval conflicts and political leaders: Elizabeth I in the age of the Armada, Churchill and D-Day. Patrick Wright, by mid-decade, could thus refer to the 'redeclared' Second World War through which the country was living (1985: 85). His own researches in *On Living in an Old Country* set the terms for a new understanding of the role of the national past, notably its rural life and stately homes, in contemporary politics and culture. Writers, artists and critics took note.

A second factor is the role of immigrant communities. As a set of islands with a long history of trading and imperial expansion, the United Kingdom had long been peculiarly permeable to migration from overseas. New waves of migration have customarily provoked hostility from existing residents, as well as, over the longer term, mingling and naturalisation, in the form of intermarriage, language or cuisine. In the 1980s the most prominent immigrant communities, whether first or second generation, were from the Caribbean, Africa and South Asia. Their extensive presence in Britain was a legacy of empire, and more recently of direct appeals from Britain for migrant workers from colonies and former colonies to fill vacant jobs, notably in the NHS and public transport, in the 1950s and 1960s. Yet like other migrant communities they frequently faced discrimination at work, in social life and from the authorities. The presence of ethnic groups visibly distinct from the white population need not make for social turmoil. Since the 1990s it has frequently been officially acclaimed, by a state committed to multiculturalism – itself, in turn, controversial for its alleged occlusion of power relations (Mulhern 2009).

In the 1980s themselves, the situation was more ambiguous. A totemic event in post-war immigration policy and ethnic relations was the Conservative politician Enoch Powell's speech in 1968 that warned against the alleged depravities of black immigrants, and infamously prophesied a future 'foaming with much blood' if immigration continued. Powell's intervention has been cited ever since in fiction and poetry by black British authors. While Powell himself might be isolated by the political class, Stuart Hall – among the most perceptive analysts of post-war Britain and himself a migrant from the Caribbean – argued that the New Right had evolved in part from Powellism, and hence that the nascent Thatcherism had racism at its roots. Thatcher's own attitudes are less important here than the political context she exploited. The broad base of support for the New Right in politics included an element of white English nationalism, which successively gave allegiance to Powell, to the extra-parliamentary threat of the National Front in the 1970s, and to the relatively authoritarian and jingoistic government headed by Thatcher. As a result, the reassertions of British pride mentioned above tended, in practice, to become entangled with a suspicion of immigrants for having diminished that pride and secure identity in the first place. The clearest political embodiment of this ideological climate was the 1981 British Nationality Act, which removed the automatic right to British citizenship from children born on British soil. The move deliberately restricted the naturalisation, and the identification as British, of second-generation minorities. The 1981 Act thus represented a regression, in terms of immigrant rights, from its 1948 predecessor in which, amid post-war reconstruction and widespread decolonisation, all citizens of the British Empire were recognised as British subjects and thus allowed entry to the United Kingdom. It is in this climate that many writings of the period – Salman Rushdie's angrily sardonic essays of the early 1980s, for instance – should be seen.

A third development is the uncertain state of the United Kingdom itself. In 1977 the Scottish leftist Tom Nairn had published *The Break-Up of Britain* and thus coined a banner slogan for devolutionary and nationalist movements within the British Isles. In Chapter Two we considered the case of Scotland, where a culturally devolutionary impulse was accompanied by the deployment of dialect in the work of Tom Leonard, James Kelman and their successors. Northern Ireland remained riven by the sectarian strife that had ignited in reaction to its Catholic civil rights movement in the late 1960s. Brenton's *Romans* reflected on the role of the British military in this scenario. Northern Ireland's most distinguished contemporary literature was in the genres of poetry and drama. The former had flowered since the mid-1960s in the 'Belfast Group' of poets – Seamus Heaney, Michael Longley, Derek Mahon – followed by Paul Muldoon's ludic brilliance. The year 1980 saw the start of operations by Field Day Theatre Company, a Derry-based collaboration between writers including Heaney, Brian Friel and Tom Paulin, the actor Stephen Rea and the critic Seamus Deane. The company aimed to suggest art's role as a 'fifth province' in Irish life – an imaginative addition to Ireland's four provinces – in which the stalemates of the Troubles might be suspended.

Field Day's first play was Friel's *Translations*, staged at Derry's Guildhall in September 1980. The play depicts relations between British soldiers and local inhabitants during the mapping of rural Ireland in 1833. The play centres on linguistic difference. In a utopian image, a British soldier and an Irish girl develop a romance despite not sharing a language. The characters are oblivious to the nuances of each others' words, but the audience hears both sides, for both actors speak English on stage. But elsewhere in the play Friel shows that translations in this context are not free, but shaped by colonial power relations. Place names, in particular, are a site of contest, as Anglicised versions are imposed on the native forms. Friel repeatedly reminds us of the loose fit between language and the world. Irish, English and indeed Latin all make claims on the real, overlapping in their meanings and proving partially, imperfectly translatable. The ageing schoolmaster Hugh notes that Irish eloquence has often been a compensation for an impoverished material reality: 'a syntax opulent with tomorrows' is 'our response to mud cabins and a diet of potatoes'. Language, he cautions the British officer Yolland, has no guaranteed accord with the real: 'words are signals, counters. They are not immortal'. Adopting the play's cartographic theme, he warns that a civilisation can become 'imprisoned in a linguistic contour which no longer matches the landscape of . . . fact' (Friel 1996: 418–19). Along with *The Romans in Britain*, *Translations* reasserted the British military presence in Northern Ireland as a major theatrical theme. It also insisted on the involvement of language and the politics of nation and ethnicity; a connection that will recur in this chapter.

At the end of Friel's play, friendly relations between the British Army and Irish populace are severed. Owen, an Irishman who arrived as a translator for the British, now declares the need to go underground and resist them. He may join forces with the Donnelly twins, who are all the more potent in Friel's play for never appearing; they only figure in the hushed reports of guerrilla reprisals against the British. The audience may be reminded of the Irish Republican Army. In 1980, as in *Translations*, the Troubles were not about to abate. A few months after the play's premiere, several Republican inmates of Belfast's Maze prison resorted to a hunger strike in an attempt to win recognition as political prisoners. Margaret Thatcher refused to blink, and ten prisoners died. But in the longer term Field Day, like the Scottish revival of the 1980s, can plausibly claim to have prepared the intellectual and affective ground for formal political legislation the following decade: Edinburgh's Parliament and the Belfast Agreement respectively. Though both developments have their limits and critics – not least the feminist observation that Field Day's three-volume *Anthology of Irish Writing* in 1991 insultingly skimped the contribution of women, prompting in turn two further volumes to make up the shortfall – both can also be viewed as episodes in which artistic work ultimately fed into political change at the level of the nation.

Over the Map of Britain

But can a literary work encompass a nation? In one sense the novel's or play's focus on a particular set of characters argues against such ambition. But the ambition remains, especially in a period when the fate of a nation is being discussed in a wider public conversation, and literature seeks ways to match it. Individual characters may be metonymic of larger groups, standing in for legions of others. The events of a narrative may allegorise a broader social process. And such broader processes may themselves be explicitly discussed by characters or by a narrative voice outside them. In such ways have fiction and drama bid to stage the state of the nation.

Howard Brenton was one of several writers who emerged from the radical stages of the 1970s to occupy the National Theatre. Another was David Hare, who has frequently used the stage to explore institutions, and sometimes by extension the nation. Hare and Brenton collaborated to produce *Pravda* (1985), a satire on the state of the media. The title suggests that Fleet Street's treatment of truth is kin to that of the more overt propaganda machines of the Soviet Union. But the play focuses less on government propaganda or censorship than on the power of commerce to distort public discourse. Its South African news baron Lambert Le Roux is a theatrical equivalent to Rupert Murdoch, who by the time of *Pravda*'s staging was proprietor of both the *Times* and the *Sun*: two apparent poles of newspaper convention figured in the fictional broadsheet *Victory* and tabloid *Tide*. Inspiring a race to the bottom among the rest of the media, Le Roux has encouraged the press as a whole to feed on scandal, jingoism and – the institution still upheld by the laureate – royalty. Again, the very commercial spirit that is officially encouraged in the 1980s undermines another aspect of the establishment. The sense that the nation is burdened by an oppressively coarse media climate is staged creatively by the series of 'Newsvendors' who precede individual scenes of *Pravda*, loudly proclaiming particular items – 'TWELVE GO-GO DANCERS FOUND IN CRATE AT HEATHROW: TWELVE EXCLUSIVES' (Brenton and Hare 1985: 9) – which refer the spectator to a generic tabloid story or to interpretations of the events of the play itself. At the same time the play borrows creatively from this world; not only with its noisy news vendors but with stagings of television press conferences (86) and even an advertisement for the *Daily Tide* (119). In this multi-media format it extends a tradition of radical cabaret, and anticipates Churchill's *Serious Money* – a play whose boisterousness was also notoriously close to the social sphere it depicts.

Pravda treats the press as a key to the integrity of the nation as such.

The play's first scene is a vision of traditional England, in which the protagonist Andrew has taken refuge from the world of Le Roux: 'A brilliant summer. The best [. . .] Everything grew. Even late in the season, the wicket did not take spin. In the village church – always fresh flowers on the altar' (7). But this peaceful vision of national life is no match for the media world subsequently depicted: by the end of this short scene, Andrew is already compulsively drawn back to Fleet Street. The rest of the play backtracks in time to show how Andrew arrived at this convalescent state. Repeatedly in the scenes that follow, the condition of the nation is shown to be equally fragile in the face of modern business. Le Roux's South African background makes him a foreign threat to British interests, along with his Australian sidekick Eaton Sylvester. His takeover of the *Victory* seems initially like a theft of the crown jewels, a foreign quarrying of England's essence. As he sarcastically puts it to a government minister: 'One small part of your country that you all say will never be for sale. An Everest of probity. Unscaleable. The only newspaper with England on its masthead. An institution, like Buckingham Palace, the Tower of London, and your two houses of Parliament. And as dismal and dreary a read as it is possible for humanity to contrive' (37). As Le Roux makes uncomfortably clear, the English 'institution' is also a player, and a prize, in the marketplace. The system that upholds these national symbols is also the one that allows him to buy them, while a British passport is procured for him at 'unusual speed'. At this point a stage direction specifies that '*his accent thickens*', making him sound more South African, even as he declares: 'I am 100 per cent English. No trace of my origins remains' (48).

But it is not South Africa that Le Roux ultimately represents, though he does talk of learning his trade there. He is rather a figure for capital without a country, driven across national borders by profit rather than patriotism. Le Roux is an exemplary allegorical figure for the era, and particularly for a challenge to the nation described by Steven Connor: 'An increasingly hostile "outside" pressed in upon Englishness, in [. . .] the ever more rampant and uncontrollable dynamisms of a capitalism organised in multinational forms not subject to the control of sovereign states' (1996: 3). Le Roux is contemptuous of an England whose resistance to him has been so puny: 'In England you can never fight because you do not know what you believe' (Brenton and Hare 1985: 118). In our one sighting of Le Roux at home, he is wearing Japanese robes and practising martial arts, as he fumes that the Establishment 'think they are England. They hate me because I'm an outsider. No old boy and old chap. I've broken their toys and now there are tantrums' (94). Le Roux is a monstrous creation, but Brenton and Hare are not concerned to defend this besieged Establishment. Its denizens – Sir Stamford Foley, Elliot Fruit-Norton, the Bishop of Putney – are weak, venal, easily swayed by money, rather than true defenders of a more equitable order. Fruit-Norton seeks to fend off Le Roux's takeover by forming a co-operative; when it is pointed out that his own editorials have celebrated the free market, he desperately asserts that it will be 'An unsocialist co-operative unhindered by egalitarian practices' (51). The one character in the play who sees through all the others is Rebecca Foley. When others who have been damaged by Le Roux seek to establish a 'one nation' newspaper to strike back at him, she pointedly refuses the idea: 'One nation? Look around you' (101). Through this lone figure of resistance, the dramatists offer a moral refusal both of the rapacious international corporation and of the unequal nation that it is in the business of undermining.

Hare would continue his ambitious project to dramatise the state of the nation, dwelling especially on the effects of Thatcherism, in his trilogy at the National Theatre at the start of the 1990s, and again in a more strictly personal form in *Amy's View* (1997), where the relations between a young woman, her mother and her film director husband are dramatised across a passage of time between 1979 and 1995. This use of middle-class domestic life as a way of tapping national consciousness through a turbulent time had also been a major strategy in the novel, as the work of Margaret Drabble demonstrates. Drabble's trilogy of novels *The Radiant Way* (1987), *A Natural Curiosity* (1989) and *The Gates of Ivory* (1991) all focus on the lives of particular women, while seeking to draw a broad context of public life around them. *The Radiant Way* is built around a trio of women, Liz, Alix and Esther, who at the dawn of the 1980s pursue their careers (psychoanalyst, prison tutor, art histo-rian) in shifting circumstances. Drabble informs us that the three central characters, given their backgrounds and occupations, 'should, therefore, be in some sense at least exemplary' (1987: 88).

The Radiant Way is a significant attempt at the sub-genre of the 'condition of England' novel. The form, Steven Connor reminds us, flourished in the nineteenth century, 'in novels the very teeming inclu-siveness of which seemed to be both an enactment of the problem of imagining the whole of a nation and a utopian prefiguring of such a vision of healing unity' (1996: 44). The novel, this implies, might convey the diversity of national life through its own range of characters, and indeed places. While no novel can feature every aspect of collective life in detail, fiction might at least provide images metonymic of that inclusiveness. *The Radiant Way* ostentatiously commences with such a strategy, in showing us Liz Headeland's New Year's party at the start of 1980. Here are a gossip columnist, a feminist, a television executive, a forensic scientist, a theatre director and even, explicitly, 'Representative Public Figure, Sir Anthony Bland'. They are talking, moreover, about the state of the nation and signs of the times: the New Year's setting allows Drabble's characters to 'formulate what, for them, had seemed to be the conventions of an eclectic, fragmented, purposeless decade' and to 'prophesy for the next', and their anxieties already include 'the science-fiction disease of AIDS' and the fate of Arts Council subsidies (Drabble 1987: 32).

From the start, the novel thus unapologetically pursues topical currency and general significance. Yet this elite gathering cannot stand convincingly for the nation as a whole. Drabble thus switches focus to another scene: 'Meanwhile, up in Northam, that figurative Northern city, the New Year had also advanced, ignored by some, welcomed by others, bringing surprises to some, and a deadly, continuing tedium to others.' The banality of the alternatives proffered in this sentence results directly from Drabble's attempt at inclusiveness: this novel wants not just to be about any given 'some' but somehow to keep in mind all those 'others' too, as 'The Other Nation, less than two hundred miles away, celebrated in its own style' (47). The novel's deliberate swing from London to Northam, South to North, one nation to Other Nation, echoes Victorian fictions of national disparity like Elizabeth Gaskell's *North and South* (1855) and Benjamin Disraeli's *Sybil, or the Two Nations* (1845), also explicitly evoked in David Lodge's own condition-of-England novel *Nice Work* (1988). *The Radiant Way* insists that the divide between two nations is not a Victorian memory but a present-day fact. In Drabble's Northam 'the age of the buildings and the neighbourhood was beginning to tell, a forlorn gust blew coldly down the empty streets, rust ate quietly at machinery, brick dust sifted from crumbling ledges, dirty glass frames slowly splintered as window frames rotted'. All this Drabble gnomically dubs 'The poetry of neglect' (151). Such passages introduce to her largely metropolitan novel that distinctive mode of post-industrial elegy that we surveyed in Chapter Two. In a significant passage, Alix is seen to pursue the essential connectedness of different lives across the nation:

> Mile after mile, ribbons of roads. What was going on, behind those closed curtains? [. . .] Alix liked to let her mind wander over the map of Britain, asking herself which interiors she could visualize, which not. She aspired to a more comprehensive vision. She aspired to make connections. (72)

The character here is also an image of the novelist.

Drabble thus proffers not just family drama but national panorama. *The Radiant Way* is punctuated by public set-pieces, announcing, for instance, that 'Fear had become normal, clumsiness of various sorts had become normal. Men wore dark suits and ties and were solemn inside them, or they shouted on picket lines. None of them made love, much, to their wives', while 'Women talked of biological washing powders and the price of beef and television commercials and operations on the gall bladder and the Royal Family' (170). Or again, as Drabble speeds past a passage of time:

> These were the years of inner city riots, of race riots in Brixton and Toxteth, of rising unemployment and riotless gloom: these were the years of a small war in the Falklands (rather a lot of people dead), and of the Falklands Factor in politics: these were the years when a new political party boldly declared that it would attempt to find a way out of the impasse of class conflict. (227–8)

Such passages move beyond some of our expectations of the novel form, in their escalation to generality. It is not Drabble's own, named characters who have become clumsy or talk of biological washing powders, but 'Men' and 'Women'. The scale of novelistic description, in the second passage, has shifted radically from the momentary pace of individual life to the surging, summarised tides of collective experience. The novel has made itself kin, in fact, to the news.

Two years after Drabble's novel appeared, D. J. Taylor published his polemical survey of contemporary British fiction, *A Vain Conceit* (1989). While calling for greater social engagement from novelists, Taylor was merciless with Drabble's attempt to provide it. After a devastating parody of the social gatherings that open her novel, he protested that *The Radiant Way* was essentially journalism masquerading as fiction: 'One could contrive a similar accumulation of scene and opinion by bringing together a month's front pages of *The Times*' (Taylor 1989: 54). We should be wary of prematurely dismissing Drabble's ambition. After all, the novel form has indeed consorted interestingly with the news, from John Dos Passos' chronicles of New York to David Peace's treatment, in *GB84* (2004), of the same turbulent period as Drabble. And those critics unimpressed by Drabble's newsy soundbites of national life also often insist that fiction should engage with contemporary history, not retreat from it to a private realm. On a generous estimate, we might turn Taylor's attack to Drabble's advantage, seeing in this hybrid of novel and news a creative version of Benedict Anderson's influential contemporary account of the modern nation. The newspaper, Anderson avers, is read by an individual reader who is nonetheless aware that this act is 'replicated simultaneously by thousands (or millions) of others'. The 'community in anonymity' of a newspaper readership is a model for the nation itself, which is bound together by such quietly collective experiences (1991: 35–6). The novel, too, Anderson suggests, offers a 'precise analogue of the idea of the nation', mirroring in its 'meanwhiles' the simultaneity of collective life in which millions of people co-exist without ever meeting (24–6). Drabble, indeed, oddly echoes this with one of her sudden links between the personal and the political: 'Meanwhile, and very much meanwhile, monetarist theories did not prevent Esther from going to Bologna' (1987: 188). Simultaneity, perceived across isolated individual actions which nonetheless fall into a broader pattern, is one of Drabble's trademarks here, as in the extended sequence in which a range of geographically distinct characters are unwittingly united in having lunch (1987: 137–55). The attempt to imagine such unrealised community, or at least to demonstrate synchronicity, is a technique that Drabble inherits from Virginia Woolf.

Yet to invoke Woolf highlights the difficulty of *The Radiant Way*, and potentially of the entire aspiration to write the 'condition of England'. Perhaps the real difficulty is one of voice. Woolf's whimsicality is picked up – Esther took a place at Cambridge in part 'because she heard an owl hoot thrice in the college garden when she retired to her narrow bed after the glass of wine with Flora Piercy' (87) – along with her cautiously ironic deployment of the portentous: 'But why had they been sitting on a table? And in whose flat? These were now mysteries known only to God' (12). This is not to query Woolf's own status. But it is to suggest that what was effectively modernist in 1927 may be riskily mannered in 1987. Drabble's narrative voice is arch, and slightly archaic. It places her at an odd angle as chronicler of the state of a nation that she herself shows to be a site of struggle. Her own awareness of the difficulty of finding a voice for that role surely contributes to the book's frequent bouts of self-consciousness. When Liz Headeland senses a secret in her own past, the narrator wonders: 'Do you know what it is? Do I know what it is? Does anybody know what it is?' (145). Perhaps most tellingly, Drabble recites the elements of the novel: 'A few families in a small, densely populated, parochial, insecure country [. . .] Where does the story begin and where does it end?' (171). The strains of voice in *The Radiant Way* are a sign, less of Drabble's own weakness, than of the difficulty of finding a form for the 'comprehensive vision' it seeks.

Conveniently Forgetting

Perhaps recognising this, other writers seeking to document the condition of England in this period would frequently relinquish the unifying narrative ambition upheld by Drabble, instead adopting other strategies. It is suggestive that among the most successful, Jonathan Coe's retrospective *What a Carve Up!* (1994), adopts (as its title hints) a montage of voices and parodies alongside a comically flawed first-person narrator, rather than announcing the state of the nation from a position external to the story. Other novelists also found insights by manipulating specific, embedded voices: most notably Kazuo Ishiguro in *The Remains of the Day* (1989), the last Booker winner of the Booker's great decade. The novel is narrated by one Mr Stevens, a butler from the fictional Darlington Hall who has embarked on a motoring trip with the stated aim of visiting the Hall's former housekeeper and persuading her to return. The narrative is produced day by day over a week in 1956, thus making this already a historical novel. But it reaches back in turn to the 1920s and 1930s, the apotheosis of Stevens' employment under his former master Lord Darlington. There are thus effectively three times in question: the inter-war period, the post-war and also tacitly the late 1980s when Ishiguro writes and publishes the novel. The ambiguous relations between these periods are central to the book. The inter-war period is sometimes misremembered from the 1950s, as the ageing Stevens produces a series of minor slips and cloudy memories. The 1950s meanwhile are being reconstructed from the 1980s, and the reader is entitled to wonder what is at stake. One telling answer is – typically, in this book – never explicitly mentioned. The year 1956 was that of the Suez Crisis, when an ill-starred military adventure into the Middle East demonstrated Britain's diminished global power in the face of the ascendant United States. The novel's geopolitical dimension is at least implicitly signalled by the arrival of an American businessman, John Farraday, as the new owner of Darlington Hall. The book's title thus takes on some public import: the remains of the British Empire, of British power or of one version of England itself are the ground in which Ishiguro digs.

Ishiguro's scenario is thus richly layered and suggestive. But his major achievement is in forging Stevens' voice. The butler is one of the great first-person narrators of his era, densely informative but also deceptively fallible and in some ways fundamentally unreliable. His motives for visiting his former colleague Miss Kenton (now 'Mrs Benn', though Stevens is reluctant to use the name in his narration) are more romantic than professional, but this inadmissible fact is inexpertly suppressed by the narration. A similar principle applies to Lord Darlington, whom Stevens defends almost to the end as a man of honour, 'a gentleman of great moral stature' (Ishiguro 1989: 126), but who gradually emerges as having campaigned to appease the Nazis in the 1930s. Stevens continues to defend his own positions with elaborate, polite locutions whose extensive attempt to appear calm comes to seem covertly frantic. After he has twice refused to admit his past association with Lord Darlington to present-day interlocutors, he reasons:

> Indeed, it seems to me that my odd conduct can be very plausibly explained in terms of my wish to avoid any possibility of hearing any further such nonsense concerning his lordship; that is to say, I have chosen to tell white lies in both instances as the simplest means of avoiding unpleasantness. This does seem a very plausible explanation the more I think about it; for it is true, nothing vexes me more these days than to hear this sort of nonsense being repeated. (126)

A curious detachment is apparent in Stevens' relation to his own motives. He professes to analyse them as though they were someone else's, seeking 'a very plausible explanation'. This could indicate an admirably heightened self-awareness, in which his own thoughts are approached with the scepticism of a professional analyst; but in fact the most pertinent psychological term is denial. Rather than affording self-knowledge, Stevens' meticulous discourse is evading it.

Ishiguro's achievement is notable for its lack of pyrotechnics. He demonstrates that great psychological subtlety can be achieved with a form that appears relatively simple beside the decade's celebrated phrasemakers and frame-breakers. The formality of Stevens' tone is slightly dated even for the 1950s, let alone the late 1980s; but this archaism is embedded in the novel, forming part of its meaning, in contrast to the pre-war pastiche that Drabble's external narrator uncertainly employs. The novel's style is closely connected to the model of professional subjectivity that Stevens advocates for a butler, as he seeks to define his ideal of 'dignity'. Stevens takes this key word from the Hayes Society's declaration that a great butler must exhibit 'a dignity in keeping with his position' (33); his ensuing discussion then tends to keep it in quotation marks, as though nervous to take it from its source without acknowledgement. With such small touches, Ishiguro indicates Stevens' wariness in approaching the 'borrowed language' (Connor 1996: 109) of English, in which he seeks to improve his facility by reading novels (Ishiguro 1989: 168). When Stevens comes to define his central term, he reasons that '"dignity" has to do crucially with a butler's ability not to abandon the professional being he inhabits'. Great butlers 'inhabit their professional role' to the utmost, and 'wear their professionalism as a decent gentleman will wear his suit'; a task in which 'We English' are at an advantage over foreigners (42–3).

Englishness is explicitly at stake in this novel. The novel may be viewed as a satire on a tradition of English reserve, amid the archetypally English scenery of the country house and the rural West Country. But its political analysis goes deeper than this. For one thing, at the time Ishiguro wrote the novel, the ideological role of that scenery was under fresh scrutiny. 'National Heritage', in Patrick Wright's analysis, 'involves the extraction of history – of the idea of historical significance and potential – from a denigrated everyday life and its restaging or display in certain sanctioned sites, events, images and conceptions': notably the country house and the greenery of 'Deep England' to which paeans to the nation all seemed to return. 'Abstracted and redeployed', Wright continues,

> history seems to be purged of political tension; it becomes a unifying spectacle, the settling of all disputes. Like the guided tour as it proceeds from site to sanctioned site, the national past occurs in a dimension of its own – a dimension in which we appear to remember only in order to forget. (1985: 69)

Wright's analysis offered a localised exemplification of Fredric Jameson's contemporaneous claim that historical consciousness was being eviscerated, even as spectacles of the past were multiplied (1991: 18). Andrew Higson (2003) has pointed to the role of the 'heritage film' in granting a bigger screen to such spectacles. Heritage films were primarily adaptations of classic English novels from the Merchant-Ivory production company. Versions of E. M. Forster's *A Room with a View* (1985) and *Maurice* (1987) were seen to enact English nostalgia. The yearning was not necessarily for empire itself. As Higson insists, the films were politically ambiguous rather than simply conservative, and their source material in Forster, for instance, was thoughtfully liberal. Yet the films did offer a past of refined manners and great houses, and thus chimed with the popularity of the heritage industry.

It is in this climate that Ishiguro's novel quietly intervenes. In narrating the spectacular sites of the heritage past from the 'below-stairs' standpoint of a butler, it offers an alternative angle on their history. And in showing Stevens' struggles with the vagaries of memory and his own repression of events, it foregrounds the very process of selective memory and useful forgetting that Wright had considered ideologically influential. More specifically, what the novel bids us remember is not simply the exclusions or quirks of Englishness, but a widespread entanglement with fascism that has been sidelined from the national past. The Second World War has been fundamental to recent ideas of British identity and integrity. Ishiguro, without giving any succour to fascism itself, troubles the clear distinction between righteous Britons and their political others. His book suggests that prior to the war, the ethics of contemporary geopolitics were less self-evident, not least among the upper classes and diplomatic elite that Stevens serves. Thus Lord Darlington orders the expulsion of two Jewish servants from the house, a decision in which Stevens – only following orders – naturally acquiesces (147). More insidiously, perhaps, Lord Darlington and his associates make the case against democracy as such, as an outdated and inefficient system:

> 'Look at Germany and Italy, Stevens. See what strong leadership can do if it's allowed to act. None of this universal suffrage nonsense there. If your house is on fire, you don't call the household into the drawing room and debate the various options for escape for an hour, do you?' (198–9)

The novel's presentation of these positions is the more effective in that they come not from a Nazi thug but from an English gentleman. And Stevens' defence of Lord Darlington protests that such views should not be viewed as exceptional: 'the most established, respected ladies and gentlemen in England were availing themselves of the hospitality of the German leaders', and 'Anyone who implies that Lord Darlington was liaising covertly with a known enemy is just conveniently forgetting the true climate of those times' (136–7). Ishiguro's history is fiction, not an infallible guide to that 'true climate'. But he bids us question whether a 'convenient forgetting' has enabled Britain's status as constant bulwark against totalitarianism. The novel ends amid the literal remains of a day, and the fading of the light is an appropriate image: not just for Stevens' or England's supposed decline, but for the failure of insight that the book carefully exposes. Unlike the brash cabaret of Brenton and Hare, or Drabble's panoramic view, Ishiguro's insight into England proceeds indirectly, through a systematically distorted vision.

Andahgroun

'Ishiguro's own position,' avers Dominic Head, 'as someone born in Japan but brought up in Britain, gives him an intriguing "semi-detached" or dual perspective' (2002: 156). To this extent he can be compared with those authors who have been much clearer about the duality of their perspectives, reflecting explicitly on the questions of identity raised by migration and resettlement. Black British fiction and poetry have repeatedly looked back over the ambivalence of the immigrant, faced with racism but also the appeal of the new country. Yet in saying this, one must also observe the changeable significance of the word 'black' itself. The term might seem to refer to the genetic 'given' of skin colour. But its purchase is in fact variable, a matter of historical context and political practicality. James Procter describes it as 'a political signifier which first became valent in Britain in the late 1960s and 1970s' (2000: 5), and adduces Kobena Mercer's assertion that '[w]hen various peoples – of Asian, African, and Caribbean descent – interpellated themselves and each other as /black/ they invoked a collective identity predicated on political and not biological similarities'. The word's connotations were thus 'rearticulated as signs of alliance and solidarity among dispersed groups of people sharing common historical experience of British racism' (Mercer 1994: 291). On this analysis, blackness is in part a pragmatic construct and coalition. Accordingly there is no guaranteed consensus about whether, for instance, Salman Rushdie is a black British author, or better labelled, say, British Asian. The most useful thing is not to impose a framework retrospectively, but to recognise that the alliances and interpellations that Mercer describes were themselves operative, and under reconstruction, in the 1980s. Thus it is characteristic that Rushdie's own essays this decade tend to invoke a broad, often besieged community of black Britain, including diverse Asian immigrants as well as Africans and Caribbeans, for which he sees himself as an advocate.

A significant example is the debate around *Handsworth Songs*, a 1986 documentary from the Black Audio Film Collective, which sought a historical perspective on a deprived suburb in Birmingham where, in two riots in 1981 and 1985, black youths had attacked shops and battled police. Rushdie reported on the film for the *Guardian*, disparaging it despite its favourable reception in *New Socialist* and *City Limits*. The conjunction of liberal and leftist media outlets involved here is characteristic, and was typical of the political culture in which Rushdie was then located. He situated himself also as part of black Britain. His complaints at the film's visual clichés came, he implied, from a member of a community frustrated at its misrepresentation, rather than from safely outside it. The first person plural is significant:

> It isn't easy for black voices to be heard. It isn't easy to get it said that the state attacks us, that the police are militarised. It isn't easy to fight back against media stereotypes. As a result, whenever somebody says what we all know, even if they say it clumsily and in jargon, there's a strong desire to cheer, just because they managed to get something said [. . .] I don't think that's much help myself. That kind of celebration makes us lazy. (Rushdie 2000: 263)

Rushdie's disparagement met a response from Stuart Hall. By 1989, in the lecture 'New Ethnicities', Hall could see a partial shift between two phases in black culture. A first moment of the assertion of black identity had provided 'the organizing category of a new politics of resistance', concerned at a cultural level with '*access* to the rights of representation by black artists' and '*contestation* of the marginality, the stereotypical quality and the fetishized nature of images of blacks, by the counter-position of a "positive" black imagery' (1997: 441–2). The newer phase Hall saw as concerned with the 'politics of representation' – with more sophisticated and open-ended textual forms, which in Hall's view included *Handsworth Songs* – and as ending 'the innocent notion of the essential black subject', displaced by a fuller sense of the diversity and constructedness of blackness. And of Britain and Britishness themselves; for despite an awareness of diaspora and diverse roots, new black art was engaged in 'contestation over what it means to be British' (447).

At least one of the writers considered below, Hanif Kureishi, was instanced as part of Hall's de-essentialising second phase. But the point here is not to allot writers to one camp or another. A review of the debates between Rushdie, Hall and others reminds us that 'black' was a contested, constructed category in the period; that writers and artists were seeking new forms to articulate it, while also subject to criticism for doing so; and that a growing tendency, in the era of second and third generation black British subjects, was to establish the Britishness of black life and explore the ways that Britain itself must thus be different. Let us consider, then, the way in which black writers were responding to this climate across different genres.

Joan Riley's novels *The Unbelonging* (1985), *Waiting in the Twilight* (1987) and *Romance* (1988) explore experiences of immigrants from the Caribbean. *The Unbelonging*'s neologistic title signals the problems at stake. Its protagonist is the schoolgirl Hyacinth who has been summoned to England by her oppressive Jamaican father. Her experience in a grey, dismal London is repeatedly contrasted with her memories of Kingston, Jamaica, to which she returns in dreams. Riley's book is a kind of *Bildungsroman*, showing the growth of her protagonist, against the odds, to her eventual graduation from university; but to the end, Riley's simple narration, third-person yet close to Hyacinth's thoughts, continues to relay the extent of the character's naivety, notably about both sexuality and politics. A form of belonging is what Hyacinth seeks, but the novel discloses this as a tortuous business, founded on imagination and fantasy. At school in England, Hyacinth considers that 'everything in this strange country was hard to believe' (Riley 1985: 15). She is isolated by her blackness, and fights another girl – 'A mixed-race child adopted by white people' who 'seemed to hate the black kids even more than the whites did' (18). Racial identities are thus denied and repressed, and Hyacinth is unable even to befriend other black children because of her shameful home life (31–2), in which she is repeatedly beaten by her father for wetting the bed. His cruelty and abuse is viscerally clear to the reader, but even after fleeing from him, Hyacinth is reluctant to report it to her white teachers and doctors – not only for fear of reprisal, but also because she fears the white establishment even more: 'her father had warned her about white people – how they hated black people, how they would trick them and kill them' (30). Hyacinth is thus left stranded between a white society she distrusts and a black identity she resents. Living in a hostel and racially abused by a white girl, she wants 'to tear the girl apart, rob her of that skin that was so much a badge of acceptance' (75). Infuriated with her own appearance, she has her hair straightened (89–90). At university, amid a politicised black movement, she refuses to be considered African: 'these people seemed more interested in going back to the primitiveness they had come from' (113). She has thus rejected some of the possible forms of belonging – English, black, pan-African – cleaving instead to the dream of her return to Jamaica. But Riley's final chapter shows Hyacinth's bewildered return to an island that does not match her memories, and where a surviving friend harshly tells her, 'Go back whe you come fram' (142). 'How many times,' Hyacinth wonders, 'had she heard that since coming to Jamaica, or was it since she had gone to England? She felt rejected, unbelonging. [. . .] But if it was not Jamaica, where did she belong?' (142). She can no longer distinguish between her rootlessness here and in Britain. Riley finally dispels the dream of a true home, and suggests a more challenging reality, in which the migrant must construct her own way of belonging.

Analogous dilemmas were also confronted in poetry. James Procter (2000: 97) sees poetry as the key genre within black British writing in the 1970s and early 1980s. Its status reflected its association with the activists Linton Kwesi Johnson and Benjamin Zephaniah, for whom poetry was not only a mode of political expression but also closely allied to music. Johnson's poetry of repeated choruses was released with musical accompaniment by Virgin records. In *Inglan is a Bitch* (1980) he addresses a series of current social issues: police brutality and stop-and-search policy, dubious arrests, unemployment, the evasiveness of Rastafarianism's 'mitalagy' (24) and the waywardness of black youth who 'gat no course' and 'don't count de caas' (11). The briefest quotation shows that Johnson was consistently working in dialect: spelling words phonetically to suggest the legacy of Caribbean pronunciation, making statements in an alternative syntax in which the usual subjects 'I', 'we' and 'us', for instance, are substituted 'mi' and wi'. So a veteran black immigrant remembers: 'w'en mi jus' come to

Landan toun / mi use to work pan di andahgroun' (26), or a prisoner recalls 'Out jump t'ree policeman, / di 'hole adem carryin' batan' (8). The directness of Johnson's political polemics – declaring of the far Right, 'we gonna smash their brains in / cos they ain't got nofink in 'em' (20) would not necessarily be matched by subsequent poets. But the use of dialect was pervasive. It can be seen in the poetry of John Agard, Jimi Rand, Marsha Prescod and Valerie Bloom, or in Grace Nichols' 'Caribbean Woman Prayer' which asks God to 'Make dem see dat de people / must be at de root of de heart / dat dis place ain't Uncle Sam backyard' (Nichols 1988: 66). Nichols, whose volumes *i is a long memoried woman* (1983) and *The Fat Black Woman's Poems* (1984) were significant introductions of a black female perspective, in fact moves in and out of dialect depending on the voices involved in a given poem. James Berry likewise writes at times in Standard English, but his *News for Babylon* (1984) presents Caribbean proverbs in dialectal form. Fred D'Aguiar has noted that Berry's revisions can take the poem still further from Standard English: thus 'Tiger wahn to eat a child, tiger sey / he could-a swear it was a puss' becomes 'tiger wahn fin yam pickney, tiger sey / he could-a swear e woz puss' (D'Aguiar 1993: 60–1). D'Aguiar presents the example in a discussion of 'creole', which he places in 'a continuum, with Standard English at one end and the most countrified creoles at the other and all the [British] city-speak in between' (1993: 59). Procter (2000: 97) notes that the use of dialect was partly inspired by Kamau Braithwaite's insistence, from the late 1960s, of the vitality of 'nation language'. Dialect poetry, like Tom Leonard's Glaswegian verse, was quickly granted political significance by critics, as a mode of resistance to Standard English. Rather than being a spontaneous expression of creole speech, such writing is arguably very self-conscious: the spellings and syntax require a whole new set of textual conventions to be constructed and maintained. For most readers, accurately to copy out a line of dialect will require closer attention to the page than to transcribe a line of Philip Larkin. Yet this densely textual mode, which makes some common cause with contemporary avant-garde poetry for its estrangement of English, paradoxically does also seek to align poetry with a certain kind of ordinary speech, in a tradition reaching back to the Romantic tradition of Robert Burns and William Wordsworth.

D'Aguiar's own work in the 1980s shows a capacity to deploy creole as part of a poem written in more orthodox English. His sequence of 'Mama Dot' poems (1985) refers back extensively to village life in his ancestral home of Guyana. The poems describe a wise old woman whose experience spans the century: when she watches films of early air shows,

'She's so old, she's a spectator in some.' The same poem values traditional custom over modern technology: when Mama Dot wants '[t]o see an ancestor, in Africa', 'Her equipment's straightforward, / Thought-up to bring the lot / To her' (D'Aguiar 2001: 11). The whole sequence presents Mama Dot as a repository of wisdom, folk recipes and balms. Her life has the dimensions of magic realism: 'The day Mama Dot takes ill, / The continent has its first natural disaster', and when she 'asks for a drink to quench her feverish thirst', '[i]t rains until the land is waist-deep in water' (15). Sometimes D'Aguiar hands his verse over to Mama Dot's own Guyanese voice. She remembers a kite flying: 'tuggin de face into de breeze / coaxin it up all de time takin a few steps back / an it did rise up bit by bit till de lang tail / din't touch de groun' (10). More often she is presented through his own supple Standard English: 'She gesticulates and it's sheet lightning on our world', 'All the crying we ever did is a roof, soaked through' (5). D'Aguiar's ability to move between registers may be read as analogous to his insistence on both his Britishness and his Guyanese background. A letter from Mama Dot – largely presented in Standard English, with a few local touches ('dey bound / Fe improve cause dem cawn get no worse!') – tells the British-based recipient that 'You are a traveller to them. / *A West Indian working in England; / A Friday, Tonto, or Punkawallah; Sponging off the state*' (13). A series of non-white archetypes are rolled together here, as the letter-writer cautions against the supposed implacability of white Britain. Yet even if the natives are suspicious even of the immigrant's next-door garden with its hints of miscegenation ('the roots of both mingling'), the letter concludes that 'You know England, born there, you live / To die there, roots put down once / and for all' (13).

Indeed, whatever the initial obstacles, D'Aguiar himself, with a degree in English from the University of Kent, became a significant broker for black British poetry: most significantly in editing a section of the collection *The New British Poetry* (1988), in which black writers were anthologised alongside women and avant-garde practitioners. D'Aguiar would repeat this gesture at a rainbow coalition by contributing a survey of black British poetry to the influential collection *The Scope of the Possible* (1993). In both these texts D'Aguiar is at pains to insist that blackness is not the only factor in any poet's life and work: 'critical attempts to isolate their work and group them together will look more and more absurd' (1993: 70), as 'Two black poets in Britain today are likely to have less in common than two poets picked out of a hat' (D'Aguiar 1988: 4). Yet the contexts of these statements make them seem premature. By the end of the 1980s, D'Aguiar clearly still considers it important to gather and represent black poets' work, as well as insisting that expressions of 'the black experience in Britain' have 'changed what it means to be British; deepened it in fact' (1993: 70).

The Other Man's Country

That statement can also be cautiously applied to one of the decade's most elaborate meditations on migration, from a writer who tended self-consciously to set himself outside ethnic groupings. V. S. Naipaul's *The Enigma of Arrival* (1987) is intriguingly parallel to Ishiguro's *Remains of the Day* in its treatment of England through the landscape of the West Country. Naipaul is a migrant from Trinidad, where his Indian ancestry had already given him a sense of marginality. He moved to England to study at Oxford from 1950. But he did not settle as a writer of English themes, or (like his contemporary Samuel Selvon) a chronicler of post-colonial London. Instead he spent the next decades, in a prolific series of novels and travel writings, primarily investigating volatile political states around the postcolonial world. *The Enigma of Arrival* is thus a new kind of arrival in Naipaul's own career. The book's genre is itself an enigma. It is presented as 'a novel in five sections': the subtitle is the more necessary as the book might easily be treated as autobiography. Its narrator seems to have had Naipaul's career, and recounts episodes from it at length. But as Michael Wood notes (2002: 89), Naipaul at once transcribes and edits his life, removing all reference to the wife who lived with him in Wiltshire. The book is also carefully structured, in four main sections of symmetrical size. Naipaul thus writes a deeply personal book while granting his experiences the simultaneously provisional and ordered quality of fiction.

Naipaul's book ranges across the spaces of his life, situating him as part of 'that great movement of peoples that was to take place in the second half of the twentieth century [. . .] a movement between all the continents' (Naipaul 2002: 154). But the book insistently returns to the Wiltshire countryside where it begins, and where a dejected Naipaul settles in the 1970s after an unsuccessful attempt to make a new home in America. In this move, Naipaul is already breaking a mould. For postcolonial British writing has more often laid its scene in the city, in an environment where the modernity of the migrant matches that of his or her surroundings, and where the 'cultural mixing' Naipaul refers to is often thoroughly in evidence. Great contemporary cities, he proposes, have become 'cities of the world' appealing to 'all the barbarian peoples of the globe', rather than insular national capitals (154).

The Wiltshire countryside's appeal is very different. It is not obviously a place of hybridity or diversity, nor of speed and spectacle. Its appeal to the visitor lies in its sense of continuity. Naipaul records not just farm buildings and cottages, but the view of Stonehenge: there could hardly be a stronger image of English antiquity. For the migrant to settle here thus presents a distinctive scenario. Naipaul, especially in the novel's first section which sets the scene in a mysteriously slow-motion fashion, acknowledges his status as a 'stranger', without ceding his right to inhabit the valley. 'After all my time in England,' he admits,

> I still had that nervousness in a new place, that rawness of response, still felt myself to be in the other man's country, felt my strangeness, my solitude. And every excursion into a new part of the country – what for others might have been an adventure – was for me like a tearing at an old scab. (6)

For this reason, his vision of Wiltshire is by no means a reprise of the paeans to Deep England that Patrick Wright had recently assembled, in which expatriates lovingly catalogued 'Long winter walks through the Wyre Forest ending at the George in Bewley', or 'a celebration of the Eucharist in a quiet Norfolk Church with the mediaeval glass filtering the colours, and the early noise of the harvesting coming through the open door' (Wright 1985: 76, 81). Naipaul's rural England is stranger, and more estranged. It lacks precisely the warm sense of home and ownership that come easily to English nostalgists. In a cold river valley where, his opening line tells us, 'For the first four days it rained' (3), the chilly climate helps to kill his neighbour Jack, and then affects Naipaul's own lungs. His gaze is equally cool. At the outset he declares: 'I saw what I saw very clearly. But I didn't know what I was looking at. I had nothing to fit it into. I was still in a kind of limbo' (5). The clarity of his immediate vision persists, even as the explanatory context for what is seen gradually modifies. Naipaul makes it his task to look closely and meticulously record what he sees: 'The downs all around were flinty and dry, whitish brown, whitish green. But on the wide way at the bottom, around the farm buildings, the ground was muddy and black. The tractor wheels had dug out irregular linear ponds in the black mud' (7).

What is most remarkable is not Naipaul's endless observation but its repetitiveness. Features of the countryside, and the phrases that Naipaul has attached to them – the droveway, the windbreak, the military firing range, Stonehenge, Jack's garden – become like mantras. The fact that he met Jack's aged father-in-law before meeting Jack himself (14) is not announced once, but repeatedly: 'The old man first, then' (15), he confirms, then a few pages later: 'It was his father-in-law I noticed first. And it was his father-in-law I met first. I met him quite early on' (21). Bruce King suggestively sees the use of repetition across the whole book as musical (2003: 142–3), with the first lines (Naipaul 2002: 3), for instance, virtually reappearing halfway through the long novel (185) as Naipaul's narrative catches up with his starting point. But the more local repetitions have a different tone. They suggest obsessiveness: an ongoing struggle to remember, incessantly updated by the reassuring recitation of pieces of information, in the manner of Samuel Beckett's fraught monologists. Reviewing the novel, Salman Rushdie diagnosed this feature as not merely a formal tic, but a direct reflection of Naipaul's theme. Rushdie recognises 'the sense of a writer feeling obliged to bring his new world into being by an act of pure will, the sense that if the world is not described into existence in the most minute detail, then it won't be there. The immigrant', Rushdie declares in unwitting anticipation of a later novel of his own, 'must invent the earth beneath his feet.' On this reading, Naipaul's Beckettian obsessiveness is a historically specific act of laying claim. 'It is a kind of extreme minimalism,' Rushdie acutely sees, 'but it becomes almost hypnotic. And slowly the picture is built, figures arrive in the landscape, a new world is won' (1991: 149).

This process of 'winning' the world of the valley is visible in Naipaul's account of his gradually shifting feelings for the place. 'Unanchored and strange', he feels that 'my presence in that old valley was part of something like an upheaval, a change in the course of the history of the country' (13–14). Naipaul is well aware of the imperial history to which the local manor house belongs, and the fact that '[f]ifty years ago there would have been no room for me on the estate; even now my presence was a little unlikely'. But rather than resisting the environment, he connects himself to it. He sees a logic, a 'clear historical line', reaching back to Indian migration to Trinidad, which has ultimately 'given me the English language as my own' (55). At the same time, Naipaul revises his view of the valley's antiquity. 'Here was an unchanging world,' he initially thinks: 'the country life, the slow movement of time'. 'But that idea of an unchanging life,' Naipaul realises, 'was wrong. Change was constant.' And his own presence in the valley, he sees, is 'an aspect of another kind of change' (32). In numerous ways, Naipaul comes to understand the landscape around him as historical, shaped by 'the hand of man' (24); and he has now become a tangible part of that process of historical change.

It would thus be misleading to see Naipaul's Wiltshire settlement as a simply conservative gesture. He has been a controversial figure amid postcolonial writing and thought, in part for placing his proud individualism over the assertion of postcolonial national identity. Naipaul sees the landscape through the English literary canon. At one point he realises that his new familiarity with the landscape has led him to an understanding of a small local reference in *King Lear* that has eluded scholars (18). This is typical of Naipaul's 'minimalist' approach, at the very time when others were proposing radical new stagings and critiques of Shakespeare in the light of postcolonialism. He might thus be viewed as a nervous 'mimic' of the English, while at the other extreme Bruce King sees Naipaul as having 'conquered' England (2003: 147). But the book's tone suggests something more modest. *The Enigma of Arrival* shows, not an attempt to be more English than the English, but a quiet, understated assertion of the migrant's right to be in England, or any-where. Its articulation of the change that thus occurs on both sides is the more persuasive for being so painstakingly slow. Naipaul's postcolonial pastoral, while uncannily showing England through weary foreign eyes, also offers a peaceful, gradualist model of cultural change. It is at the slowest pace that, in Naipaul's own later description (Jaggi 2001), the book 'sets ideas about country life on their head'.

Here to Change Things

Naipaul's themes were shared, if differently addressed, not only by Rushdie but by the other most celebrated British Asian writer to emerge since Naipaul, Hanif Kureishi. Rushdie's first fame, we have already seen, arose from his novel of India *Midnight's Children* (1981). But like the writers we have already considered here, he and Kureishi were insist-ently concerned with the state of Britain. Both supplemented their fic-tional narratives with polemical essays in which they addressed current issues – the representation of the Raj in TV drama, the racism of British institutions – through personal anecdote as well as historical research. In this respect they contributed to the national conversation. Rushdie, in particular, assumed something of the bardic role in his essays of the 1980s, unashamedly using his status as a novelist as licence to discuss the constitutional pressure group Charter 88 or to assail Margaret Thatcher's Britain in apocalyptic terms (Rushdie 1991: 159–65). When he and Kureishi wrote of Britain, they wrote for the most part of urban England: above all London.

Kureishi would revisit his youth in the novel *The Buddha of Suburbia* (1990), but he began as a dramatist. His first plays belonged to the local and left-wing theatre of the early 1980s. *Borderline* (1981), developed with the Joint Stock theatre company, explored the anxieties and pres-sures on British Asians, specifically in the London suburb of Southall. Its themes of urban racism and intergenerational conflict would resound not just through Kureishi's further work, but through much black British writing. *Outskirts* the same year, a study of two old schoolfriends, was also characteristic of Kureishi in its rewriting of his own past amid suburban youth culture, though this play approaches National Front violence from the point of view of the perpetrators rather than the victims. The play's scenario in which two former schoolboys are uncertainly reunited would be reprised in Kureishi's real breakthrough to both popular and critical success: the film drama *My Beautiful Laundrette* (1985). The film gained a theatrical release, but was made with money from Channel Four, the new outlet for alternative programming since 1982. Like Bleasdale's *Blackstuff*, the film is an instance of how public service television could both support significant writing in the 1980s and broadcast it to iconic status. *My Beautiful Laundrette* is a typical Channel Four production of the 1980s in its dramatisation not just of ethnic minority life but of homosexuality. The protagonist Omar, like most of the characters, is of Pakistani ancestry. His uncle Nasser inducts him into business as the owner of a laundrette. Crucial in Omar's success is Johnny, an unemployed squatter and former schoolfriend whom Omar hires as handyman. Johnny's history includes racist activism, but he and Omar now become lovers, and remain together at the film's end despite tangling with Johnny's thuggish former friends.

Kureishi's film is insistently concerned with England, which is seen primarily through the battered housing estates and railway lines of south-east London. Two views of England emerge. One emphasises the racism that the Pakistani characters have had to endure. Omar's father, a decrepit idealist and intellectual, tells him that 'They hate us in England'; 'We are under siege by the white man. For us education is power' (Kureishi 1996: 25, 18). Another businessman, Zaki, asks, 'What chance has the racist Englishman given us that we haven't torn from him with our hands? Let's face up to it' (21). Even Salim, a ruthless businessman whose money comes from drugs, ultimately laments of Johnny's friends that 'they abuse people [. . .] Our people'. To Johnny himself he declares, 'All over England, Asians, as you call us, are beaten, burnt to death. Always we are intimidated' (61). Within the film, these recurrent statements are corroborated by the behaviour of most of the white characters we encounter. Omar remembers Johnny and his friends marching through Lewisham, 'with bricks and bottles and Union Jacks', in the 1970s (43). Now, in the 1980s, the same whites demand of Johnny: 'Why are you working for them? For these people? You were with us once. For England. [. . .] I don't like to see one of our men grovelling to Pakis' (38). All this could make for a drama primarily about racial discrimination and violence. It echoes Kureishi's own analysis, outside the film, of a 'continual struggle against racism' faced by black and Asian

Britons: 'the pig's head through the window, the spit in the face, the children with the initials of racist organizations tattooed into their skin with razor blades, as well as the more polite forms of hatred' (100).

Yet Kureishi's writing goes beyond this vision. His film is primarily about Asians in business, where Nasser and Salim are shown as assured operators whose work has brought them great wealth in England. Salim's luxurious home is decorated with paintings by the great Indian painters he 'patronizes' (27), and is the venue for genteel dinner parties for numerous 'well-off Pakistani friends' (32). Nasser's great house in Kent is the scene of parties and business meetings in which other wealthy Pakistanis defer to the host. Clearly, despite the racism described elsewhere, it is possible for Pakistanis to prosper in Kureishi's England. The two facts are even related, the first making a necessity of the second: as Salim grimly puts it, '[W]e're nothing in England without money' (48). Financial success can even be presented as a properly English form of belonging. In the background of one of Nasser's gatherings a tacky electronic version of 'Land of Hope and Glory' plays. Margaret Thatcher's name is repeatedly invoked, as Nasser jovially suggests that his success in business is in tune with her Britain: he tells Omar, '[W]e'll drink to Thatcher and your beautiful laundrette', which go together 'like dall and chapatis' (37). Nasser refuses to think of modern Conservatism as a racist restraint: declaring himself a professional businessman rather than a professional Pakistani, he insists that '[t]here's no race question in the new enterprise culture' (41). Not only do British Pakistanis dominate the film and display wealth, they frequently take a poor view of white people. Salim's wife Cherry considers England a 'silly little island off Europe' which could never truly be home (19). When Salim himself scornfully asks, 'What the hell else is there for them in this country now?' (37), he seems to mean Johnny's people, as though the white English have become an enfeebled, outdated underclass. 'Everyone has to belong' (43), insists the racist youth Ghengis, but in this text it is whites like him who seem to be finding it a problem. England, Salim thinks, is 'tilted in favour of the useless [. . .] The only positive discrimination they have here' (21). The ex-colonials, it seems, have beaten the former imperial masters at their own game: this Wildean inversion underpins much of Kureishi's comedy.

Thus Omar tells Johnny, 'I'm not going to be beat down by this country. When we were at school, you and your lot kicked me all round the place. And what are you doing now? Washing my floor. That's how I like it. Now get to work' (51). For the bullied Pakistani proudly to issue orders to the National Front thug might be an aspiration, but in this context, where Johnny has done Omar a favour in taking on a job in the first place, it lacks reality. So does Omar's father's calm disdain for Johnny's fortunes (53). In both scenes Johnny, apparently the film's most physically indomitable character, is humbly acquiescent in his treatment. The script's implausibilities point to the element of fantasy in this work – which is already signalled by the 'beautiful' laundrette itself, bedecked with neon like a vintage cinema. Kureishi rightly describes his drama as 'an amusement, despite its references to racism, unemployment and Thatcherism' (5). In a curious irony, the film's apparent pursuit of the most 'realistic' contemporary themes – race relations and homosexuality – actually makes for a uniquely fanciful allegory. The story, which ends with the Pakistani and his former NF persecutor lovingly flicking water over each other, is less a report from the front line than a utopia; a work that gathers marginal, persecuted experiences from the period and wilfully celebrates them. Kureishi's script was rare among major works of the 1980s in inspiring a pop song. Lloyd Cole's version of Johnny's story was brief and enigmatic, but in equating 'my beautiful laundrette' with 'my beautiful escape' he captured a crucial aspect of this text.

If any work of the 1980s treated migration, ethnicity and the state of Britain under the sign of fantasy, it was Salman Rushdie's *The Satanic Verses* (1988). Rushdie's novel also became the most notorious of all time, as in the months after its September publication it was increasingly denounced and burned by Muslim activists, and in February 1989 the religious leader of Iran declared a *fatwa* or death sentence on Rushdie. Their ire related mainly to the large portions of the book depicting the origins of Islam, in which the prophet Mohammed is shown as humanly fallible and a flock of prostitutes take on the personae of his wives for commercial gain. The fundamentalist reaction was that all Muslims had a duty to kill the novelist, who was forced into hiding under Special Branch protection. The literary 1980s, worldwide as well as in Britain, thus ended in an unprecedentedly ominous atmosphere. Writers took up Rushdie's cause in petitions, essays and statements. Booker Prize winners for years to come would declare their solidarity with him as they claimed their awards. Debates over free speech had retained some currency during the relatively authoritarian climate of the Thatcher years, but the Rushdie crisis ignited them anew. Liberal values were abruptly confronted with a theocratic opposition, different in source, motive and intensity from more familiar forms of conservatism (like the puritanical campaign that had targeted *The Romans in Britain*). Meanwhile Britain's Muslim community itself, whether for or against Rushdie, suddenly became more visible. Kenan Malik, in a retrospective history (2008), sees the episode as a significant step on the path to a form of multiculturalism in which religious and ethnic groups became entrenched and endorsed in their distinction from one another. By the twenty-first century, with a global 'clash of civilisations' announced in the wake of the 9/11 attacks and Anglo-American invasions of the Middle East, *The Satanic Verses* could look like the harbinger of an era. Rushdie's explicit treatment of fundamentalism in the novel (1988: 205–15), while based on the earlier Parisian exile of the very Ayatollah who would sentence him to death, would also appear prophetic in an age when the Western world would live in fear of Islamic terrorist cells.

Yet Rushdie was also dealing with more local and timely matters. Despite its ill repute as an irreverent treatment of historical Islam, *The Satanic Verses* is at least as much a portrait of contemporary London, specifically the migrant communities and their struggles with a prejudiced police force and a suspicious state. The book's major protagonists, the Bollywood actor Gibreel Farishta and the Anglophile Indian Saladin Chamcha, are both effectively immigrants to England. After miraculously surviving an air crash, they experience contrasting fates in London. Much of the novel revolves around the Shandaar Café and its attendant rooming house, where Chamcha is sheltered amid a community of first and second generation immigrants. These include the café owner Muhammad Sufyan; his daughters who are as engaged with Western popular culture as with their Indian ancestry; the community activist Hanif Johnson (conceivably a nod to the streetwise Kureishi); and the poet Jamshed 'Jumpy' Joshi. Beyond them is a wider social context in which the controversial black activist Uhuru Simba dies in police custody. In the incendiary atmosphere that follows, a riot rips across Rushdie's fictional district Brickhall.

The novel is thus crowded with talk of the politics of ethnicity, in both abstract and concretely local terms. The poet Joshi appropriates Enoch Powell's imagery to argue that 'humanity is a river of blood': 'Reclaim the metaphor, Jumpy Joshi had told himself. Turn it; make it a thing we can use' (187). Uhuru Simba likewise reclaims a despised racial image, taking on 'the old and honourable role of the uppity nigger', to tell a court that England's immigrant population is 'here to change things', having themselves been changed by migration: 'We have been made again: but I say that we shall also be the ones to remake this society, to shape it from the bottom to the top' (414). Rushdie has resonantly, but rather vaguely, called the novel 'a love-song to our mongrel selves' (1991: 394). More specifically, and among many other things, it is a partisan tribute to the secular, left-wing black activism of the 1970s and 1980s, which would be eclipsed both by the travails of socialism and by the rise of 'faith-based' and sectarian forms of community organisation towards the turn of the century.

Yet the vessel in which Rushdie casts all this pressingly 'realistic' material is no naturalistic work. The realities of ethnic discrimination and struggle are framed by complex layers of fantasy and alternate worlds. Chapters on contemporary London alternate with those describing Islam's origin hundreds of years before. The latter chapters, which primarily provoked the *fatwa*, are linked to the present by being presented as the dreams of Gibreel Farishta. But the relations between dream and reality, past and present, are ambiguous. Farishta's theological dreams do not stay safely bracketed by his real life, but seem to have a historical reality and formative influence of their own. Meanwhile, the contemporary sections are not insulated from magic and mysticism, but suffused with them. The first event in Rushdie's 'real' world is Farishta and Chamcha's tumble from an exploded airliner, in which they fall safely to earth while talking to each other. Rushdie's narrator admits that 'it was impossible for them to have heard one another', characteristically adding 'let's face this, too: they did' (6). This will thus be a fictional world in which the 'impossible' happens, including the two men's mutation into respectively an angel and a devil. This enchantment of the real is arguably matched by a certain demystification of the medieval, early-Islamic world, in which religion is seen to arise from fallible human needs and social contexts: thus the worldly and the fantastical mingle from both sides. Farishta, possessed with angelic powers, sees a 'metamorphosed city' of 'essences instead of surfaces' (320–1); another character believes that 'the world of dreams was leaking into that of the waking hours [. . .] the seals dividing the two were breaking' (304).

Rushdie's England thus has a peculiar status. Like his London 'visible but unseen' it has a dual character, at once grittily present and fabulously allegorical. Rushdie constantly insists on its contemporaneity (a room is strewn with 'the *Voice* newspaper and feminist science-fiction novels' [173], racial violence is now committed on Thatcherite principles [284]), but simply to record the world of the 1980s is inadequate to this author: it must also be warped by fantasy. It is as though the presence of angels, devils and miraculous events afford Rushdie the critical difference he seeks from the real. They offer him an ostentatious way of symbolising forces and ideas, which become larger and gaudier than life, and also the subject of authorial commentary and narrative transformation. Thus Chamcha's mutation into a devil destroys any conventional prospect of verisimilitude, but also represents the demonisation of immigrants by the British state and population. He is goaded and abused in a police van (157–64) and incarcerated in a detention centre full of monsters, including a manticore who explains that 'They have the power of description, and we succumb to the pictures they construct' (168). Chamcha's diabolical aspect subsequently becomes a totem among London's black community, in another instance of revaluation: 'an image white society has rejected for so long that we can really [. . .] reclaim it and make it our own' (287). Chamcha thus becomes a symbolic figure in the public mind – but only because he was already luridly symbolic, made over into a walking emblem by his author. Symbolism, in this novel, goes all the way back: its characters tend to be the exaggerated embodiments of ideas. This goes for the ostensibly secular, non-fantastical characters too – the Thatcherite bigot Hal Valance is an obvious example (266–70) – but their stereotypical quality is perhaps excused and framed by the fantasy around them. In this novel, even the real people are unreal.

In this fictional world, unbuckled from naturalism, Rushdie can sport with ideas, and interject grand metaphorical statements at the level of action. Most emblematic of all is Gibreel Farishta's fury with London, whose offences he identifies with its weather: '"City," he cried, and his voice rolled over the metropolis like thunder, "I am going to tropical- ize you"' (354). Rushdie produces a long list of the cultural effects of climate: the implication is of a 'reverse colonization' in which England will be made like India (355). The scene is archetypal of Rushdie's book, taking licence to unleash compensatory magic on an unwelcoming Britain, and to offer an image for the whole postcolonial remaking of the nation (Israel 2006: 83–4). Decried by Muslims the world over, Rushdie has also been celebrated for granting postcolonial Britain another dimension: an imaginary surplus to reality in which oppressive realities could be allegorised, parodied and disassembled. It is striking that two of the texts that reflected most extensively on the matter of Britain, at either end of the 1980s, were also the two to provoke the greatest fury.

Chapter Five

Commitments

Common Parlance

'It is 1988 and I no longer feel I know what "feminist" means': thus Gillian Allnutt commenced her selection of 'quote feminist unquote poetry' in the crowded, four-part anthology *The New British Poetry*. The hedging section title tries to have it both ways, announcing feminism as the guiding theme but casting doubt on it in the same breath. Allnutt worried that the word that 'has been part of common parlance in this country for the past twenty years' has now lost its status, becoming an embarrassment even on the political Left (1988: 77–8). She registered a historically specific impression, in which feminism was beginning to be presented as part of the recent past, with the present defined by 'post-feminism'.

Writing at the same time, Cora Kaplan also recognised feminism as already a historical matter. If the second wave of the women's movement had begun in the late 1960s, it was now twenty years old. The conservative political climate of the 1980s, Kaplan proposed, was not congenial to celebrating this history. Some of the connections between imaginative writing, cultural criticism and practical politics that were naturally made in the 1970s had now diminished (Kaplan 1989: 22–3). As Lynne Segal had written, the women's movement of the 1980s had lost some of the purposive unity it had known in the previous decade (1987: xii).

Yet none of these writers was ultimately out to concede defeat. Feminism might be declared an anachronism by the 1990s, but this rhetorical tactic was largely a way of denying its unsettled claims. 'Many younger women would not call themselves feminists,' Helen Carr observed, 'even though they express what in the 1970s would have been thought feminist views' (1989: 5). Feminism might be organisationally fragmented, but this equally reflected its percolation into diverse millions of everyday lives. As Kaplan saw, popular television drama now deployed a 'women's language', staging gendered struggles for an audience now readily capable of thinking in such political terms (1989: 19–20). It has become a truism that the new experiences associated with the 1960s – of free love or casual drug use – were really more widely experienced in the following decade. We can likewise say that many of the struggles of the women's movement in the 1970s were still bearing fruit and shaping ordinary lives, for both sexes, in the decade discussed by this book.

This chapter is concerned with the conjunction of feminism and literature in the 1980s, in a number of ways. The women's movement had emphasised gender as a significant category of analysis, a modality of experience shaping social life, let alone art. Gender will be a recurrent focus here: from certain prominent political uses of it to its treatment in fictional narrative. The organisational networks of the women's movement sought to create spaces for women's writing; these will be considered in relation to both theatre and the novel. Feminism is not, of course, only a matter for women. Some male writers reacted to it directly. Finally, we will consider gay writing in the 1980s. Gay culture has its own independent trajectories, but gay liberation and expression have also been significantly tied to the feminist movement, which has encouraged understanding of desire and affect. This chapter's title refers primarily to the political commitments of feminism, which informed much of the writing we are about to see. But the word, in the sense of emotional commitment, is also pertinent to the sphere of personal relations that feminism has done much to transform.

Advances and Retreats

The women's movement of the 1970s had proliferated into different strands and political emphases. Distinctions were drawn between 'liberal' feminists concerned for women to gain equality of opportunity, pay and advancement, and socialist feminists who asserted that the structures of patriarchal oppression were inseparable from economic exploitation and class inequality. Different again was the assertion of 'radical' feminism that men were inherently violent, that heterosexual intercourse was inevitably a form of domination, and that women must sever connections with men and create their own relationships apart from the so-called 'malestream'. The construction of cultural institutions dominated by women indeed proved valuable. Ideologically, however, radical feminism could also carry the stronger implication that female and male identity were fundamentally, perhaps biologically distinct, and that authentically female values and experiences must be reclaimed.

The advent of Margaret Thatcher might have undermined any stable gender dichotomy. A woman was among the most fearsomely single-minded political leaders in modern British history, proud of her inflexibility, scornful of the language of nurture or co-operation. Here was prominent empirical evidence that the conventionally gendered characteristics of masculine and feminine could in fact be found in either sex. Yet this fact has often tended to be rolled back into a reassertion of gender norms, with Thatcher labelled an honorary male. She becomes the exception that proves the rule, not a demonstration of the open-endedness of gender identity but simply an aberration. Reviewing a biography of Thatcher in 1990, Martin Amis followed one of her statements with the mock-exasperated 'Women!', then asked: 'But *is* she one? Well, yes and no' (Amis 2001: 21).

Amis' ambivalence reproduces an ambiguity around Thatcher herself. We saw in the Introduction that Thatcherism thrived on, or despite, apparent ideological contradiction. This much was likewise true of Thatcher's own gendered persona. The Iron Lady could also deploy softer modes. In *Monuments and Maidens* (1985) the novelist and cultural critic Marina Warner assessed Thatcher as one of a series of female icons including Joan of Arc and Britannia. Thatcher could appear the reincarnation of this British heroine, Warner proposed, 'not because she is a battle-axe like Boadicea, but because she is so womanly, combining Britannia's resoluteness, Boadicea's courage with a proper housewifely demeanour' (Warner 1985: 51). The cliché that Thatcher 'wears the trousers', Warner observed, was tellingly inaccurate. It was not just that, in literal fact, 'she never wears trousers' (51), but that the cultivation of a feminine appearance and qualities contributed significantly to her political power.

In November 1984, deep into the miners' strike, Thatcher used a television interview with Miriam Stoppard to praise 'women's special qualities' and 'suggest her own greater integrity, sincerity and depth of feeling' (Segal 1987: 246). In 1986 she appeared on *The English Woman's Wardrobe*, guiding viewers through the outfits she had worn on different political occasions. She wielded a handbag as a constant prop, identifying her with the responsible housewife. Through the decade her apparel became more grandly regal: the fashion journalist Brenda Polan observed that Thatcher had discovered a form of 'power dressing' typical of the time. Her biographer John Campbell insists that this was no masculinising move: her achievement 'was in managing to look powerful and feminine at the same time'. As often with Thatcher, the effect is a paradox: 'hard-faced femininity' (Campbell) or 'Florence Nightingale with a blowtorch' (Denis Healey) (Campbell 2003: 472–6). Although Thatcher's attainment of unprecedented power might indicate what a woman could now achieve in Britain, she gave scant ground to feminism. Her cabinets were almost exclusively male. She showed little inclination either to promote women colleagues or to promote sexual equality through legislation. Marion Bowman observed in 1989 that 'It's almost as if, as a woman, Margaret Thatcher represents no one but herself' (2007: 17).

The ambiguous conjunction of femininity and power represented by Margaret Thatcher was significant in the cultural imagination of the period. The image of the ruthlessly successful woman, achieving individual goals rather than part of a female collective, informed bestselling popular fictions of business and sexual adventure. Julie Burchill's *Ambition* (1989) is a pastiche of this mode. We will shortly see this image of contemporary womanhood explored in the theatre. Still more directly, the representation of the prime minister herself would form a significant sub-genre of literary content. Inevitably the matter of Thatcher's gender often arose in such work. Amis' John Self in *Money* (1984) concocts an apology for her inattention to the inner cities: 'Sorry, boys, the PM has PMT' (1984: 155). In Salman Rushdie's *Satanic Verses* the immigrant community delights 'at least three times a week' in burning a waxwork effigy of Thatcher, complete with '[h]er perma-waved coiffure, her pearls, her suit of blue' (1988: 293). Elsewhere in the novel the vulgar businessman Hal Valance reveres her 'revolution' while also apparently denigrating her as 'Mrs Torture', 'Maggie the bitch' (266, 269). The sadistic overtones of Rushdie's renaming echo the 'powerful sexual ambivalence' that John Campbell finds in numerous responses to her (2003: 472). Ian McEwan's *The Child in Time* (1987) coyly hints at Thatcher's presence in featuring a prime minister whose sex is never specified. The tactic allows McEwan to suspend the question of whether the present premier is still running his near-future society; it also extends the view of Thatcher as a contradictory compound of the sexes, or as removed from the limits of gender by power itself. Other male writers would extend the novel's fascination with the prime minister: from Mark Lawson's *Bloody Margaret* (1991) and Philip Hensher's *Kitchen Venom* (1996), focused around the latter days of her reign, to Iain Sinclair's caricatured portrait of her as 'The Widow' in *Downriver* (1991).

But Margaret Thatcher was not the only significant version of womanhood available in the 1980s. Marina Warner counterposed to her the very different manifestation of female power on view in the protests at

Greenham Common, an air base in Berkshire where the United States Air Force had been stationed throughout the Cold War. In June 1980 it was announced that cruise missiles would be housed at the base, as a deterrent against a nuclear strike from the USSR. The weapons arrived in November 1983, and remained until 1991, when the Berlin Wall was down and the Soviet Union itself on the brink of disintegration. The base became an iconic site in the period, thanks to the female protesters who began to picket the site from September 1981. They were the decade's most enduringly visible manifestation of feminist activism. Some protesters proposed a specifically female activism, both in the method of protest and in the values being defended and decried. It was suggested that women, as the potential or actual bearers of children, had a peculiar status in defending life and denouncing the engines of death within the base. Pregnant women were part of the protest, and at least one child was born in the peace camp. That event, as Marina Warner records, demonstrated 'a shared need to show that women on their own can deliver life as well as give birth, and do not need obstetricians and hospitals, identified with the impersonal, mechanistic male world' (1985: 59). That mechanistic world was most intimidatingly represented by the contents of the Greenham base itself: missiles, bomber jets and military personnel, behind concrete and barbed wire.

Figure 8   The Bomb That Will Bring Us Together: protesters encircle Greenham Common, early 1980s

Greenham's image will recur in several texts considered in this chapter. It was a movement with political goals, but also a cultural process: it involved singing, dancing, craft. The protesters wove webs of coloured wool, hung ribbons from bushes and fences, painted images of lunar goddesses and martyred women. Warner admired the campaigners' indomitability. She nonetheless registered concern that 'the archaic, all-encompassing mother of creation' celebrated by some protesters might be 'the most dangerous and intractable patriarchal myth of all' (60). The radical commentator Judith Williamson made a parallel observation. Citing the words of protesters in the volume *Greenham Women Everywhere*, she observed that '[t]here is an emphasis on motherhood, the family, woman as nature and as provider – exactly the myths about femininity that the women's movement has tried to question' (Williamson 1987: 213–14). Leaflets asserted that women were 'springs' that could become 'rivers' into 'an ocean of women's energy', and even that a 'full moon festival' at Greenham would produce a female 'rainbow dragon' to travel around the world. Williamson found here an uncomfortably mystical 'relation between women and ecology' (217–18). Yet, she acknowledged, the movement had been successful in capturing media attention; the nuclear family was one way to tap popular sentiments against nuclear war.

Lynne Segal maintained a level head in the face of essentialism and the temptations of separatism. In 1987 she looked back over the fortunes of feminism in the 1980s and argued that feminists had too often promoted a vision of unchanging femininity. The notion of 'sexual difference' could be reified into an absolute. Masculine and feminine principles were viewed as essential rather than as the historically contingent constructions that many in the women's movement had sought to uncover and disassemble. Feminist analysis, Segal proposed, had mistakenly come to emphasise 'the inevitability of men's violence and competitive power-seeking', contrasting it with 'a more nurturant, maternal, co-operative and peaceful "female" psychology and behaviour' (1987: ix). The protests at Greenham Common, though politically heroic, had fuelled this dualistic mode of thinking.

Yet the reality of women's experiences in the 1980s, Segal asserted, had little to do with such binaries. The balance of power in gender relations and roles had already been shaken and shifted in ways so radical that essentialism was simply atavistic. Feminism might be mutating, but it endured through diverse contemporary manifestations:

The 'deconstructing' feminist academic studying the multiple meanings of 'femininity', the Cosmo journalist promoting greater choice in the lives of career women, the women in community struggles fighting the withdrawal of choice in their lives through the closure of nurseries, working-class women fighting the impact of 'privatisation' and its deteriorating job conditions, or Black women fighting heightened racism generally and increasingly racist regulations in welfare provision, all reflect the advances and retreats in the lives of different groups of women in recent years. (x–xi)

It is this diverse, historically mutable terrain that we will now see explored in creative works.

Meeting Spaces

The collective structures of the women's movement might have frayed by the mid-1980s. Yet the legacy of feminist organisation remained significant for creative production and publication by women, not least in the theatre. Its inherently collective character had made it a cultural site for the movement from the early 1970s. At the same time, the institutions of theatre and the need for space, capital and publicity to produce it meant that women could not simply create spontaneously and in isolation, but needed to engage with structures of finance and influence – and hence to struggle with male-dominated hierarchies within the theatre.

Feminist theatre had developed through numerous independent companies: Women's Theatre Group, Women's Company, Monstrous Regiment. Clean Break, Spare Tyre and the lesbian group Siren were all founded in 1979. New writers emerged from their ranks: Clair Chapman wrote plays for Spare Tyre, Tasha Fairbanks for Siren. Gay Sweatshop, formed in 1976, followed the model of the feminist companies, as a significant independent group developing work by gay writers and actors. These fringe companies were often forced to use impromptu spaces and resources: 'community centres, women's meeting spaces, or schools' (Aston and Reinelt 2000: 12). Through the 1970s Arts Council funding for fringe theatre increased considerably, finally comprising up to 12 per cent of its budget: from £7,000 to £1.5 million between 1971 and 1978 (Wandor 2000: 60–1). The 1980s changed this scenario. Sharp cuts were made early in the decade to alternative theatre companies. The socialist company 7:84 (England) lost its grant in 1984 and disappeared. Feminist initiatives were likewise squeezed. This was among the most direct ways in which the dominant political tendency of the decade was able to affect the state of cultural production.

New ventures were nonetheless made within the 1980s. The Women's Playhouse Trust was founded in 1980. Its artistic director Jules Wright, an Australian socialist-feminist, stated that the organisation's aim was 'to redress the balance between men and women working in British mainstream theatre by ensuring that the principal artists – writers, directors, choreographers, composers – employed by the WPT were women' (Goodman 1996: 107). The Trust's first production was of *Lucky Chance* by Aphra Behn, a seventeenth-century woman writer who was being revisited by feminist literary historians. The Trust continued to revive older works (including plays by men like Ibsen, with strong female parts) and to support plays in translation, as well as new plays by British writers including Winsome Pinnock and Sarah Daniels. Pinnock was one of the most significant talents to emerge from black women's theatre, which developed its own institutions during the decade. Theatre of Black Women was founded in 1982: among the founders was Bernadine Evaristo, who would achieve acclaim as a poet. Lacking a physical space of its own, Evaristo has reflected, the company could not be a broader cultural centre, but it did work to introduce more black women to practical work as directors, stage managers and designers: 'We enabled black women to take control of the creative process of making theatre, from start to finish' (Goodman 1996: 133, 136). Another associate of the new body was Yvonne Brewster, who in 1982 became the first black woman to serve as drama officer for the Arts Council. Theatre of Black Women survived for the rest of the 1980s, staging the early work of Jackie Kay among others. Another black women's theatre organisation, Talawa, was founded in 1985. To its pleasant surprise Talawa received a grant of £85,000 from the left-dominated Greater London Council, a year before that body was abolished by central government. Meanwhile another initiative developed in Wales. Magdalena '86 was an international festival of women's experimental theatre in Cardiff, which subsequently became established as The Magdalena Project. Susan Bassnett notes that the application of the term 'feminist' to the event was contested, and that participants did not necessarily agree about the quest for a shared 'feminine' aesthetic. In 1987 its workshop 'A Women's Language in Theatre?' was opened to delegates of both sexes. Though Bassnett records that few men attended, the shift was arguably typical of a move away from women-only forums as the 'radical' feminism of the 1970s was marginalised into the 1990s (2000: 75). Relatively mainstream venues were also becoming available for feminist work. David Edgar (2009) notes that the Royal Court theatre, with Max Stafford-Clark as artistic director, was a significant venue for new writing by women in the 1980s.

Sites for feminist theatre continued to appear, then, even in unpromising circumstances. One of their goals was to encourage new writing by women. Michelene Wandor records that a collaborative ethos had initially tended to encourage collective work even in playwriting, with a 'strong notion that the individual fictional voice was somehow reactionary' (2000: 58). This is one reason why the emergence of prominent individual playwrights from the women's movement was, as Wandor also states, belated (57). Another reason is the discrepancy between what was written and performed, and what was published. Published plays by women at the start of the 1980s were relatively few. Wandor herself took the initiative of editing the first four volumes of a series of *Plays by Women* for Methuen, starting in 1982. By the 1990s Methuen were at last granting women playwrights their own individual collections alongside Pinter, Stoppard or Brecht. This was significant for making further performances more feasible, and in making the writers available to study: it contributed to the reformation of the theatrical canon. In the latter half of the 1980s, the Royal Court theatre made another contribution to this process by selling programmes that included the text of the play in question. Sarah Daniels, Timberlake Wertenbaker and Clare McIntyre were published in this way (Goodman 1996: 97). The tactic was the more necessary as the only woman to win a volume of collected plays from Methuen before 1990 was Caryl Churchill.

Critical work nonetheless began to appear. Wandor's own volume *Carry On, Understudies* (1986) gave an account of the emergence of feminist, gay and lesbian theatre from political movements and the experimental stage since 1968, while her study *Look Back in Gender* (1987) scanned the post-war British stage from a consistently feminist standpoint. It gradually became plausible to talk of a canon of contemporary women's playwrights. Jules Wright observed in 1994 that since the 1970s, a British feminist theatre 'which initially emphasized collective approaches has become more individualized' (Goodman 1996: 113). David Edgar (2009) suggests that an 'individualization' of attention also highlighted new women writers through the decade, proposing that before the 1980s, Pam Gems and Caryl Churchill were Britain's only truly 'nationally known' woman playwrights, but '[by] the end of the decade, there were two to three dozen'.

Gems, born in 1925 to a working-class background, was a relative latecomer to writing for the theatre. In the 1970s she became involved with the women's movement and its theatrical cognates; she was a founding member of the Women's Playhouse Trust. She has worked extensively as an adaptor of canonical works: her versions of major plays by Ibsen and Chekhov appeared in the 1980s. Several of Gems' own plays have also involved the rewriting of traditional texts and the staging of historical figures and stories. These include *Queen Christina* (1977) and most famously *Piaf*, staged by the Royal Shakespeare

Company in 1978 but subsequently successful in the West End and even on Broadway. *Piaf* is exemplary of feminist concerns in reimagining a female icon, whose lowly class origins are demonstrated by the colloquial English dialect Gems has her speak. The show was a celebration of a strong woman, but also a revisionist consideration of the restrictive conditions that shaped her career. Gems continued to offer large parts for women, sometimes older actresses, in work that reanimated female figures of the past. *Camille* (1984) retells Alexandre Dumas' story of a consumptive courtesan and her doomed romance in nineteenth-century Paris; subsequent plays depicted the life and the filmic legacy of Marlene Dietrich. Yet Gems also staged her feminist concerns in a setting much closer to home. *Loving Women* (1984) was developed from her earlier work *The Project* (1976). The play juxtaposes scenes from 1973 and 1983 in the same London flat. The stage directions record a passage from youthful radicalism – 'Political or ethnic posters, including Che and Mao' – to 1980s domesticity: 'retro, with Thirties lamps, and some pictures of old movie stars in plastic frames' (Gems 1985: 159, 186). The activist Susannah worries that the contraceptive pill which allowed her to 'beat nature' has in fact cheated her out of motherhood, while the hairdresser Crystal has borne babies and had affairs. They vie for the affection of the socialist Frank, and the play concludes with the two women developing a friendship. But Gems does not promote separatism or misandry. Frank is a decent, committed figure, one of a generation of men who has sought to adapt to feminism even in a political 'cold climate' (193).

Aces

If Gems was one exemplary figure for women playwrights, any consideration of women's writing for the theatre in the 1980s must also take proper account of Caryl Churchill. Along with *Serious Money* (1987), in the 1980s her major work included *Fen* (Almeida, 1983), a quasi-sociological exploration of the inhabitants of Britain's Fenlands, and *Softcops* (written in 1978 but first staged at the Barbican in 1984), a study of eighteenth-century punishment. Along with the pancopticon scene in Angela Carter's *Nights at the Circus*, *Softcops* was explicitly inspired by the French historian Michel Foucault, an indication that the latest Parisian research could shape political theatre as well as feminist fiction. One of Churchill's most significant plays was a product of the new conjuncture of the early 1980s: *Top Girls* (Royal Court, 1982). The play directly assesses the prospects for women, and different versions of female identity and success, in the context of Margaret Thatcher's first term as prime minister.

Top Girls' content is relatively simple, yet its dramatic structure is intriguingly distinctive. The long first scene shows a dinner party in a London restaurant. It is hosted by Marlene, recently promoted to a managerial post at the Top Girls employment agency. The guests are five women from widely disparate historical periods and locations: a thirteenth-century wandering Buddhist; a woman who donned male disguise to hold the office of pope in the mid-ninth century; a Victorian traveller; a character from Chaucer; and a figure from a Breughel painting in which she leads a crowd of women in an invasion of hell. All have dared to do things unaccustomed to their sex.

The other two Acts are naturalistic in content. In Act Two we witness the Top Girls agency at work, and learn how Marlene has been promoted ahead of a male colleague, whose traumatised response culminates in a heart attack. Meanwhile Marlene's teenage niece Angie runs away from home in East Anglia and arrives at the agency, seeking sanctuary with Marlene. In another narrative swerve, Act Three shows the scene a year before when Marlene visits her sister Joyce and Angie. The play concludes with the revelation that Angie is Marlene's daughter, brought up by Joyce as Marlene fled the constraints of family, and with the two sisters arguing about Britain's political direction. *Top Girls* thus moves first from one ontological or theatrical plane to another, then from one moment in time back to another which complicates and troubles, rather than simply explaining, the first. Our sense of where the play's implicit values lie, what judgements we are encouraged to make, is not straightforward.

Thus Act One implies that the professional success possible to a woman in the early 1980s is on a par with history's 'top girls'. The play might be seen to celebrate the women's achievements, as Marlene proposes a toast: 'We've all come a long way. To our courage and the way we changed our lives and our extraordinary achievements' (Churchill 1990: 67). But much of their conversation is a downbeat record of the limits of their freedom. Lady Nijo is unrepentant about her devotion to the young emperor whom she served as a concubine: 'I belonged to him, it was what I was brought up for as a baby' (57). The women mourn dead friends and lovers, and share the memory of feeling that their life is over, being 'dead already' (65, 61). Pope Joan recalls giving birth to a baby in public, and accordingly being stoned to death (71). Griselda retells the tale from Chaucer in which her husband removes her children for over twelve years as a test of her loyalty (76–9). The hardships casually imposed on the women testify to many centuries of almost unchallenged oppression. If one character has escaped the melancholy of her peers it is Breughel's figure Dull Gret, who speaks in monosyllables, relishes simple food and concludes the dinner party by gleefully recounting her battle with devils (82). Her tale culminates an arc of shared lamentation which has concluded in anger.

The actors playing these historical figures return to play contemporary parts in subsequent scenes. This gesture suggests a continuity between past and present, perhaps even implying that the struggles of the women of the past are reincarnated and replayed in the 1980s. A related tactic was used in Timberlake Wertenbaker's *New Anatomies*, written for the Women's Theatre Group in 1981, in which four of the five women in the cast each play three or more roles, covering both sexes and both European and Arab characters. The ostentatious shuffling of roles within performance is a provocation to the spectator to draw connections between them. Marlene, however, is present in all three Acts of *Top Girls*. Act Two shows us her professional authority, while her agency's interviews with prospective clients also repeatedly indicate the challenges that women face in pursuing careers. Marlene advises the secretary Jeanine not to tell prospective employers she is engaged to be married as the prospect of pregnancy would deter them. She insists that Jeanine must plan ten years ahead. Jeanine responds that 'I might not be alive in ten years.' While deferring to Marlene's expertise, she also protests a desire to live in the present (85–6).

In another interview, the businesswoman Louise describes the workplace inequality that has held her back: 'I've seen young men who I trained go on, in my own company or elsewhere, to higher things. Nobody notices me, I don't expect it, I don't attract attention by making mistakes, everybody takes it for granted that my work is perfect.' Louise is unapologetic about voicing her experiences in the interview: '[I]t's your job to understand me, surely' (106–7). The third interviewee, Shona, proves to be a fantasist, aged twenty-one and posing as twenty-nine, spinning a yarn about her executive lifestyle selling fridges. Her fantasy life is subtly comic in its dreams of travelling '[s]traight up the M1 in the fast lane to where the clients are' and staying in hotels that serve 'fillet steak and mushrooms'. But it also voices an irrepressible aspiration. Accused of having done no jobs in the past, she concludes: 'I could though, I bet you' (117). In different ways, all the applicants insist on their aspirations, even as their female interviewers try to dampen them. The agents themselves, in other contexts, also proclaim their options. Win's suggestion 'You could marry him and go on working' is trumped by Nell's 'I could go on working and not marry him' (102).

Marlene is confronted by the wife of her erstwhile rival for promotion, who asks: 'What's it going to do to him working for a woman?' and accuses Marlene of being 'one of these ballbreakers'. Marlene's response is impressively unflappable. At this point the play seems supportive of her professional rise against the odds, which has also led another woman to address her misogynistically. Yet the third Act shifts the sense again. Marlene's argument with Joyce dramatises a dilemma between escaping, as Marlene did to the USA – 'on into the sunset' (137) – and remaining rooted, as Joyce has done in her provincial terrace, raising Angie alone. Marlene's decision may seem understandable, even to Joyce (136). But the sisters' debate finally becomes explicitly political, as Marlene praises Thatcher's agenda for the 1980s and Joyce rejects it in the name of her inherited class affiliation. Marlene sees her own rise paralleled by the country's: 'Get the economy back on its feet and whoosh. She's a tough lady, Maggie. I'd give her a job. She just needs to hang in there [. . .] First woman prime minister. Terrifico. Aces.' Joyce responds, 'I suppose you'd have liked Hitler if he was a woman' (138). The exchange sums up Thatcher's ambiguity for feminism. The play thus culminates with the accusations against the 'ballbreaker' Marlene curiously re-emphasised, and given new endorsement by her crass New Right rhetoric. Marlene has succeeded in a patriarchal environment by excelling at the 'masculine' virtues, while also tactically maintaining gender distinctions: 'I don't wear trousers in the office' (62).

Given Churchill's own politics, the conclusion of the play might seem clear enough. She has stated that the play arose from her bewilderment at American feminists' approval of women's success in capitalism, where in her British experience 'feminism tends to be much more connected with socialism and not so much to do with women succeeding on the sort of capitalist ladder' (Aston 2001: 38). Yet the play's complexity belies straightforward condemnation. Elaine Aston scorns the veteran critic John Russell Taylor for being uncertain whether or not Marlene was a heroine. Aston insists instead that 'Marlene's male-identified subject positioning is an unequivocal indexing of Churchill's critique of bourgeois feminism' (2001: 40–1). But Taylor's uncertain view reflects the play's richness. The dramatic structure in which we move back in time means that even as the concluding scene gives us more information, it is hardly final; rather an alternative perspective on Marlene and her world. *Top Girls'* Acts seem to make contrasting points, but one cannot be said to cancel out or resolve the others. The play is animated, too, by local qualities that make it more than polemic. The theatrical coup of the restaurant scene is one such; so is the extraordinary ear for colloquial dialogue that Churchill's script displays, not least between the teenaged Angie and her precocious friend Kit. *Top Girls* has become a canonical feminist play because it raises so directly contemporary issues of female achievement. It also endures for the vivid particularity of its author's imagination.

Bomb or No Bomb

Sarah Daniels belongs to the next generation. Born in 1957, she could name as contemporaries Clare McIntyre, Debbie Horsfield and Kay Adshead, all in their twenties as the decade began, and Andrea Dunbar, who was only nineteen when *The Arbour* was staged at the Royal Court in 1980. Their plays addressed contemporary gender relations head-on. In McIntyre's *Low Level Panic* (Royal Court, 1988), three women in a bathroom articulate their fear and anger at a culture seemingly saturated in pornography, which is also seen as inciting sexual violence. Other writers' documentation of changing working-class communities in the North of England echoed that of the British New Wave around 1960, but with a gendered perspective that at that earlier moment only Shelagh Delaney had offered. The unemployed teenage girls of Horsfield's *Red Devils*, written for Liverpool Playhouse, are outdone by the delinquent estate-dwelling youths of Dunbar's *Rita, Sue and Bob Too* (1982), adapted to the screen in 1986. Adshead's *Thatcher's Women*, staged at London's Tricycle Theatre in 1987, offered another take on the prime minister's significance for gender politics. The play portrays northern women who, in order to provide for their families after the industrial decline of the early 1980s, travel to London to work as prostitutes.

Daniels herself unapologetically used the stage to assess gender relations and to make arguments. She was accordingly branded a shrill, embittered misandrist, a sign that she was hitting her targets (Sierz 2001: 28). Her first play *Ripen Our Darkness* (Royal Court Theatre Upstairs, 1981) shows a housewife, Mary, cracking up from marriage to a condescending church warden. Presented with an ultimatum to go into state care, she commits suicide; her note informs her husband, 'Your dinner and my head are in the oven.' In an extraordinary leap beyond naturalism, Mary then wakes in an all-female paradise, though her supernatural guardian's first comment to her is about the kind of gas used in her cooker. The female deities dismiss the Bible as a 'libellous load of crap', then apply the same description to *Star Trek* (Daniels 1997: 64–7). Daniels' sharp tone and quick exchanges of dialogue, flavoured with vinegar wit, would remain recognisable – for instance in *Masterpieces* (Royal Exchange, 1983), which became one of the world's most performed feminist plays (Goodman 1996: 99). Like *Low Level Panic*,

Masterpieces investigates the psychic effects of pornography, displaying a society of misogynistic banter and abuse. Through the play we witness the character Rowena's trial for killing a man whom she has pushed in front of an Underground train. The play reconstructs the context of psychic violence that produced this reaction to the fear of rape. When Rowena looks at a series of pornographic magazines, a tape plays the three monologues of women explaining why they went into nude modelling. 'Once in this game,' one voice remarks, 'it's harder than you would imagine to get out' (Daniels 1997: 203–4). Daniels, like other feminists of the era, is seeking an analysis of the motives behind the exploitative industry, as well as its effects. The commercial use of female sexuality is seen to be all-pervasive. Rowena tells her police psychiatrist that 'I felt assaulted every time I went out – adverts for everything from oranges to Opfels, all sold with women's breasts' (207). The scene between the two characters (206–9) is almost archetypally representative of feminist concerns in the period. Rowena complains of objectification and exploitation with the uncompromising clarity of a theorist, the very tone that led feminism to be called humourless. The psychiatrist tries to demote Rowena's feminist discourse through various tactics of dismissal: stating that her crime could be attributed to pre-menstrual tension, expressing surprise that a woman wearing a skirt should be 'fanatical' in her attitudes, and accusing her of losing her sense of humour. On the contrary, Rowena says: he's inadvertently made her laugh twice. She culminates the play with a description of a snuff movie, the apotheosis of the male violence whose numerous forms the play has explored. Rowena tells a policewoman that she will now 'have a long time to think about it'. The sense of the conclusion is that life in a women's prison will be preferable to the male company she has experienced (230): a grimmer equivalent of Mary's female paradise.

Daniels' play *The Devil's Gateway* (Royal Court Theatre Upstairs, 1983) resembles her other early works in its domestic setting, interest in the overlooked figure of the housewife, and attempt to connect different forms of oppression and resistance. It is also of unusual interest in addressing the most prominent feminist action of the decade: the Greenham Common peace camp. Contemporaneously with Daniels, David Edgar's radical history play *Maydays* (Barbican, 1983) presented Greenham as the proper successor to the emancipatory movements of the past. Daniels, however, when encouraged to write about Greenham by the director Annie Castledine, found herself able to do so only indirectly. Her play describes the tentative, growing interest in Greenham of Betty, a working-class mother in East London. We see the limits of Betty's world, her uncertainty about public issues from the news, and her husband Jim's mockery of her ignorance. Her naivety allows her to ask important questions. When television news sparks a family discussion of nuclear weapons, she '*innocently*' remarks, 'I don't see why anyone's got to have them.' Jim's response, concluding 'we are living in a highly civilised age of technology, thank God' (82), places him on the side of patriarchal knowledge and asserts the housewife's inability to understand global affairs. When Betty makes a speech remarking that she has had to pick up the pieces after her husband's redundancies, and sarcastically stressing her task in maintaining the home – 'nothing of any worth except cook and clean and keep everything bloody together' – it is audible to us, but not to Jim (101). Yet the play gradually works to undermine his superiority and value her experience. It shows the poignantly hesitant growth of Betty's political consciousness.

Daniels remains interested in the supportive bonds between women. These are the more plausible because they are imperfect and uneven. Betty and her long-standing best friend Enid are temporarily estranged during the play, but restore their friendship over an unexpected toke of marijuana and shared secrets. Carol, Betty and Jim's daughter, is trying to establish herself in a higher class, 'Stripped pine Islington' (89) setting, creating a tension with her parents who disdain her new airs and graces. But she finally returns to the family home having been at least verbally abused by her husband. At the same moment Enid arrives, having hit her own abusive spouse with a chip pan and left home: 'Bomb or no bomb I got round to thinking I ain't waiting around for it, biding me time stuffing a crew of big-bellied boozers' (157). The play thus gathers various female relationships into a final, fanciful unity, as the women set off from the domestic setting which has dominated the play for Greenham Common, Bognor or both. Just as important is Betty's aged mother Ivy, who fights her own corner with barbed wit, but also repeatedly insists that Betty stand up to Jim. She is given a monologue late in the play, which takes the audience of the nuclear age back to the years of the Blitz. The Second World War changed 'sod all' for the better, she opines, though it had shown women how strong they were (139–40). Her presence in the play suggests that the determined feminist politics of the present are the proper descendant of a grittily stoical female outlook in the past.

The Devil's Gateway insistently addresses the vexed intersections of social class, feminism and the peace movement. Some characters assert that only middle-class women concern themselves with such matters. Enid dismisses them as distant from the hardships she and Betty have known: 'Where were they when we were fighting for our kids' lives? If this [the bomb] is the only thing that threatens their lives then I'm glad'

(97). This is a repeated rhetorical strategy, counterposing the distant threat of nuclear annihilation with the supposedly more concrete realities of local struggle. Enid's daughter Linda likewise reacts to the idea of a Greenham eviction: 'What about all the people what get evicted round here? Who's fighting for them?' (104). Linda tries to diminish the peace movement by comparison with the feminist crusade. She has already made a radical break from her upbringing, entering a lesbian relationship with the social worker Fiona. The two characters voice a debate over the articulation of feminist and peace movements that was current at the time. As Lynne Segal records, some radical feminists deemed Greenham Common 'co-option on a mammoth scale'. But many more activists applauded the links that the campaigners had made between feminism, anti-militarism and the need for a healthier geopolitical dispensation (Segal 1987: 164). Fiona in *The Devil's Gateway* promises 'creativity' on the Common, and reads from a pamphlet that articulates the two struggles: 'The women's peace camp is dealing with the tip of the iceberg . . . Cruise missiles, and at the same time, the base of patriarchy.' Daniels gives voice to scepticism, and uses Linda to dismiss any jubilant gender essentialism: 'I ain't going dancing through no woods painting myself with menstrual blood' (1997: 105). But the play's movement insists on the validity of linking the different struggles; those who deny it seem churlishly strained. Likewise, Betty finally dares to bridge the gap between East End housewife and peace campaigner. When Jim refuses to give her the money for the journey, Ivy hands it over. The very old, she says earlier, share with the peace campaigners a preoccupation with death (98).

Daniels' greatest achievement is to treat such imposing issues without resorting to solemnity. Aware of the stereotype of the joyless feminist, she ceaselessly belies it in a writing that mixes agit-prop with sit-com. From Ivy's instant putdowns (one of Jim's tirades is dismissed 'Shut it, Brian Clough' [79]) to Enid's string of malapropisms, a play about the country's most fearsomely pressing threat is fuelled by almost constant one-liners and badinage. Daniels joins a certain tradition of homely black comedy about the bomb's effects. Tom Lehrer's 1953 refrain 'we'll all go together when we go / all suffused with an incandescent glow' was echoed in Brendan Behan's *The Hostage* (1958), where a cheery song proclaims that 'The South and the North poles are parted [. . .] Till the H-bomb will bring them together' (1978: 170). The refrain would be picked up in Daniels' own era by the Smiths' pop record 'Ask' (1986), where 'if it's not love, then it's the Bomb that will bring us together'. An incongruous gap looms between local troubles and the deadly weaponry whose awful power might at least clear the slate: Linda and Fiona speculate that it would take a bomb to change Betty and Enid's apparently predictable lives (Daniels 1997: 139). Fiona and Linda are in this play what Raymond Williams (1977: 121–7) called the 'emergent' element, a new social agent: young, already world-weary, savvy, independent feminists, who spend a night spraying protests on a sex shop then talk their way out of an encounter with a police constable (Daniels 1997: 148–50). But they share their wit and resilience with their mothers and grandmothers.

Herlands

Historically, as Cora Kaplan (1989) notes, feminist literature and publishing have found intellectual grounding in feminist cultural criticism. Feminist criticism in the 1980s was a major force within the literary academy, and also an influence on wider perceptions of culture in the media and the reading public. A significant strain of work was the revisionist critique of primarily male writers. Through the 1980s, academic feminist critics reconsidered effectively the entire English canon, from Chaucer to Yeats and far beyond. Their political commitments to gender justice produced readings with quite different priorities from earlier literary criticism. Sometimes attention was applied to texts, moments or characters that had previously seemed marginal, though canonical narratives and cruxes were equally subject to new scrutiny. With new principles of judgement in play, the canon as a whole looked different, and established reputations – those of D. H. Lawrence or T. S. Eliot, Kingsley Amis or John Osborne – were challenged on new grounds.

Feminism also sought to reclaim art and writing that had countered this hegemonic history. Virginia Woolf's celebrated essay *A Room of One's Own* (1929) made the case for such retrieval, grimly imagining the likely fate of Shakespeare's sister in comparison to the playwright himself. Woolf's work itself became a touchstone for later feminist intellectuals. The American critic Elaine Showalter outlined the new field of 'gynocriticism': the retrieval of and commentary on women's writing as a contribution to the cultural resources of the feminist movement. The bid to reclaim lost creative traditions was reflected in literary publishing. In 1973 Virago Press had been founded by the Australian feminist Carmen Callil and her colleagues in feminist journalism, aiming to provide a publisher for '52% of the population'. A 'virago' was a female warrior, conveying the qualities of 'irreverence and heroism' that Callil sought (Callil 2008). While feminist criticism concentrated its fire on the hitherto unrecognised misogyny of the existing canon, Virago led a crusade to republish works by women, many of them forgotten. From

1977 its Reprint Library published history, memoir and social documentary. From 1978 the Virago Modern Classics imprint featured dozens of works from the past. The list included the American writers Willa Cather and Edith Wharton, the mid-century fiction of Rosamund Lehmann, the Irish novelists Molly Keane and Kate O'Brien, and the neglected British modernists May Sinclair and Dorothy Richardson. All these works predated the 1980s by a distance, but their rediscovery forms a notable part of literary publishing in the decade. The re-establishment of this body of women's fiction shifted the prevailing sense of what the canon was; for readers and publishers, and also for writers now producing new work.

Virago also published new writing outside fiction, notably feminist social analysis from such critics and historians as Sheila Rowbotham and Juliet Mitchell. Dorothy Thompson edited the collection *Over Our Dead Bodies: Women against the Bomb* (1983), exemplary of contemporary anger and activism at the threat of nuclear war in Europe. Beatrix Campbell self-consciously retraced the journey of George Orwell's *The Road to Wigan Pier* (1937) in *Wigan Pier Revisited* (1984), aiming to restore the female experience of work and motherhood that Orwell had neglected. Elaine Showalter's flagship of gynocriticism *A Literature of Their Own*, a history of British women novelists, received a revised Virago edition in 1982.

The older women writers being rediscovered were matched by a younger generation – among them A. S. Byatt, Margaret Drabble, Angela Carter and the Canadian novelist Margaret Atwood – who commended them to the editorial board and in some cases wrote new introductions to their work. Equally important were Virago's publications of work from abroad: notably Maya Angelou's celebrated memoirs of black American life commencing with *I Know Why the Caged Bird Sings* (1984); Atwood's science fiction allegories; and the voluminous works of Joyce Carol Oates. Virago's work was emulated by The Women's Press, founded in 1978; its logo was an iron, an image of the domestic labour habitually undertaken by women. Like Virago, the press published works from the past, such as Charlotte Perkins Gilman's feminist utopia *Herland*, and gave them a new audience. It also published new writing, from such authors as Joan Riley (whose *The Unbelonging* we considered in the previous chapter), and from 1985 it made recent American science fiction available in Britain. Joanna Russ and Marge Piercy's works of the 1970s, like Atwood's *The Handmaid's Tale* (1985), extrapolated pressures around gender politics from the present into putative futures. As well as science fiction, the feminist detective story was a significant sub-genre, practised by Val McDermid and Joan Smith.

Virago would repeatedly come under fire for having sold out to mainstream publishing, but it was equally criticised for the opposite failure of staying too true to its worthy roots. By the late 1980s Nicci Gerrard considered both Virago and The Women's Press 'locked into identities that are beginning to feel slightly out-of-date' (1989: 24). We have come full circle, to Gillian Allnutt's fears that feminism itself was *passé*. If it is remarkable that after several millennia of gender inequality it should take only fifteen years for a feminist press to seem outmoded, the shift is testimony to the rapid success of the movement itself, and also of the speed with which ideas and images were circulated and discarded by the late twentieth century. Gerrard did not seek to invalidate feminist publishing *tout court*. She noted that new presses had already emerged in the 1980s. These included Pandora, established by Philippa Brewster as the feminist trade imprint of Routledge and Kegan Paul in 1983; and Serpent's Tail, a left-field publishing house founded in 1986. While several major feminist novelists in the 1980s published with mainstream houses – Michèle Roberts at Methuen, Angela Carter with Chatto & Windus – the establishment of new feminist presses gave a distinctive space to the next generation. Thus Pandora published Jeanette Winterson's first novel in 1985, and the American Leslie Dick published her intellectually dense debut *Without Falling* (1987) with Serpent's Tail. Second-wave feminist publishing had commenced in the atmosphere of grassroots collectivism and consciousness-raising typified by the feminist journal *Spare Rib*. New outlets were still appearing in the age of *I-D* and *The Face*, a climate where increasing importance was given to marketing and design.

To Join the Human Race

A British writer who essayed several genres was Zoe Fairbairns. On the eve of the 1980s Virago published *Benefits* (1979), a dystopian narrative in which an authoritarian government seeks to retrench traditional gender roles by law. Fairbairns' vision drew on the climate, both political and meteorological, of the 1970s, but was subsequently hailed by some as prescient of official attitudes to family in the 1980s. She looked back as well as forward, in the historical family saga *Stand We At Last* (1983), which charted generations of struggle from the nineteenth century to the 1970s. If these genres gave Fairbairns conventions to address past and future, she also addressed the present more directly, in *Here Today* (1984) and *Closing* (1987). The latter treats the very current theme of women's increasing involvement in business, with its attendant political ambiguities. *Here Today* is also concerned with women's experience of work, primarily the world of the temporary secretary. 'Here Today' is the name of the employment agency at which the protagonist Antonia begins. As in *Top Girls*, this setting illustrates the newly familiar situation of women at work but also their transience and poor conditions; indeed the feminist Catherine sets up a union for temps. *Here Today* is also a kind of detective story. Antonia finds herself seeking the truth about another temp's fate, and closes the novel by picturing a new career as a private investigator.

The novel's title indicates the temps' transience: Antonia is sick of hearing the riposte 'gone tomorrow' (Fairbairns 1984: 25). It also suits the novel's depiction of the texture of the present – in its working conditions, sexual mores, package holidays and popular culture. Disc jockeys play Kate Bush and Ottawan's 'Hands Up' (100, 77). A boy battles with his Rubik cube (49). Antonia jokes that she has a high-powered job in mind, but that Margaret Thatcher has already claimed it (54). The leftist Catherine belongs to 'her women's group, Teachers Against the Tories and Amnesty International', reads Virago Modern Classics and considers writing an article for *Spare Rib* (31, 39, 40). While her beliefs might resemble the author's own, Fairbairns allows them to be sublimated into the narrative. Upheld by a particular character, feminist principles are placed in dialogue with others, even affectionately mocked. In particular Catherine's initially virginal inno-cence must co-exist with the worldly experience of Antonia, who is uninterested in abstract feminist principles but lives out the pains and pleasures of female independence.

The novel noticeably engages with change as the secretaries' world is destabilised by new technology. The efficiency of the word proces-sor, it is claimed, could make numerous office workers redundant. Antonia distrusts the new machines, but is declared 'a natural' in her first encounter with one (99–102). She later commandeers a computer to expedite her escape from a Spanish resort, and finally dreams of using a hospital computer to secure a life-saving drug (234). Fairbairns thus dramatises a continuing ambiguity in the relations between women and technology. Excluded from many forms of work and education, women have also often been positioned as belonging to a natural sphere, happily distant from technology. Yet as the professional typists of *Here Today* remind us, women have been leading users of some technologies. Fairbairns unobtrusively implies that they can continue to be so in the microchip era. While entirely engaged with women's experience, the novel is bracingly free from any regressive essentialism about it.

Fay Weldon also used forms of apparently realistic – though ulti-mately, daringly, far-fetched – fiction to dramatise the epoch and impact of second-wave feminism. Repeatedly she represented the duplicity, weakness and manipulativeness of men, and a variety of ways in which women might respond to their predicament. One of Weldon's most extreme answers appeared in *The Life and Loves of a She-Devil* (1983). Adapted for television in 1986, the story would become one of the best-known narratives of feminism as a threat to male privilege – produced by a feminist rather than a misogynist. The book's protagonist Ruth Padgett experiences a fate specific to an older woman, become unglamorous, unvalued and betrayed by her husband. The character responds not with capitulation or forgiveness, but by wreaking a prolonged, deliberate vengeance. She burns down the family home and, in a striking rejection of the ideological and emotional claims of motherhood, leaves the children with her husband and his new lover. That the mistress is also a romantic novelist makes Ruth's mission a revolt against the imprisoning cultural falsifications of romance as well as male power. She also promotes female solidarity by establishing an employment agency in which she provides downtrodden women a new start. Where Churchill's Top Girls agency is viewed as thoroughly compromised by masculine imperatives, Weldon's version recalls the interest in establishing female institutions which had ranged from radical feminism to new theatre companies and publishing houses. Yet her protagonist is only ambiguously a feminist heroine. Ruth's most extraordinary decision is to undergo plastic surgery, whose details she carefully specifies to the doctors, in order to be transformed into an attractive woman who can win back her husband. In fact she becomes the mirror image of her rival, the romantic novelist Mary Fisher. Weldon's story joins other feminist writing of the time in highlighting the artifice of femininity. Beauty is figured here as a Frankenstein creation, not natural but man-made, rather as Angela Carter depicted a radical feminist sect changing a man into a perfect woman (*The Passion of New Eve*, 1977) or the 'freak' bird-woman on the edge of humanity in *Nights at the Circus* (1984). Indeed Weldon's redeployment of Mary Shelley's image of monstrous creation places her book in the field of feminist Gothic as well as marital drama. In Weldon's story, the feminist revenge against male venality is curiously combined with a determined repetition of the very versions of femininity that have contributed to gender iniquity in the first place. If *Top Girls* considered the risks of women adopting a supposedly masculine aggression to succeed, Weldon's *She-Devil* offers the even more alarming spectacle of an unabashed quest for power that involves the calculated mimicry of conventional femininity.

Yet it is part of Weldon's significance to be untroubled by such apparent tensions. Her feminism aims not for theoretical correctness but for a freedom in which women can act as irresponsibly and egotistically as men. Retrospectively she defended her character's decisions thus:

> I'm on Ruth's side though I get a lot of tut-tutting from right-minded readers. Irresponsible. Dangerous. Ruth should have done what she *ought* [. . .] But that's always said of women, isn't it; they're expected to carry the moral burden of the world, allowing men to walk free. And now in novels too. [. . .] Nobody tells men writers, I suspect, what their characters *ought* to do. (Newman 1993: 199)

The statement is emblematic of Weldon's place in literary culture. She has been prepared to attack the entire opposite sex far less guardedly than most of her feminist contemporaries: in 1982 she told John Haffenden that 'it's every woman's right to hate men if she wants', while equivocating over her own feelings on the matter. Yet she also insisted that her women characters were 'terrible creatures', just as bad as the males. Weldon's deadpan observation that '[o]ne wishes women to join the human race' means that they deserve the right to be as guiltlessly imperfect as their counterparts (Haffenden 1985: 312–13). Weldon's own persona – fluent, fearless, barbed, inconsistent – exemplifies her demand: what seems eccentric or outrageous from her has long been viewed as normal enough from her male contemporaries.

A different persona was projected by Anita Brookner, though she also professed admiration for Weldon's writing. Brookner was a successful art historian at the Courtauld Institute when she turned to fiction in 1980. Already fifty-two, she ventured into literary creation in an attempt to battle a sense of drift in her life (Haffenden 1985: 59). The experiment was successful; with the efficiency more readily associated with a writer of genre fiction, she went on to deliver a novel a year for the rest of the decade, and several more beyond it. Brookner was a literary phenomenon of the 1980s, a novelist seemingly arrived from nowhere who attracted considerable popularity and critical respect. The latter was sealed when *Hotel du Lac*, her fourth novel, was awarded the Booker Prize in 1984. It tells the story of Edith Hope, a woman on the verge of middle age who has jilted her unsatisfactory fiancé in London and is now undergoing a penitential exile at a Swiss hotel. During the novel she interacts with other guests and tries to understand their characters and motives – notably Philip Neville, a wealthy businessman who proposes to her a marriage of convenience. Edith flees this prospect too, returning at last to England. The narrative has been regarded as typical of Brookner's work, at least in this period. She indeed returned repeatedly to the dilemmas of isolated woman protagonists, like the lecturer Kitty Maule in her second novel *Providence* (1982), in stories that circle around feelings of desire, alienation and regret yet less often partake of the pleasures of plot and unexpected action. Brookner could be viewed as a 'woman's novelist', analogously to the classical Hollywood 'woman's picture' (*Stella Dallas*, *Now Voyager*) which also rested on emotional dilemmas rather than shoot-outs. She can be placed in a modern lineage with such mid-century women novelists as Rosamund Lehmann and Molly Keane, several of them republished by Virago; indeed *Hotel du Lac* is dedicated to Lehmann. Yet Brookner was not universally popular with feminist readers. Pensive, regretful, uncertain, her heroines hardly lived up to Edith Hope's surname. This model of female subjectivity was viewed as needlessly passive after the struggles lately waged for women's agency.

Brookner did not battle to win over her feminist critics. 'You'd have to be crouching in your burrow to see my novels in a feminist way', she declared: 'I do not believe in the all-men-are-swine programme' (Haffenden 1985: 70). Yet her prolific output and wide popularity may have worked to obscure her distinctiveness. Brookner was not, after all, a cosily English writer. The daughter of Polish Jews, she declared herself out of place in England, and her protagonists tended to have similarly divided backgrounds. Kitty Maule in *Providence* is not only the child of a French mother and English father, but was also partly raised by her grandfather, a Russian acrobat and couturier. Introduced as 'difficult to place', she declares herself 'not anywhere at home' (Brookner 1982: 88). Edith Hope is likewise the offspring of an Austrian mother and a prematurely dead English father, and even before leaving for Switzerland considers herself 'out of place' in England (Brookner 1984: 10). At the hotel itself she is more literally exiled, a constant refrain in the novel: Brookner refers to 'the melancholy of exile' (52), but gives little hint that home would be happier. Of her own life she declares 'one can't go home again' (Haffenden 1985: 60), a sentiment directly mirrored in Hope's telegram to her married English lover upon leaving the Hotel du Lac: having written 'Coming home', she replaces the word with the cooler 'Returning' (Brookner 1984: 184).

Edith Hope is also in one way a metafictional figure, for she has a second life as a romantic novelist under the name Vanessa Wilde. It is made clear that her style of writing is becoming outmoded next to the more sexually explicit narratives that will appeal to readers of *Cosmopolitan*, 'those multi-orgasmic girls with the executive briefcases' (28). Brookner might be wryly reflecting here on her own position, as an author who does not indulge in the casual descriptions of sexual activity by now prevalent in fiction. Yet her novel's identification with the romance genre is only partial. The contrast between Vanessa Wilde's romances and Edith Hope's reality makes romance implausible: the genre does not answer to the condition of exile that Brookner takes as inescapable. It is slightly misleading that an air of middlebrow sedateness should have become attached to one of the most desolate writers of the era, a woman who could proclaim that she was 'walking about with the mark of Cain on my forehead': 'the world's loneliest, most miserable woman', who believed that her own parents 'should never have had children' (Haffenden 1985: 75). Kitty Maule speaks of a mode of writing in which 'extremely dry language' should contain 'the most uncontrollable sentiments': 'even if the despair is total, the control remains' (Brookner 1982: 34). It could be another self-referential statement. Conceivably Brookner's bleak vision would have been taken more seriously from a male writer. In this respect at least, she might have found a reason to make common cause with feminism.

An Emerging Refusal

The mission, exemplified by Virago, to reclaim lost accomplishments by women helped to prompt a further literary development, in new writing that took earlier literature as its starting point. The practice of rewriting earlier fictions was widespread in the late twentieth century, involving both homage to earlier works and a critical questioning of their assumptions. Feminism significantly informed such critique and rethinking. Sue Roe's novel *Estella: Her Expectations* (1982) returns to the materials of Dickens' *Great Expectations* and rearranges them from the point of view of its young female character, in a changed and unspecified setting. A recentring of attention and agency, and decentring of the original male point of view, is thus effected, while Roe's language moves dramatically away from that of the original to become self-referential and question the workings of fiction itself. A similar effect, though not so evidently experimental in tone, can be identified in Emma Tennant's *Two Women of London* (1989), which transposes the characters of Jekyll and Hyde into a compound of two female selves. Ms Jekyll is here the ideal feminine figure that the troubled Mrs Hyde is able to become, partly by taking the drug Ecstasy. This last is a strikingly contemporary reference, as the drug entered public consciousness around 1988 during the explosion of the Acid House subculture. A still more pointed updating is the suggestive comparison that Tennant draws between the late Victorian society depicted in Robert Louis Stevenson's novel and the 'new Victorian values' of the Thatcher era (Tennant 1989: 121). The Victorian social pathologies that are condensed in Stevenson's image of a divided self are echoed, Tennant hints, in a contemporary Britain where the division between haves and have-nots has once again been encouraged to expand, and stark boundaries of self and other are once more drawn as an ideological result. More directly, the novel's twin female characters indicate a tension in the public expectations of female life, between the burdens of domesticity and the glamour of worldly ambition. In this sense Tennant's reworked tale from one *fin de siècle* is also a significant feminist allegory for another.

A critical replay of the canon would also be seen in A. S. Byatt's *Possession* (1990), where the nineteenth-century poets Robert Browning and Elizabeth Barrett Browning were refigured in fictional guise, complete with pastiche poetry. Byatt's Victorians are framed by the scholarly investigations of 1980s academics whose lives parallel those of their literary quarry. The academic setting allows Byatt to express scepticism about the very milieu of literary theory that has accompanied the era of revisionist fiction. The revision of the past was also a persistent force in the writing of Michèle Roberts. Partly raised in French Catholicism, Roberts has repeatedly returned to Christian imagery with a mission to restore carnal plenitude to its puritanical outlines. Her work thus combines religion with sexuality and an area traditionally entrusted to women: food. *The Wild Girl* (1984) offered a 'secret gospel' of Mary Magdalene, returning to the Bible yet also, by supplementing it, refusing its absolute authority and envisaging a Christianity in which the sexes are equal. In *The Book of Mrs Noah* (1987) Roberts again reflected irreverently on theological history, this time via a wife's fantasies of being 'Mrs Noah' and the supportive 'sibyls' she dreams up. The novel refers heavily to the Old Testament but also to a range of other sources. Its babel of multiple stories and voices can break up into a 'Litany of the Blessed Virgin', then into another column of eulogistic terms representing 'the feminist Roman Catholics opening their mouths wide to praise the Great Mother' (Roberts 1987: 42–3). The book's voices make numerous explicit arguments about the cultural repression of women: thus the narrator recalls Virginia Woolf's indignation that the libraries are full of books by men about Woman, but never the reverse (132), and one of the sibyls argues that the word 'feminine' needs to be reinvented to reclaim it from its allegedly negative connotations (141). Roberts' novel, while textually playful, is one of the most uncompromising of the period in its rigorous pursuit of the feminist ideals established in the 1970s. Roberts would also figure in a further revisionist project: the twin volumes *The Seven Deadly Sins* (1988) and *The Seven Cardinal Virtues* (1990). Edited by Alison Fell, and published in Serpent's Tail's *Masks* series, both books contained the same seven woman writers responding to one of the key words with a short story. The venture was characteristic of feminist culture, not only in its collaborative character, but in its re-use of ancient source material in irreverently contemporary tones.

That combination was also characteristic of Angela Carter and Jeanette Winterson. Carter's retelling of fairy tales in *The Bloody Chamber* (1979) did much to establish this paradigm, while Winterson's use of the Bible in *Oranges are Not the Only Fruit* was comparable to Roberts' in turning a patriarchal source to subversive ends. We considered these writers earlier under the rubric of postmodernism, but they were also part of feminist culture, and have become canonical on both counts. Dominic Head plausibly complains that Carter and Winterson have been overrated at the expense of more traditionally realist writers (2008: 26). Indeed, we have seen that women writers in the 1980s adopted numerous strategies including, as in Fairbairns or indeed Margaret Drabble, the attempt to track the contemporary via the realist novel. Head's view that critics have privileged experiment over tradition promises a fruitful alternative to academic orthodoxy. But the ascendancy of Carter and Winterson was not only a matter of scholarly retrospect. It also reflected the desires of the time. Thus Nicci Gerrard's inclusive 1989 survey of feminism and contemporary writing culminates by celebrating *Nights at the Circus* and *The Passion* as part of 'an emerging refusal to succumb to the dispiriting climate of the 1980s': 'They absolutely refuse to succumb to the times in which they are written, and instead fire the grey stuff of daily life with passion and wide intelligence' (1989: 166). Their ability to incorporate the fantastic offered a space apart from the given, even as – in Carter's salty disrespect for essences or Winterson's debt to northern camp – they also engaged polemically or comically with the real world. Notwithstanding the precise content of Carter's circus or Winterson's Venice, the novels' readiness to exit the normal laws of biology or facts of history stood in itself as a utopian promise of political possibility, or of literature's own transformative capacity.

Winterson can claim another considerable distinction. She is arguably the first popular, established British writer to write consistently and openly from a lesbian perspective. That Winterson herself (1996: 118, 103) can disavow the label of 'lesbian writer', expressing distaste for Radclyffe Hall and admiration for T. S. Eliot, in fact testifies to her success in making the taboo seem an antiquarian matter. Of course, her ascent to the contemporary canon coincided with a change in attitudes and cultural norms as rapid as the progress of feminism itself. Winterson could expect a sympathetic readership in feminist circles where lesbianism had often been promoted as a political decision. But the mid-1980s mainstream into which she sailed was not so propitious. In a society virtually bereft of publicly prominent lesbians, *Oranges*' story of the struggle to inhabit such a sexual identity in an authoritarian setting was not merely a happily distant memory. The young Jeanette's first sexual encounter with her friend Katy is implicitly compared to the storming of the Winter Palace (Winterson 1991: 87). Yet this revolutionary relationship eventually fizzles out, and Katy returns to the heterosexual fold. Even if men are 'beasts' one would not want to touch (71–2), lesbian love in Winterson is as potentially transient and fraught as its straight counterpart. She would not devote her career to asserting the superiority of any sexual preference: her later novels involve shifting, bisexual or ambiguously androgynous protagonists. But to attain this fluidity required her first to break the mould: an achievement redoubled by the BBC's 1990 adaptation scripted by Winterson herself. *Oranges* detonated a false normativity while retaining its cool self-possession and deadpan humour. It stands as one of the decade's great liberating works of art.

Make it Softer

In 1982 Fay Weldon was asked if the time had come for 'post-feminist writing in which the men might be liberated'. 'It's astonishing,' she replied, 'the way men depend on women to write it for them [. . .] Let the men liberate themselves, it's time they did it' (Haffenden 1985: 313). One major male author to make the attempt was Ian McEwan. He had told the *New Review*'s forum in 1978 that the insights of the women's movement would shape fiction's future. In the 1980s he attempted to make them integral to his own work. His 1981 television screenplay *The Imitation Game* depicts a woman, Cathy Raine, seeking to contribute to the military effort of the Second World War; first by work in munitions on the home front, then by enlisting as a code-breaker at the Bletchley intelligence facility. McEwan's portrait of the nascent feminist drew on his interviews with women who had served during the war, who explained that despite the perils of the period it had brought them an independence from which they did not want to return to patriarchal domesticity. Cathy Raine is victimised for transgressing the bounds of her gender, and concludes that women's exclusion from war is an ideological necessity: if women fought, then male soldiers would have 'no one to fight for' and war's savagery would be stripped of its saving illusions (McEwan 1981: 142).

War preoccupied McEwan. His script for Richard Eyre's film *The Ploughman's Lunch* (1983) explores Britain's cultivation of fantasies about its past: revisionist discussions of the Suez crisis take place against the current military activity in the Falklands. But conventional warfare is less ominous than what threatens to succeed it. The film's dislikeable, opportunistic protagonist also encounters a peace camp in Norfolk. The occupants' friendliness 'progressively disorientates' him. Though he works for BBC radio news, he does not see the protest as inherently newsworthy: 'It might help if you could get yourselves attacked by the police' (McEwan 1989: 83–4). McEwan's own sympathies are with the campaigners. He had travelled to Greenham while planning the film and felt 'great admiration' for its protestors (Haffenden 1985: 184). Indeed Greenham's linkage of gender and peace is fully articulated in McEwan's other work outside prose fiction at this time. *Or Shall We Die?* is the text he wrote for Michael Berkeley's oratorio, performed in February 1983 and released on record. The text was published with *The Ploughman's Lunch* in 1989, indicating that the two works – which amounted to a 'move abroad' from the novel form – derived from the same period of reflection. McEwan explains the full extent of his thinking in this volume.

The nuclear arms race had become a prevailing fact of life in the early 1980s, and deeply infiltrated McEwan's fears and dreams. Like many dissident commentators he was frustrated by its Wonderland logic: 'That this madness, which threatens not only human life, present and future, but all life on the planet, should be presented on our television screens as sanity, as responsible deliberation on "defence" policy by calm, authoritative men in suits, gave the matter the quality of a nightmare; either they were completely mad, or we were' (1989: 4). McEwan's analysis reaches beyond the weapons themselves. He sees them as enabled by a cast of mind, evolved by the end of the Second World War, which was hardened to mass destruction. By Hiroshima technological innovation had gained its own deadly momentum: a rationalist scientific pursuit had generated the irrational prospect of Armageddon. McEwan connects this to a scientific world-view that distinguishes between subject and object, observer and world. Against this, he asserts that the new physics of the twentieth century have already collapsed such distinctions:

> To bind intellect to our deepest intuition, to dissolve the sterile division between what is 'out there' and what is 'in here', to grasp that the *Tao*, our science and our art describe the same reality – to be whole – would be to be incapable of devising or dropping a nuclear bomb. (14)

For McEwan this is also a matter of gender. In a series of binary distinctions, he associates nuclear weapons with a commonsensical

'Newtonian' science and with masculine aggression, while resistance to
them implies an 'Einsteinian' universe and feminine nurture. The two
attitudes to reality are 'a male and female principle, yang and yin'. In
the oratorio a man and woman voice stark versions of these positions.
In a satire of the prevailing order, 'Pure thought alone describes the
universe' and '[t]he weak-hearted, the effeminate, the disloyal / must
know nothing'. A woman addresses the 'derided womanly moon' and
proposes that everything in 'our virile times' suggests 'the metaphor
of rape' (20, 23). The question of human survival is gendered. W. H.
Auden's counsel that we must love one another or die is updated to the
question that gives McEwan his title: 'Shall there be womanly times, or
shall we die?' (15).

In fact McEwan's gendering of the debate is tendentious. He does
not argue for it, but lets it rest on received ideas which were themselves
under practical challenge from many of the same people campaigning
against the arms race. McEwan's essentialism lags behind feminism
itself. But he at least establishes a broad intellectual context for his paci-
fism, in contrast with Martin Amis' treatment of the same perils in his
collection of stories *Einstein's Monsters* (1987). McEwan dedicates his
oratorio to 'all children', and maintains that those who 'had children in
their lives' are especially affected by the bomb (2, 5). In his polemical
essay 'Thinkability' Amis similarly announces that fatherhood helped
awake him to the threat (1987: 5). To this extent he acknowledges
his own gender as part of his position. Yet this does not prove a very
progressive move, as Adam Mars-Jones' stinging polemic on contemporary masculinity *Venus Envy* (1990) would show. Amis' assertion of
paternal feeling apparently qualifies him as a 'new man', liberated into
a nurturing role. But it also amounts to an erasure of women, including
the female peace campaigners who had long pre-empted his polemic.
As Mars-Jones acutely sees, Amis' very style, bristling with combative brilliance, is peculiarly unsuited to the promotion of peace. Above
all, he neglects to integrate his rejection of nuclear weapons into any
account of the system that has produced them: 'There is no suggestion
that anything about nuclear weapons corresponds to anything in the
world before them' (Mars-Jones 1997: 135). By comparison, McEwan's
attempted holism seems creditable.

McEwan's major work of the decade emerged from the ideas he had
explored in other genres. *The Child in Time* (1987) combines diverse
elements. In the mid-1990s, the Conservative government continues
its fourth term with authoritarian policies extrapolated from the mid-
1980s. Stephen Lewis, a writer of children's books, is in protracted
mourning for his abducted young daughter Kate. The abduction has led

his equally grief-stricken wife Julie to separate from him. Stephen serves on a committee tasked to produce a report on childcare methods, but it finally emerges that this is a fig-leaf for the authoritarian report that the government has already prepared. Charles Darke, the report's author and Stephen's friend, indulges a fantasy by moving to the country and regressing to childhood. His own wife Thelma is a physicist who keenly explains new theories of time and the universe. Stephen turns to these in attempting to understand an uncanny, hallucinatory moment in which he steps back in time several decades and witnesses his own parents in a pub, debating whether to abort his own foetus. His elderly mother later tells him that her own vision of him at the same moment persuaded her to keep the baby, thus making the whole story possible. Finally Stephen is summoned to visit Julie, and finds her pregnant from their last encounter. Their baby is born at the novel's close.

As that summary shows, *The Child in Time* is an eccentrically diverse book. While motifs recur, the story's strands do not necessarily cohere. McEwan states that it emerged from his entranced image of the single scene at the pub (1989: xxv), and this perhaps accounts for the elusiveness of its unity. Equally, the scene's slippage through time clearly chimes with the new views of time explicated by Thelma. She hopes that 'quantum mechanics would feminise physics, all science, make it softer, less arrogantly detached, more receptive to participating in the world it wanted to describe' (McEwan 1987: 43). The opinion precisely replicates McEwan's own. Thelma dismisses commonsense views of linear time, which are associated with an older physics. More complex views belong with the new science, in which 'the clever boy was on his way to becoming the wise woman'. If McEwan apparently signs authority over to womankind here, he also claims a little back. Though Thelma is disdainful of art's ignorance of science, her examples of complexity include 'the elaborate time schemes of novelists' (120). *The Child in Time* features many instances of time subjectively experienced: the perpetual present of the child, the 'redeemed' time of sexual love, the slow motion of a motor crash (33, 64, 94). Its inclusion of a slip in time through which past events can be influenced may be viewed as a practical illustration of Thelma's progressive science, though it also recalls the cinematic blockbuster *Back to the Future* (1985), which was released while McEwan wrote the novel.

As in his screenplay and libretto, McEwan seeks to articulate connections between private and public spheres. The nuclear threat is fleeting in the novel, only briefly flaring after a controversy at the Olympics (35). But the calamitous state of the world is insistent. In this future Britain the police are armed, licensed beggars patrol the streets, traffic is gridlocked, schools are for sale, and the state sponsors an all-day channel of trash TV. 'The art of bad government,' Stephen reflects, 'was to sever the line between public policy and intimate feeling' (8–9). The government is also trying to intervene in the intimate realm through its new *Authorised Childcare Handbook*, from which extracts appear at the head of each chapter.

Stephen's views as a committee member are uncertain: he comes to see that views of childcare are historically variable (80). But there is no doubt about his feelings for Kate. Through Stephen's obsessive memory McEwan renders scenes of tender interaction between father and daughter, while the numbing effects of loss are tellingly observed. In itself this is distinctive. McEwan is exploring a new generation of paternity, in which fathers (primarily middle-class professionals) are closely involved in childrearing and emotionally and physically involved with their children. Mars-Jones sees the novel as hijacking women's parental role, but unlike his decimation of Amis this critique remains unconvincing. The novel seems rather to investigate the relatively new dispensation in which men's right to be more involved with their children brings corresponding responsibilities. Stephen is indeed implicated in parenthood to a peculiar degree. His appearance at the pub effectively ensures his own birth – though this amounts to a new conviction on his mother's part (175). And finally, in the absence of a midwife, he is closely involved in his new child's birth. He remembers his role at Kate's birth as essentially 'symbolic', but is now of more practical use. Even so, he insists on 'the mother's absolute right to order her own domain', sees Julie in her labour as 'alone' despite his presence, and perceives just 'how active and generous' the verb 'to give birth' is (216, 218, 219). The scene pays extensive tribute to motherhood, while also trying to envision a more collaborative approach to childrearing. McEwan's suspension of the baby's sex – the novel ends just as the parents decide to investigate it – suggests a symbolic eschewal of gender's roles and hierarchies, in the temporary state of promise before the family 'rejoins' the world (220).

The Last Summer

The legal and social recognition of homosexuals in Britain is a story of liberalisation that roughly parallels the era of second-wave feminism. Sexual acts between males over twenty-one years of age were decriminalised in Britain in 1967. But the road of gay liberation would not prove altogether straight. In the late 1980s gay people were faced with a new challenge from the state, in the legislation known as Clause 28, later Section 28, of the Local Government Act 1988. Its Conservative sponsors fulminated at what they saw as the indulgence of gay and lesbian rights by local authorities; notably the presence in schools of children's books that appeared to present gay and lesbian partnerships as normal and acceptable. Most notorious was *Jenny Lives with Eric and Martin*, translated from Danish in 1983. Aside from *The Satanic Verses*, Susanne Bosche's book was perhaps more embroiled in public controversy than any other work of fiction this decade. The legislation galvanised Britain's gay community. New political networks were established, as the 'Clause' gave campaigners a focal point for protest against homophobia at large.

But the gay population of Britain, and indeed the developed world, had already been provoked into solidarity earlier in the 1980s, with the arrival of AIDS. The HIV virus was communicable by sexual intercourse or blood transfusion. It could lie undetected for years before developing into a form that would kill the infected within months. Its modes of transmission meant that statistically, intravenous drug users and those engaged in promiscuous, unprotected sex were at high risk; in addition, anal intercourse carried a higher risk of infection than other sexual practices. HIV took a heavy toll on a gay population whose sexual lives were unburdened by the need to prevent pregnancy, and unconstrained by the institution of marriage from which they were legally excluded. Lifestyles changed. Caution and contraceptive use increased, among the heterosexual as well as the gay population. AIDS drew a cultural response, notably from gay artists. The film-maker Derek Jarman learned in 1986 that he was infected, and devoted the rest of his life to documenting the danger, elegising his past and lambasting official homophobia. Gay Sweatshop's production of Andy Kirby's play *Compromised Immunity* (1985) was one of several theatrical responses.

In fiction a strikingly direct treatment came in *The Darker Proof: Stories from a Crisis*, published by Faber in 1987 and expanded a year later. Adam Mars-Jones shared the volume with the American writer Edmund White. Mars-Jones had already made his name, and won a place in 1983's *Granta* pantheon, via the short story form with the playful volume *Lantern Lecture* (1981). In *The Darker Proof* he demonstrated how literary realism could still offer the emotional resources to respond to a calamity both public and intimate. The stories offer subtly different perspectives on the crisis. Thus 'Slim' and 'Remission' are narrated by men with AIDS, while 'An Executor' reverses the angle to dramatise the tasks of a man close to the deceased, and 'A Small Spade' depicts the comparatively cloudless relationship between an HIV carrier and his boyfriend as they make a trip to Brighton. The collection shows that 'living with HIV' is not only a matter for those carrying the virus. Others' lives adapt in the processes of care, precaution and bereavement. Mars-Jones frequently conveys this in a kind of comedy of manners. Thus the 'executor' Gareth (whose legal title echoes the work of the disease itself) is repeatedly faced with matters of etiquette. At the deathbed of his former lover, he and the dead man's mother are unsure who should fetch a nurse: 'Gareth was very willing to take the cowardly option, but could not at the minute remember which it was.' He makes tea for the bereaved family, reflecting on the value of tea and coffee 'in crisis, as generators of trivial catechism'. Telling another friend of the death, he wonders whether to begin '"I'm afraid I have bad news"', then rejects this as 'usurping the medical style' (Mars-Jones and White: 1988: 35, 38, 41). Mars-Jones is not making light of death. His closely observed narrative tracks the myriad details through which people live with its excruciating reality. The business of making tea or finding words is not even truly a welcome distraction from death, but part of the business it brings in its wake. The living go agonisingly on through these fruitless acts.

The tone most hospitable to Mars-Jones' characters is gallows humour. One sufferer says of a former lover that '"If the virus has missed out on him, it's missed a great opportunity. [. . .] And that seems out of character"' (1988: 23). 'Slim"s narrator inhabits a new world of euphemism in which, compared to his actual condition, the once unmentionable cancer becomes a socially acceptable disease: 'Cancer. That I can live with' (8). He has 'learned that there is a yoga of tears': the 'stupid tears' that take most energy are 'very more-ish' (5). He shows us that illness creates a new somatic economy, in which energy must be rationed and used with a care that the unafflicted would never consider. Writing cheques in full has been a waste of time, he now sees: 'If I could have right now all the energy I've wasted writing every word on my cheques, I could have some normal days, normal weeks' (6). Mars-Jones persistently records these subtle, profound changes to a normal life easily taken for granted. In 'A Small Spade' Neil's HIV is not yet at crisis point, though his partner Bernard wonders 'if perhaps at some stage he and Neil would have to decide whether "antibody-positive" was not now an understatement of Neil's condition' (87). The lengthy sentence, gathering ever more qualifying words to douse its menace, subtly renders Bernard's reluctance to air his fears. As they breakfast in a café, Neil's finger catches a splinter. What would be a painful nuisance to most becomes a more sombre concern. Bernard worries at the risk that a drop of blood might pose to other customers, and that a borrowed safety-pin must be disinfected – but at the further risk of offending Neil. Blood has 'acquired a demonic status over the few previous years', 'taken back its seriousness as a stuff' (108–10). Mars-Jones' slow-moving narration follows the minute progress of such everyday events, quietly showing that the everyday is suddenly not what it used to be. His authorial position might finally be identified with the medical staff who repeatedly appear in his stories: expertly informed, not cheerful but too responsible for fear, facing the worst of a new era with cool dedication.

The decade's most acclaimed gay novel swerves around AIDS in the act of alluding to it. Will Beckwith, the narrator of Alan Hollinghurst's *The Swimming Pool Library* (1988), mentions at the outset that his story takes place in the summer of 1983, 'the last summer of its kind there was ever to be' (1988: 3). The characters are oblivious of the virus that will change their lives, let alone the battles with government homophobia that would be in train when Hollinghurst, having written the novel alongside years of book reviewing for the *TLS*, finally published it. As usual, a tag like 'gay novel' looks reductive. But, as with Winterson's *Oranges*, to tear off the label is prematurely to disregard the specific social pressures into which the book emerged, and hence the defiance it presented. In Hollinghurst's case, it would also perversely ignore the book's substance. For *The Swimming Pool Library* really is a determinedly gay novel in every way available.

One way is sex. Undoubtedly a tradition of gay writers has existed in English, and many were being reclaimed at this time. Hollinghurst explicitly thematises this. Yet the literary canon does not thereby include many explicit depictions of gay sexuality. In a curious inversion of latent and manifest contents, while Oscar Wilde's actual homosexual desires were well attested, his plays must be combed for symbolic references to them. Acts that had only lately been decriminalised were largely invisible in the canon – though not, of course, in pornography, which Will readily samples in the novel. In this context Hollinghurst's boldest gesture is his utterly unabashed rendition of gay male desire. As though deliberately eliminating any ambiguity or hint of reluctance over this, Hollinghurst makes his protagonist startlingly promiscuous, endlessly appetitive and almost invariably able to procure whatever sexual favours he seeks. This brings in turn a stream of descriptions of the male body, often eyed up in the showers at a swimming pool. In this novel it is commonplace to read 'His sleek, heavy cock, cushioned on a tight, crinkled scrotum, stuck out from beneath a roll of fat' (15), or 'It was a sumptuously heavy thing, purpling up with blood as the cock-ring bit into the thickening flesh' (274). When Will and his most consistent partner Phil have sex, 'I slipped my hands between his legs and squeezed his balls, and watched his eyes widen as he overcame his inhibition.'

Once Phil has urinated all over the floor, Will recalls, he 'fucked him in it like a madman' (163).

The novel is probably the most sexually graphic and prolific text considered in this study. Amis' John Self looks timid beside it. It can plausibly be said that the extent of its libido reflects the shattering of a taboo: that Hollinghurst cranks desire to such a pitch as a kind of compensation for centuries of repression, and to leave no doubt that gay sex is here to stay. Yet Will is a dubious hero. His promiscuity may represent the real habits of a subculture on the eve of AIDS, but it does not seem admirable. He is outraged by Phil's dalliance with an older man, though he has casually cheated on Phil in the same hotel a few minutes earlier (276). It seems that promiscuity is only for oneself; monogamy is required in others. While Will serves as an explosive device in the midst of mainstream fiction, he also presents a hedonism that seems morally unsustainable whatever one's sexual preference.

This heedless hedonism is countered and contextualised by a second major strand: an extensive inquiry into the history of gay life and its representation. This is driven primarily by Lord Nantwich, an elderly gay peer who asks Will to write his biography. We accordingly read lengthy passages from his diaries, detailing a hidden gay culture through the early twentieth century. Nantwich's cellar contains a Roman swimming bath decorated with erotic art that suggests an ancient world of free homosexuality; the image is echoed in the public-school swimming pool in which Will explored his own sexuality as a boy. Will's enquiries – lending the novel a touch of the detective genre – lead to various other sources, like a boxing club sponsored by Nantwich and the trove of portraits held by the seedy photographer Ronald Staines. Near the novel's close Staines screens rare amateur footage of the writer Ronald Firbank, on whom Hollinghurst himself wrote a dissertation. Firbank is one member of an assortment of gay artists to whom the novel refers, along with the composer Benjamin Britten and the novelist E. M. Forster. They suggest a canon alternatively conceived, a cultural history parallel to the norm. But the historical theme is further deepened when it emerges that Nantwich was entrapped by police and imprisoned for gross indecency in 1954. He has tried to enlist Will as his biographer as a kind of restitution or moral education, because Will's own grandfather was pivotal in the 'gay pogrom' (278) of that era and was rewarded with a seat in the House of Lords. Even the feckless Will Beckwith is troubled by the past, and especially by his culpable ignorance of 'that period just before one was born' (279). The novel's implicit insistence on taking historical responsibility gains urgency because repression turns out not to be all in the past. Will's closest friend James, a doctor whose gay desires are largely unrequited, is himself entrapped and held in custody as Nantwich was thirty years earlier. Even the idle Will can see that the homophobia of the 1950s is 'really not another world [. . .] it's going on in London now almost every day' (265).

It is in one way incongruous to conclude a discussion of feminism's impact with so androcentric a novel as Hollinghurst's debut. But it has a place beside the literature of the women's movement in its elegant, unflinching announcement of alternative desires. The 1980s do not appear the most propitious time for progressive politics. The architects of the period's rightward shifts mostly had scant sympathy for those struggling to be liberated from oppressions based on gender and sexuality. Yet to review the literature of the period is not only to find a creative richness engendered by those commitments. It is also to perceive how far they succeeded, in achieving liberties that will not be lightly relinquished.

Conclusion

'We are at the end of an age. The greatest decade in the history of mankind is nearly over.' The words were spoken in the 1980s, but refer to the 1960s. The stoned prophet at the end of Bruce Robinson's film *Withnail and I* (1987) notes that the decade has just ninety-one days to run. The imminent ending is not merely calendrical. The commercial appropriation of the counterculture – 'they're selling hippy wigs in Woolworths' – signals to him the close of an era.

The 1960s is the most fabled of all decades. Ian Jack (2009) considers that the potency of that decade's projections of itself has determined our entire contemporary tendency to slice time in ten-year cycles. The mythologies also produce mourning. Few decades have been publicly reviewed so often. We observed in the Introduction that the New Right defined itself against the 1960s, as an era whose permissiveness needed to be revoked. Among those with a more positive stake in the 1960s, the decade also provokes regret; not that it happened, but that it had to end. This can involve pure nostalgia for a lost garden of youth and innocence. Or it can more ambivalently register the failures of the decade, as *Withnail*'s hippy does, positing the end as the time when the decade went wrong. Joan Didion, who had made much of her reputation as a chronicler of the era, could write in the 1970s about 'the morning after the Sixties', and debate whether they had ended in 1969 with Charles Manson's murders, or in 1971 when, less traumatically, Didion moved house (1979: 205, 47). If you remember the 1960s, the slogan says, you weren't there. But faced with the impossibility of being there any longer, many people have spent decades remembering them.

Can anything similar be said of the 1980s? The idea seems incongruous. Emotional investments in the idea of this decade are different. The 1960s is associated with a flowering of popular culture and a generation of youth in revolt against ossified hierarchies. Its young inhabitants, the post-war Baby Boomers, could claim a long intoxication from a cocktail of cultural originality and political righteousness. Politically, the equivalent for the 1980s might be the Conservative Party constituency secretary proudly dusting a fading photograph of the prime minister's visit. Victories over trade union militancy or the privatisation of public utilities have their critics and defenders, but in popular memory they do not shed the rosy glow of the civil rights movement or May 1968. Even artistically, across many fields – cinema, visual arts, popular music – the decade looks intriguing, but less immediately, consensually distinguished than its gilded precursor.

Yet remembering the 1980s has been a significant element in recent cultural life. Even before the decade's close, literature can be found in an attitude of commemoration. *The Swimming Pool Library* may announce novelties, but it is also already retrospective. Its 1983 setting placed even the novel's first readers at a distance from its events. As we have seen, this brings a specifically elegiac feeling: the novel looks back across the frontier of the AIDS crisis. But even without this factor, Hollinghurst's exquisite style renders the early 1980s as a poignant memory of overcast April days and metropolitan high summer. A similar project underlies Dyer's *The Colour of Memory*, in which the events of 1986–7 have already become precious Polaroids, fragile snatches of passing time. The novel treasures the kind of moment 'which, even as experienced, is obscurely touched by the significance with which it will be invested by the future, by memory: this is how I was, this is how we were; this is how we spent our time, wasting whole afternoons and not caring because it was winter and there were so many afternoons still ahead' (1989: 86). As these writers demonstrate, it was possible to be nostalgic for the 1980s while they were still going on. But this was only the beginning of a tide of remembrance.

In the realm of popular narratives and iconography, one of the 1980s' major developments was the growth of retro culture. Cultural retrospection, in which a period adopts the styles of an older one, is not new. But the forms and extent of such revivalism are intimately connected with the media of the moment. In the late twentieth century, cinema, television, advertising, recorded and transmitted music, and electronic technologies of the image were combined with commercial imperatives to make aspects of the past prominent in the landscape of the present. The cycle in which a cultural style became past enough to be revivable significantly accelerated. In the post-war period, the 'Teddy Boys' of the 1950s styled themselves on a version of Edwardian clothing from the century's start. The 1970s witnessed a Teddy Boy revival. In the 1980s, images of the 1950s remained in extensive circulation, from typefaces and clothes to domestic interiors. The bulk of this imagery was American. That does not diminish its appeal to a British imagination. On the contrary, it demonstrates the gradual tendency of much British culture, from at least the 1950s on, to enter a merger with its larger transatlantic counterpart. Several Hollywood films – *Back to the Future* (1985), *Peggy Sue Got Married* (1986), *Stand By Me* (1987) – not only depicted the earlier period, but explicitly thematised the distance between past and present through time travel and frame narratives. Their British counterparts include *Wish You Were Here* (1987), a seaside coming-of-age drama, and *Absolute Beginners* (1985), an adaptation of Colin MacInnes' 1959 novel that ambitiously attempted to give London's 1950s the glamour of America's. That glamour was more reliably tapped in the television and billboard advertisements for Levi's jeans from 1986 on: miniature dramas in downtown laundrettes and Greyhound buses played out against soul records of the 1960s.

The foundation of so much cultural production on performances of the past produced an increased self-consciousness – among ordinary television audiences, let alone artists or writers – about period flavour. A given decade could evidently be summoned and represented with a certain combination of signs and sounds. The very idea of the decade as a coherent unit of culture and feeling was, as Ian Jack indicates, stronger than ever before. This seemed one of the legacies of the 1980s. What was less evident, as the decade passed away, was that it would soon be subject to the same logic.

'It could be said that we haven't had any new popular culture in the 1990s,' averred Michael Bracewell, 'we've simply had the recent past again, focusing on a selective memory of the 1970s' (2002: 204). Jonathan Coe's *The Rotters' Club* (2001) is the best-known literary contribution to, or reflection on, this rerun. But the 1980s too turned out to be both a decade ago and just around the corner. Writing in early 2010, Simon Reynolds reckoned that a 1980s revival had now been taking place in popular music for longer than the decade itself. How long such a process can last is debatable. One could logically assume that such a revival will exhaust itself. But retro time, unlike the calendar, seems to work less by succession than by accretion. Each revived era is added to an expanding library, which remains available. We cannot reliably forecast the ways that the 1980s will be remembered in future. But we can note the prevailing forms of cultural remembrance at the start of the twenty-first century.

Across various media, two kinds of revivalism can be identified: the simple revival of existing texts or items, and the redeployment of elements of the past into new work. The first, 'replay' category includes seasons of films from the decade or discos devoted to its popular music. That music has also been repeatedly repackaged in compilations, television and radio programmes, while becoming part of the register of familiar 'oldies'. Into a world in which these replays are already the norm come 'remakes': fresh works that bundle their elements into new combinations. In music, Reynolds cited a series of acts and movements – some obscure, some as commercially successful as Daft Punk, The Strokes and Franz Ferdinand – which had spliced their sound from scenes now two or three decades old. In Hollywood cinema, *The Wedding Singer* (1998) takes place in a day-glo 1985 (and was revived as a Broadway musical in 2006); *13 Going on 30* (2004) inverts the movement of *Back to the Future* to send a girl from 1987 into the twenty-first century present and back; *Donnie Darko* (2001) takes the US election cycle of 1988 as backdrop to its grimly fantastic events. In Britain, *The Business* (2005) and *The Firm* (2009) respectively depict gangsters and football hooligans in the 1980s. *Billy Elliot* (2000) restages the picket lines of the miners' strike as the backdrop to its tale of a working-class Geordie ballet dancer. *This is England* (2006) commences with a montage of early-decade news to introduce its story of skinhead thugs at the time of the Falklands War. Historical interest is added: the audience recognises, and sometimes finds comedy in, the look, object-world or iconography of the 1980s, while also, in more serious films, being asked to reconsider the decade as a period of recent social history. Something similar applies to *Ashes to Ashes* (2008), a BBC series in which a police officer from the present travels back to the 1980s. As the shameless sequel to an equivalent series set in the 1970s, *Life on Mars*, the programme demonstrates the fluidity of the retro continuum. The period element here is rather like a sauce that can be added to a dish to add instant appeal: set a police drama two or three decades in the past and it assumes a new dimension and cultural status.

All these screen narratives depend heavily for effect on both visual and aural cues for the period. They are full of versions of 1980s fashion (as well as cars, telephones, stereos and the like) and popular music. Thus 1980s' sartorial styles – leg-warmers, leggings, jackets with rolled-up sleeves in the mode of the US television series *Miami Vice* – have been regularly revived since 2000, in the rarefied domain of the catwalk but also, in many cases, as part of the currency of fashion in ordinary life. All the replayed material was prominently gathered in a further genre: television retrospectives devoted entirely to items and phenomena of the recent past. The flagship here is the BBC's *I Love* format, which allocated an episode, and a relevant guest presenter, to each year. *I Love the 1970s* (2000) was followed by *I Love the 1980s* in 2001; *I Love the 1990s* (2002) seemed to have arrived prematurely. These series, already lightweight, encouraged trashier imitators on other channels.

The aspects of the past being revived are primarily those that appealed to the young. The revival occurs when that generation has not only grown up, but in many cases ascended to positions of influence in the media. The children who watched *Bagpuss* find themselves scheduling Saturday night television; the teens who first encountered computers via the ZX Spectrum are now designing websites. Contemporary retro is also fuelled by affluence, and by the demographic shift in which, for an increasing proportion of the population of developed countries, childrearing takes place later. Childhood itself can thus become prolonged or fondly replayed. All this is facilitated by technological advance. The digital age is an archival age. In film and television, for instance, the sheer abundance of material from the recent past now available for consumption makes the 1980s themselves look comparatively bereft. Despite the decade's fascination with the 1950s and 1960s, the actual material available was scant and elusive next to the 2000s, when virtually every minor situation comedy from the last fifty years seemed to be repackaged for sale on DVD. The other great shift of the 2000s was the arrival of the internet's interactive 'Web 2.0' phase, dominated by user-generated content. In early 2010 the photographic site Flickr, hosting billions of amateur photographs, contained user groups including '80s Nostalgia', '1980s Prom', 'Great Taste from the 80s', 'My 80s Bedroom – 1980–1989', 'The 1980s BRAIN DRAIN Nostalgia Train', and 'I love the 80s' competing with 'I♥80s', among many others. The replay/remake distinction applies here too: while some pages are dedicated to images from the 1980s themselves, scanned in from photographic originals, other users take the trouble to create neo-1980s images and videos deploying the objects, colours and sounds that the culture has agreed upon as triggers of the decade. The shift from the 1980s is again worth remarking. Where retro culture was once directed by a handful of Baby Boomers gaining access to Hollywood budgets, it can now be readily generated and broadcast to the entire globe by millions.

Much of this retrospection seems wilfully apolitical. One can forge a pastel 1980s bleached of strife. Yet specific political events are in fact regularly retrieved for analysis by the media. This is not only a compulsively retrospective culture, but an anniversarial one, in which, for instance, the fact that twenty-five years have passed since the Falklands War is apparently newsworthy in itself. In late 2009 the commemorative cycle reached the great wave of European emancipations that closed the 1980s. The fall of the Berlin Wall was re-enacted as the former Soviet leader Mikhail Gorbachev and Polish trade unionist Lech Walesa, among others, symbolically toppled a line of giant dominoes. The recent past is not only an item for commemoration but also a political token or weapon, to be deployed according to convenience. Margaret Thatcher's admonition of the 1960s was an instance of this. The 1970s remain a byword for sagging corporatism, union power, economic decline under social-democratic supervision. The 1980s themselves, however, are rarely available in twenty-first century political discourse as a positive point of comparison. Even on the political Right, the confrontations that Thatcher relished and won may be revered but are of limited rhetorical use in the present. 'Tory cuts pave the way for a return to 80s dole queues' is the headline over a column by the progressive commentator Polly Toynbee (2010), who reminds readers that '1980s signing-on offices – think the queue in *The Full Monty* – with their plastic seats bolted down to linoleum floors, offered a brief interview from behind a scratched reinforced window with bad-tempered, harassed staff who pushed people into pretty useless training or compulsory work schemes that led nowhere.' *Boys from the Blackstuff* thus remains the originary text for one politically significant version of the decade. On this reading, the 1980s are to subsequent years what the 1930s were to the 1940s. The memory of mass unemployment is a cautionary tale: the listener shudders and vows not to go back.

One might concede the potency of all this, yet maintain that it has little to do with literature. But this distinction will not hold. At the National Theatre, David Eldridge's *Market Boy* (2006) depicted traders in Romford Market from 1985 to 1991. Pop songs of the era punctuated the action; costumes prompted audience laughter. The programme contained an essay on the era's politics by the former Conservative minister Edwina Currie, alongside three pages of retro lists and advertising slogans. A garish Margaret Thatcher descended from the gods on Union Flag wings to take the acclaim of her Essex heartland. The stage musical of *Billy Elliot* featured a Thatcher avatar driving a miniature tank. The real Thatcher's public visibility was diminished after she suffered strokes in 2002; caricatures like these filled the gap. The gleeful anticipation of her death became a public pastime for some. Pop songs contemplating the event comprise a small sub-genre. *Maggie's End* (Shaw Theatre, 2009) dramatised the imagined aftermath of her demise in summer 2010.

But it is the novel that has most subtly quarried the remains of the 1980s. Significant fictional accounts of Thatcherism had already appeared in the 1990s (Sinclair 1991, Bracewell 1992, Coe 1994), but the post-millennial retrospect is another category again: the neo-1980s novel. (In the terms proposed above, such novels are remakes, while a run on Fighting Fantasy Gamebooks or early Anita Brookner would amount to a replay.) Nicola Barker's *Five Miles from Outer Hope*

(2000) is a grotesque coming-of-age story set around the Devon coast in 1981. Its temporal setting has little real bearing on the plot, but does allow for one of fiction's purest essays in the pop-memory mode of *I Love the 1980s*:

> And there will be riots in Brixton, and Royal marriages and the space shuttle Columbia: flying and orbiting. And somehow they'll check-mate the Yorkshire Ripper, and baseball will strike, and air traffic controllers, and McEnroe will win the US Open, and Karpov will reign as World Chess Champion. (Barker 2000: 11)

Similar impulses are more subtly diffused through David Mitchell's *Black Swan Green* (2006), whose thirteen-year-old protagonist Jason Taylor provides a month-by-month narrative of 1982. The novel is littered with period details. The Human League's 'Don't You Want Me?' plays 'dead loud' on the first page, and a climactic disco allows Mitchell to catalogue the year's chart hits (2006: 1, 346–7). *Chariots of Fire* is in cinemas and *Superman II* is on television, along with Paul Daniels' magic show and 'a glittery new quiz show called *Blankety Blank* presented by Terry Wogan' (40–1). Jason buys the *2000AD* summer special for 40p, 'a packet of Letraset and a TDK C-60 cassette to tape the best songs in the Top 40 off Radio 1 on Sunday' (212). The retro culture limned earlier seems a significant context for this novel. Mitchell might not so relentlessly light on such details if the media had not already established them as the primary model of remembrance for this period. Yet they can also plausibly convey the priorities of a child: the latest challenge that Mitchell, a formidable technician, had set himself.

Unlike Barker, Mitchell connects his story to larger historical events, as a local boy sails for the Falklands and dies in battle. Yet *Black Swan Green*, a reconstruction of childhood's travails, does not primarily aim to be a state of the nation address. That task is unambiguously assumed by Tim Lott's *Rumours of a Hurricane* (2002). The novel tells of the printer Charlie Buck, from election day 1979 to his decline and suicide in the recession of the early 1990s. Almost everything in Lott's tale is blatantly charged with historical meaning. Charlie buys his council flat, celebrates victory in the Falklands, and joins the picket line in Wapping as police battle the old print unions. He moves to Milton Keynes (a new town whose attractions were extensively advertised on television in the early 1980s), establishes a small business and avoids a sexual encounter because of his fear of AIDS. The novel is so freighted with historically symptomatic events and actions that, as Andy Beckett (2002) observed, a given page 'almost expires under the weight of symbolism'. Once more we inhabit a mode of recollection that overlaps with *I Love the 1980s*.

Lott often dishes his history raw, or with minimal cooking: 1979 means 'Inflation, decimalization, the three-day week, industrial chaos, oil-price hikes, Irish terrorists taking their deadly suitcases and shopping bags to the streets and litter bins of England' (Lott 2002: 15). Charlie's political position is later elucidated: 'He voted for Margaret Thatcher in the last election, following her triumph over the Argie menace. It made the Prime Minister swell in Charlie's imagination, it made him respect her. And there was more money appearing in his pay packet as income tax shrank' (210).

Few fictions of the 1980s have been so unabashedly explicit in presenting their historical analysis. Though Lott's narrative is cast in the present tense, his novel is openly a retrospect from a moment where a degree of consensus has been established about the decade's trajectory. Its occasional clumsiness is the cost of a real ambition: to articulate the whole span of the 1980s in a fiction that indicates the historical significance of individual acts. In the mid-twentieth century the Marxist thinker Georg Lukàcs proposed that the historical novel should present a narrative which exemplifies and connects up with history's main current. It should realise a parallel between individual and general, contingently local and socially typical. Literature, Lukàcs writes in *The Historical Novel*, 'must disclose the social foundations of politics by portraying living human destinies, individual destinies which concentrate in their individual uniqueness the typical, representative features of these connexions' (1969: 158). Charlie Buck, the skilled manual worker who turns Tory and attempts to integrate into a changed Britain, is plainly intended to be such an individual. The doubt voiced by Beckett questions not only Lott's technique but the persuasiveness of this very form of historical fiction, in the wake of the modernism that Lukàcs distrusted. Yet fiction found other ways to represent the decade's dynamics.

Probably the most distinguished neo-1980s novels to date were published within a month of each other, in spring 2004. Hollinghurst's *The Line of Beauty* and David Peace's *GB84* contrast so drastically that they effectively divide the decade between them. Hollinghurst depicts a young, gay Oxford graduate and aesthete inhabiting the house of a grand Tory family in West London; Peace narrates the year of the miners' strike, touring the back roads between battered Yorkshire towns. Where Peace covers every week of 1984 to 1985, Hollinghurst wilfully leaps over this, offering three sections in 1983, 1986 and 1987. The hungry, unemployed and dispossessed who haunt Peace's pages are absent from the Tory balls and dinner parties of *The Line of Beauty*, though the novel does directly confront the spectre of AIDS that *The Swimming Pool Library* strategically avoided. Hollinghurst is fascinated by the private lives of those in power; Peace shows the machinations of the secret state, but spends more time amid the miners' union as it is harassed and legislated almost out of existence. The books' styles, too, emphatically contrast. But both seek a way to narrate recent history.

Peace offers a chronicle history, a week-by-week record of the strike. His research is so thorough that most pages of the book could be cross-checked against the press archives of the time. The book's main narrative, labyrinthine in itself, is punctuated by occasional pages in tiny type that meticulously record the voices of two picketing miners as their lives slowly collapse. In the primary narrative, real figures – not least Arthur Scargill and Margaret Thatcher – are heard uttering the speeches they actually made at the time. The novel comes close to the news. We have observed the ambitious, but sometimes uneasy attempt by novelists like Lott or Margaret Drabble to incorporate contemporary history into the realist novel. Peace transcends this strategy by taking it to an extreme. His maniacal documentation simply discards traditional considerations of novelistic balance. Peace's style also eschews the manners of mainstream fiction. His telegraphic monotone speeds through events, yet still leaves the reader trudging through a tragedy whose end never seems in sight. Peace makes repetition central to his relentless effect, in an incantatory prose that rarely reaches the right-hand margin. The style is openly indebted to the American crime writer James Ellroy, though it delivers thoroughly English material. The crime connection is significant. Peace's use of the genre signifies that society is under suspicion. His attention is both forensic and judgemental. Peace has commented that 'crimes take place in society, not in a vacuum' (Marqusee 2004), but this formulation understates the implication of *GB84*, in which crime is integral to the very working of 'society'.

The narration that flows around Hollinghurst's protagonist Nick Guest is elegant, languid, yet indefatigably precise in rendering his myriad perceptions of mid-1980s London. The novel's method is a neo-Impressionism, a moment-by-moment stream of nuance and observation. Its most explicit precursor is Henry James. Nick is enrolled for a PhD on James and style at University College London. At a dinner party in 1983 a guest asks him what James would have made of the present company. Hollinghurst's novel is an implicit answer to that question. James, it prompts us to think, would have studied the manners and nuances of the dominant class of the age; teased at the relations between money and taste, power and style; used an ostensibly narrow social remit to seek insight into a whole era. A recurrent concern is the relation of the aesthetic to a political world from which it seems detached. Nick, a devotee of antique furniture, art and classical music, offhandedly sees modern Conservatism as having an 'aesthetic poverty' (2004: 104). Margaret Thatcher herself, arriving at a party, seems to bear him out: '[S]he moved in her own accelerated element, her own garlanded perspective, she didn't give a damn about squares on the wallpaper or blue front doors – she noticed nothing, and yet she remembered everything' (385). To 'notice nothing' makes Thatcher the opposite of the Jamesian standpoint adopted by Nick and the novel itself, to which 'noticing' is fundamental. Yet Nick is available as a hired 'aesthete' for a Thatcherite millionaire (209), whose arrogantly cruel son Wani is also Nick's lover; and Wani and Nick produce a magazine, *Ogee*, which is emblematic of the luxuriant aestheticism of the 1980s style press. Hollinghurst writes beautifully, which makes all the subtler his investigation of the complicity of beauty with power.

The 1980s, Hollinghurst declared upon winning the Booker Prize, intrigued him because they seemed 'to have determined so many things about the way we live now' (Moss 2004). David Peace meanwhile viewed the miners' strike as pivotal in producing the neo-liberal present: 'Now it's carte blanche, full-on privatisation, deregulation, trickle-down'. In Peace's view, the political and economic dispensation established in the 1980s has continued and been more entrenched over subsequent decades. The Labour Party's return to power in 1997 need not dent this case. The party's transformation, involving the renunciation of many of its former core policies, is in large part Thatcher's legacy. If the miners' strike was critical in this historical process, Peace views Britain's moral invoice as still blighted by the event: 'I didn't want the book to offer a sense of redemption, because as a country we haven't got it. And we don't deserve it' (Marqusee 2004). For both writers, the fictional return to the 1980s is a search for clues to the contemporary.

History is honeycombed with transitions, whose relative significance depends partly on the analyst's agenda. But the most interesting fictional returns to the 1980s tend to endorse the sense, expressed by Margaret Thatcher as she took power in May 1979, that a watershed was being crossed (Campbell 2003: 47). In the early twenty-first century the 1980s have been a pivotal centre of attention, for various reasons: from sheer personal nostalgia, through the artistic possibilities that the decade's raw materials offer, to a determination to understand its role in shaping the political present. On election day 1987, Hollinghurst's character Catherine feels that the 1980s are going on forever. In fact they would end on time three years later. But in the early twenty-first century, it can feel as though they never went away.

Bibliography

Acker, Kathy (2002), 'Alasdair Gray Interviewed by Kathy Acker: 1986', in Moores (ed.), *Alasdair Gray*, pp. 45–57.

Ackroyd, Peter (1985), *Hawksmoor*, London: Hamish Hamilton.

Allen, Graham (1983), *Thatcher's Britain: A Guide to the Ruins*, London: Pluto / New Socialist.

Allnutt, Gillian (1988), 'Quote Feminist Unquote Poetry', in Allnutt et al. (eds), *The New British Poetry*, pp. 77–9.

Allnutt, Gillian, Fred D'Aguiar, Ken Edwards and Eric Mottram (1988) (eds), *The New British Poetry*, London: Paladin.

Allport, Alan (2003), 'Mrs Thatcher's Liberties', in Pugliese (ed.), *The Political Legacy of Margaret Thatcher*, pp. 29–40.

Amis, Kingsley [1986] (1987), *The Old Devils*, New York: Harper and Row.

Amis, Martin (1978), 'The State of Fiction: A Symposium', *New Review* 5:1 (Summer), 18.

—(1981), *Other People: A Mystery Story*, London: Jonathan Cape.

—(1984), *Money: A Suicide Note*, London: Jonathan Cape.

—(1986), *The Moronic Inferno and Other Visits to America*, London: Jonathan Cape.

—(1987), *Einstein's Monsters*, London: Jonathan Cape.

—(1989), *London Fields*, London: Jonathan Cape.

—(2000), *Experience*, New York: Hyperion.

—(2001), *The War Against Cliché: Essays and Reviews 1971–2000*, London: Jonathan Cape.

—(2004), 'Capo di Capi', *Guardian*, 6 March, *Review* section, 4.

Anderson, Benedict (1991), *Imagined Communities*, 2nd edn, London: Verso.

Anderson, Perry (1998), *The Origins of Postmodernity*, London: Verso.

—(2007), 'Jottings on the Conjuncture', *New Left Review* 48, (November/ December), 5–37.

Aston, Elaine (2001), *Caryl Churchill*, 2nd edn, Tavistock: Northcote House.

Aston, Elaine and Janelle Reinelt (eds) (2000), *The Cambridge Companion to Modern British Women Playwrights*, Cambridge: Cambridge University Press.

Auden, W. H. (1979), *Selected Poems*, ed. Edward Mendelson, London: Faber.

Barker, Francis (1984), *The Tremulous Private Body*, London: Methuen.

Barker, Nicola (2000), *Five Miles from Outer Hope*, London: Faber.

Barker, Pat (1982), *Union Street*, London: Virago.

—(1984), *Blow Your House Down*, London: Virago.

—[1986] (1996), *Liza's England*, first published as *The Century's Daughter*, London: Virago.

Barnes, Julian (1984), *Flaubert's Parrot*, London: Jonathan Cape.

—(1989), *A History of the World in 10½ Chapters*, London: Jonathan Cape.

Barnett, Anthony (1984), 'The Failed Consensus', in Curran (ed.), *The Future of the Left*, pp. 138–47.

Barry, Peter (2000), *Contemporary British Poetry and the City*, Manchester: Manchester University Press.

Bassnett, Susan (2000), 'The Politics of Location', in Aston and Reinelt (eds), *The Cambridge Companion to Modern Women British Playwrights*, pp. 73–81.

Baudrillard, Jean (1983), *Simulations*, trans. Paul Foss, Paul Patton and Philip Beitchman, London: Semiotext(e).

—(1987), *Forget Foucault*, trans. Nicola Dufresne, London: Semiotext(e).

Beckett, Andy (2002), 'Thatcherism for Beginners', *Guardian*, 2 February 2002, at http://www.guardian.co.uk/books/2002/feb/02/fiction.whitbreadbooka-wards2002

Behan, Brendan (1978), *The Complete Plays*, London: Methuen.

Belsey, Catherine (1985), *The Subject of Tragedy: Identity & Difference in Renaissance Drama*, London: Methuen.

Bertens, Hans (1995), *The Idea of the Postmodern*, London: Routledge.

Bleasdale, Alan (1983), *Boys from the Blackstuff: Five Plays for Television*, St Albans: Granada.

Bourdieu, Pierre (1993), *The Field of Cultural Production*, ed. Randal Johnson, Cambridge: Polity.

Bowman, Marion [1989] (2007), 'The Iron Lady made flesh and blood', *Guardian*, *G2*, 18 July, 18.

Bracewell, Michael (1988), *The Crypto-Amnesia Club*, London: Serpent's Tail.

—(1989), *Divine Concepts of Physical Beauty*, London: Martin Secker and Warburg.

—(1992), *The Conclave*, London: Martin Secker and Warburg.

—(2001), *Perfect Tense*, London: Jonathan Cape.

—(2002), *The Nineties: When Surface was Depth*, London: Flamingo.

Bradbury, Malcolm (ed.) (1977), *The Novel Today: Contemporary Writers on Modern Fiction*, Glasgow: Fontana.

Bradford, Richard (2007), *The Novel Now: Contemporary British Fiction*, Oxford: Blackwell.

Brannigan, John (2005), *Pat Barker*, Manchester: Manchester University Press.

Brenton, Howard (1989), *Plays: 2*, London: Methuen.

Brenton, Howard and David Hare (1985), *Pravda: A Fleet Street Comedy*, London: Methuen.

Brooker, Joseph (2004), *Joyce's Critics*, Madison: Wisconsin University Press.

Brookner, Anita (1982), *Providence*, London: Jonathan Cape.

—(1984), *Hotel du Lac*, London: Jonathan Cape.

Brophy, Sarah (2005), 'Working-Class Women, Labor and the Problem of Community in *Union Street* and *Liza's England*', in Monteith et al. (eds), *Critical Perspectives on Pat Barker*, pp. 24–39.

Brown, Stephen (ed.) (2006), *Consuming Books: The Marketing and Consumption of Literature*, London and New York: Routledge.

Buford, Bill (1980), 'Introduction', *Granta* 3, 7–16.

—(1993), 'Editorial', *Best of Young British Novelists 2*, *Granta* 43 (Spring), 9–16.

Burchill, Julie (1989), *Ambition*, London: The Bodley Head.

Burgess, Anthony (1980), *Earthly Powers*, London: Hutchinson.

—(1989), *Any Old Iron*, London: Hutchinson.

Byatt, A. S. (1990), *Possession: A Romance*, London: Chatto and Windus.

Callil, Carmen (2008), 'The stories of our lives', *Guardian*, 26 April 2008, at http://www.guardian.co.uk/books/2008/apr/26/featuresreviews.guardian review2

Campbell, Beatrix (1984), *Wigan Pier Revisited: Poverty and Politics in the 80s*, London: Virago.

Campbell, John (2003), *Margaret Thatcher. Volume Two: The Iron Lady*, London: Jonathan Cape.

Carr, Helen (ed.) (1989), *From My Guy to Sci-Fi: Genre and Women's Writing in the Postmodern World*, London: Pandora.

Carter, Angela [1984] (2006), *Nights at the Circus*, London: Vintage.

Chapman, Ian (1993), 'Paperback Publishing', in Peter Owen (ed.), *Publishing Now*, pp. 48–56.

Childs, Peter (2005), *Contemporary Novelists: British Fiction since 1970*, Basingstoke: Palgrave.

—(2006), 'Householders: Community, Violence and Resistance in Three Contemporary Women's Texts', in Gerry Smyth and Jo Croft (eds), *Our House: The Representation of Domestic Space in Modern Culture*, Amsterdam: Rodopi, pp. 176–95.

Churchill, Caryl (1990), *Plays: 2*, London: Methuen.

Coe, Jonathan (1994), *What A Carve Up!*, London: Viking.

—(2001), *The Rotters' Club*, London: Viking.

—(2002), '1994, Janine', in Moores (ed.), *Alasdair Gray*, pp. 59–66.

Collins, Andrew (2002), *Still Suitable for Miners – Billy Bragg: The Official Biography*, London: Virgin.

Connor, Steven (1996), *The English Novel in History 1950–1995*, London: Routledge.

—(2007), 'Steven Connor', at http://www.stevenconnor.com/bio.htm

Crozier, Andrew (1983), 'Thrills and Frills: Poetry as Figures of Empirical Lyricism', in Alan Sinfield (ed.), *Society and Literature 1945–1970*, London: Methuen, pp. 199–233.

Crozier, Andrew and Tim Longville (eds) (1987), *A Various Art*, Manchester: Carcanet.

Curran, James (ed.) (1984), *The Future of the Left*, Cambridge: Polity Press and New Socialist.

D'Aguiar, Fred (1988), 'Black British Poetry', in Allnutt et al. (eds), *The New British Poetry*, pp. 3–4.

—(1993), 'Have You Been Here Long? Black Poetry in Britain', in Hampson and Barry (eds), *The Scope of the Possible*, pp. 51–71.

—(2001), *An English Sampler: New and Selected Poems*, London: Chatto and Windus.

Daniels, Sarah (1997), *Plays: 1*, London: Methuen.

Davies, Alistair and Alan Sinfield (eds) (2000), *British Culture of the Postwar: An Introduction to Literature and Society 1945–1999*, London: Routledge.

DeLillo, Don (1984), *White Noise*, Harmondsworth: Viking Penguin.

Didion, Joan (1979), *The White Album*, London: Weidenfeld and Nicolson.

Diedrick, James (2004), *Understanding Martin Amis*, 2nd edn, Columbia: South Carolina University Press.

Dollimore, Jonathan and Alan Sinfield (eds) (1985), *Political Shakespeare: New Essays in Cultural Materialism*, Manchester: Manchester University Press.

Drabble, Margaret (1987), *The Radiant Way*, London: Weidenfeld and Nicolson.

Durham, Martin (2003), 'The Thatcher Government and the Politics of the Family', in Pugliese (ed.), *The Political Legacy of Margaret Thatcher*, pp. 238–251.

Dyer, Geoff (1989), *The Colour of Memory*, London: Jonathan Cape.

—(1999), *Anglo-English Attitudes: Essays and Reviews 1984–1999*, London: Abacus.

Eagleton, Terry (2000), *The Idea of Culture*, Oxford: Blackwell.

Edgar, David (1984), 'Bitter Harvest', in Curran (ed.), *The Future of the Left*, pp. 39–57.

—(2009), 'Clare McIntyre obituary', *Guardian*, 2 December 2009, at http://www.guardian.co.uk/stage/2009/dec/02/clare-mcintyre-obituary

Edwards, Ken (1988a), 'Some Younger Poets', in Allnutt et al. (eds), *The New British Poetry*, pp. 265–70.

—(1988b), 'Sunny Murray Trio, *Live at Moers-Festival*, Moers Music 01054: Geraniums, South London', in Allnutt et al. (eds), *The New British Poetry*, pp. 295–7.

English, James F. (ed.) (2006), *A Concise Companion to Contemporary British Fiction*, Oxford: Blackwell.

English, James F. and John Frow (2006), 'Literary Authorship and Celebrity Culture', in English (ed.), *A Concise Companion to Contemporary British Fiction*, pp. 39–57.

Fairbairns, Zoe (1979), *Benefits*, London: Virago.

—(1984), *Here Today*, London: Methuen.

Farndale, Nigel (2005), 'Shifts in the Ether' (interview with Julian Barnes), 16 July, at http://www.theage.com.au/news/books/shifts-in-the-ether/2005/07/15/11 20934403847.html

Fiedler, Leslie A. (1972), *Cross the Border – Close the Gap*, New York: Stein and Day.

Fisher, Allen (1988), 'Birdland', in Allnutt et al. (eds), *The New British Poetry*, pp. 164–7.

Franklin, Dan (1993), 'The Death of the Hardback?', in Peter Owen (ed.), *Publishing Now*, pp. 23–9.

Friel, Brian (1996), *Plays: 1*, London: Faber.

Frith, Mark (ed.) (2006), *The Best of 'Smash Hits': The '80s*, London: Sphere.

Galloway, Janice (1989), *The Trick is to Keep Breathing*, Edinburgh: Polygon.

Gasiorek, Andrzej (1995), *Post-War British Fiction: Realism and After*, London: Edward Arnold.

Gems, Pam (1985), *Three Plays: Piaf / Camille / Loving Women*, Harmondsworth: Penguin.

Gerrard, Nicci (1989), *Into the Mainstream: How Feminism has Changed Women's Writing*, London: Pandora.

Gifford, Terry (2009), *Ted Hughes*, London and New York: Routledge.

Golding, William (1980), *Rites of Passage*, London: Faber.

Goodman, Lizbeth (1996), *Feminist Stages: Interviews with Women in Contemporary British Theatre*, Amsterdam: Harwood.

Gray, Alasdair (1984a), *1982 Janine*, Harmondsworth: Penguin.

—(1984b), 'Why Writers Write', *The Editor*, at http://www.alasdairgray.co.uk/q_02.htm

—[1981] (1985), *Lanark: A Life in 4 Books*, rev. edn, Edinburgh: Canongate.

—(1994), *A History Maker*, Edinburgh: Canongate.

—(2002), 'How *Lanark* Grew', at http://bookhugger.co.uk/2009/09/how-lanark-grew-in-alasdair-grays-own-words/

—(2007), *Old Men In Love*, London: Bloomsbury.

Haffenden, John (1985), *Novelists in Interview*, London: Methuen.

Hall, Stuart (1988), *The Hard Road to Renewal: Thatcherism and the Crisis of the Left*, London: Verso.

—(1997), 'New Ethnicities', in David Morley and Kuan-Hsing Chen (eds), *Stuart Hall: Critical Dialogues in Cultural Studies*, London: Routledge, pp. 441–9.

Hampson, Robert and Peter Barry (eds) (1993), *New British Poetries: The Scope of the Possible*, Manchester: Manchester University Press.

Harrison, Tony [1985] (1989), *v.*, Newcastle-upon-Tyne: Bloodaxe.

Harvey, David (1990), *The Condition of Postmodernity: An Enquiry into the Origins of Cultural Change*, Oxford: Blackwell.

Harvie, Christopher (1994), *Scotland and Nationalism*, London: Routledge.

Hattersley, Roy (1997), *Fifty Years On: A Prejudiced History of Britain since the War*, London: Little, Brown.

Head, Dominic (2002), *The Cambridge Introduction to Modern British Fiction, 1950–2000*, Cambridge: Cambridge University Press.

—(2006), 'The Demise of Class Fiction', in English (ed.), *A Concise Companion to Contemporary British Fiction*, pp. 229–47.

—(2008), *The State of the Novel: Britain and Beyond*, Chichester: Wiley-Blackwell.

Heaney, Seamus (1983), *An Open Letter*, Derry: Field Day.

—(1990), *New Selected Poems 1966–1987*, London: Faber.

—(2002), *Finders Keepers: Selected Prose 1971–2001*, London: Faber.

Hebdige, Dick (1988), *Hiding in the Light: On Images and Things*, London: Comedia.

Hewison, Robert (1987), *The Heritage Industry: Britain in a Climate of Decline*, London: Methuen.

—(1988), *Too Much: Culture in the Cold War 1945–60*, rev. edn, London: Methuen.

Higson, Andrew (2003), *English Heritage, English Cinema*, Oxford: Oxford University Press.

Hofman, Michael (2000), 'Raine, Raine, Go Away', *Guardian*, 3 December, at http://www.guardian.co.uk/books/2000/dec/03/poetry

Hollinghurst, Alan (1988), *The Swimming Pool Library*, London: Chatto and Windus.

—(2004), *The Line of Beauty*, London: Picador.

Hopkins, Eric (1991), *The Rise and Decline of the English Working Classes 1918–1990*, London: Weidenfeld and Nicolson.

Hughes, Ted (1992), *Rain Charm for the Duchy and other Laureate Poems*, London: Faber.

—(1995), *New Selected Poems*, London: Faber.

Hutcheon, Linda (1988), *A Poetics of Postmodernism: History, Theory, Fiction*. New York and London: Routledge.

—(2002), *The Politics of Postmodernism*, 2nd edn, London: Routledge.

Ishiguro, Kazuo (1989), *The Remains of the Day*, London: Faber.

Israel, Nico (2006), 'Tropicalizing London: British Fiction and the Discipline of Postcolonialism', in English (ed.), *A Concise Companion to Contemporary British Fiction*, pp. 83–100.

Jack, Ian (1996), 'Editorial: Whatever Happened to Us?', *Granta* 56, 7–8.

—(1997), *Before the Oil Ran Out: Britain in the Brutal Years*, rev. edn, London: Vintage.

—(2009) 'Downhill from here', *London Review of Books* 31: 16 (27 August), 7–10.

Jaggi, Maya (2001), 'A singular writer', *Guardian*, 8 September 2001, at http://www.guardian.co.uk/education/2001/sep/08/artsandhumanities.higher education

James, Clive (1983), *Brilliant Creatures*, London: Jonathan Cape.

James, Henry (1968), *Selected Literary Criticism*, ed. Morris Shapira, Harmondsworth: Penguin.

Jameson, Fredric (1991), *Postmodernism, or, the Cultural Logic of Late Capitalism*, London: Verso.

Johnson, B. S. (1990), 'Introduction' to *Aren't You Rather Young To Be Writing Your Memoirs?*, in Malcolm Bradbury (ed.), *The Novel Today: Contemporary Writers on Modern Fiction*, Glasgow: Fontana, pp. 165–83.

Johnson, Christopher (1991), *The Economy under Mrs Thatcher 1979–1990*, Harmondsworth: Penguin.

Johnson, Linton Kwesi (1980), *Inglan is a Bitch*, London: Race Today.

Joyce, James [1916] (1992), *A Portrait of the Artist as a Young Man*, ed. Seamus Deane, Harmondsworth: Penguin.

Kaplan, Cora (1989), 'Feminist Criticism Twenty Years On', in Carr (ed.), *From My Guy to Sci-Fi*, pp. 14–23.

Keay, Douglas (1987), 'Aids, Education and the Year 2000!', *Woman's Own*, 31 October, 8–10.

Kelman, James (1983), *Not Not While the Giro and Other stories*, Edinburgh: Polygon.

—(1984), *The Busconductor Hines*, Edinburgh: Polygon.

—(1985), *A Chancer*, Edinburgh: Polygon.

—(1989), *A Disaffection*, London: Secker and Warburg.

—(1992), *Some Recent Attacks: Essays Cultural & Political*, Stirling: AK Press.

King, Bruce (2003), *V. S. Naipaul*, 2nd edn, Basingstoke: Palgrave.

Kravitz, Peter (ed.) (1997), *The Picador Book of Contemporary Scottish Fiction*, London: Picador.

Kureishi, Hanif (1990), *The Buddha of Suburbia*, London: Faber.

—(1996), *My Beautiful Laundrette and Other Writings*, London: Faber.

Kureishi, Hanif and Jon Savage (eds) (1995), *The Faber Book of Pop*, London: Faber.

Lawson, Mark (1991), *Bloody Margaret: Three Political Fantasies*, London: Pan.

Leader, Zachary (ed.) (2002), *On Modern British Fiction*, Oxford: Oxford University Press.

Lee, Alison (1990), *Realism and Power: Postmodern British Fiction*, London: Routledge.

Leonard, Tom (1984), *Intimate Voices: Selected Work 1965–1983*, Newcastle upon Tyne: Galloping Dog Press.

Leys, Colin (1984), 'The Rise of the Authoritarian State', in Curran (ed.), *The Future of the Left*, pp. 58–73.

Lochhead, Liz (1984), *Dreaming Frankenstein and Collected Poems*, Edinburgh: Polygon.

—(1989) *Mary Queen of Scots Got Her Head Chopped Off and Dracula*, Harmondsworth: Penguin.

Lodge, David (1988), *Nice Work*, London: Secker and Warburg.

Lott, Tim (2002), *Rumours of a Hurricane*, London: Viking.

Lukàcs, Georg (1969), *The Historical Novel*, trans. Hannah and Stanley Mitchell, Harmondsworth: Peregrine.

Lyotard, Jean-François (1984), *The Postmodern Condition: A Report on Knowledge*, trans. Geoff Bennington and Brian Massumi, Manchester: Manchester University Press.

MacInnes, Colin [1959] (1986), *Absolute Beginners*, Harmondsworth: Penguin.

Malik, Kenan (2009), *From Fatwa to Jihad: The Rushdie Affair and its Legacy*, London: Atlantic.

Malins, Steve (2005), *Duran Duran: Notorious – The Unauthorised Biography*, London: Sevenoaks.

Marquand, David (1996), 'Moralists and Hedonists', in Marquand and Seldon (eds), *The Ideas that Shaped Post-War Britain*, pp. 5–28.

Marquand, David and Anthony Seldon (eds) (1996), *The Ideas that Shaped Post-War Britain*, London: Fontana.

Marqusee, Mike (2004), 'David Peace: State of the Union Rights', *Independent*, 5 March, at http://enjoyment.independent.co.uk/books/features/story.jsp?story=497787

Mars-Jones, Adam (1997), *Blind Bitter Happiness*, London: Chatto and Windus.

Mars-Jones, Adam and Edmund White (1988), *The Darker Proof: Stories from a Crisis*, rev. edn, London: Faber.

Marsden-Smedley, Philip (ed.) (1991), *Britain in the Eighties: The Spectator's View of the Thatcher Decade*, London: Paladin.

McEwan, Ian (1978), 'The State of Fiction: A Symposium', *New Review* 5:1 (Summer), 50–1.

—(1981), *The Imitation Game: Three Plays for Television*, London: Jonathan Cape.

—(1987), *The Child in Time*, London: Jonathan Cape.

—(1989), *A Move Abroad: Or Shall We Die? and The Ploughman's Lunch*, London: Picador.

McHale, Brian (1987), *Postmodernist Fiction*, London: Methuen.

McIlvanney, Liam (2002), 'The Politics of Narrative in the Post-War Scottish Novel', in Leader (ed.), *On Modern British Fiction*, pp. 181–208.

Mercer, Kobena (1994), *Welcome to the Jungle*, London: Routledge.

—(2000), 'Back to My Routes: A Postscript to the 1980s', in Procter (ed.), *Writing Black Britain*, Manchester: Manchester University Press, pp. 285–93.

Middleton, Peter (1993), 'Who Am I to Speak? The Politics of Subjectivity in Recent British Poetry', in Hampson and Barry (eds), *The Scope of the Possible*, pp. 107–33.

Millington, Bob (1993), '*Boys from the Blackstuff* (Alan Bleasdale)', in George W. Brandt (ed.), *British Television Drama from the 1980s*, Cambridge: Cambridge University Press, pp. 119–39.

Mitchell, David (2006), *Black Swan Green*, London: Sceptre.

Monteith, Sharon, Margaretta Jolly, Nahem Yousaf and Ronald Paul (eds) (2005), *Critical Perspectives on Pat Barker*, Columbia: University of South Carolina Press.

Moores, Phil (ed.) (2002), *Alasdair Gray: Critical Appreciations and a Bibliography*, Boston Spa and London: British Library.

Morrison, Blake and Andrew Motion (eds) (1982), *The Penguin Book of Contemporary British Poetry*, Harmondsworth: Penguin.

Mort, Frank (1996), *Cultures of Consumption: Masculinities and Social Space in Late Twentieth-Century Britain*, London: Routledge.

Moss, Stephen (2004), 'I don't make moral judgments', *Guardian*, 21 October, at http://books.guardian.co.uk/bookerprize2004/story/0,14182,1332083,00. html.

Mottram, Eric (1993), 'The British Poetry Revival 1960–75', in Hampson and Barry eds, *The Scope of the Possible*, pp. 15–50.

Muldoon, Paul (2001), *Poems 1968–1998*, London: Faber.

Mulgan, Geoff (1996), 'Culture: The Problem with Being Public', in Marquand and Seldon (eds), *The Ideas that Shaped Post-War Britain*, pp. 195–213.

Mulgan, Geoff and Ken Worpole (1986), *Saturday Night or Sunday Morning? From Arts to Industry – New Forms of Cultural Policy*, London: Comedia.

Mulhern, Francis (2009), 'Culture and Society, Then and Now', *New Left Review* 55 (January – February), 31–45.

Naipaul, V. S. [1987] (2002), *The Enigma of Arrival: A Novel in Five Sections*, London: Picador.

Nairn, Tom (1981), *The Break-Up of Britain*, rev. edn, London: NLB.

Newman, Jenny (1993), '"See Me as Sisyphus, But Having a Good Time": The Fiction of Fay Weldon', in Robert E. Hosmer Jr (ed.), *Contemporary British Women Writers: Texts and Strategies*, Basingstoke: Macmillan, pp. 188–211.

—(2005), 'Souls and Arseholes: The Double Vision of *Liza's England*', in Monteith et al. (eds), *Critical Perspectives on Pat Barker*, pp. 101–14.

Nichols, Grace (1988), 'Caribbean Woman Prayer', in Allnutt et al. (eds), *The New British Poetry*, pp. 65–6.

O'Brien, Sean (1998), *The Deregulated Muse: Essays on Contemporary British and Irish Poetry*, Newcastle: Bloodaxe.

—(2002), *Cousin Coat: Selected Poems 1976–2001*, London: Picador.

Oliver, Douglas (1988), 'The Infant and the Pearl (extract)', in Allnutt et al. (eds), *The New British Poetry*, pp. 219–22.

Oliver, Douglas, Denise Riley and Iain Sinclair (1996), *Penguin Modern Poets 10*, Harmondsworth: Penguin.

Orwell, George (1970), *The Collected Essays, Journalism and Letters of George Orwell, Volume 2: My Country Right or Left 1940–1943*, Harmondsworth: Penguin.

—[1941] (1982), *The Lion and the Unicorn: Socialism and the English Genius*, Harmondsworth: Penguin.

Osment, Philip (ed.) (1989), *Gay Sweatshop: Four Plays and a Company*, London: Methuen.

O'Sullivan, Maggie (1988), 'Busk, Pierce', in Allnutt et al. (eds), *The New British Poetry*, pp. 320–2.

Owen, Peter (ed.) (1993), *Publishing Now*, London: Peter Owen.

Palmer, William J. (1993), *The Films of the Eighties: A Social History*, Carbondale and Edwardsville: Southern Illinois University Press.

Peace, David (2004), *GB84*, London: Faber.

Powell, Neil (2008), *Amis & Son: Two Literary Generations*, London: Macmillan.

Procter, James (2000) (ed.), *Writing Black Britain 1948–1998: An Interdisciplinary Anthology*, Manchester: Manchester University Press.

Pugliese, Stanislao (ed.) (2003), *The Political Legacy of Margaret Thatcher*, London: Politico's.

Raine, Craig (1984), *Rich*, London: Faber.

Redhead, Steve (ed.) (2000), *Repetitive Beat Generation*, Edinburgh: Canongate.

Reynolds, Margaret and Jonathan Noakes (2003), *Jeanette Winterson: The Essential Guide*, London: Vintage.

Reynolds, Simon (1989), 'Against Health and Efficiency: Independent Music in the 1980s', in Angela McRobbie (ed.), *Zoot Suits and Second-Hand Dresses*, Basingstoke: Macmillan, pp. 245–55.

—(2010) 'The 1980s revival that lasted an entire decade', *Guardian*, 22 January 2010, at http://www.guardian.co.uk/music/musicblog/2010/jan/22/eighties-revival-decade.

Riley, Joan (1985), *The Unbelonging*, London: The Women's Press.

Roberts, Michèle (1987), *The Book of Mrs Noah*, London: Methuen.

Rorty, Richard (1989), *Contingency, Irony and Solidarity*, Cambridge: Cambridge University Press.

Rushdie, Salman (1981), *Midnight's Children*, London: Jonathan Cape.

—(1988), *The Satanic Verses*, London: Viking.

—(1991), *Imaginary Homelands: Essays and Criticism 1981–1991*, Harmondsworth: Granta / Penguin.

—(1992), 'Angela Carter 1940–92: A Very Good Wizard, a Very Dear Friend', *New York Times Book Review*, 8 March, 5.

—(2000), 'Songs Doesn't Know the Score', in Procter (ed.), *Writing Black Britain*, pp. 261–3.

Samuel, Raphael (1998), *Island Stories – Unravelling Britain: Theatres of Memory, Volume II*, London: Verso.

Sansom, Ian (2004), 'Whamming', *London Review of Books*, 2 December, at http://www.lrb.co.uk/v26/n23/sans01_.html

Segal, Lynne (1987), *Is the Future Female? Troubled Thoughts on Contemporary Feminism*, London: Virago.

Sheehan, Paul (2002), *Modernism, Humanism and Narrative*, Cambridge: Cambridge University Press.

Shepherd, Simon and Peter Womack (1996), *English Drama: A Cultural History*, Oxford: Blackwell.

Sherzer, Dina (1991), 'Postmodernism and Feminisms', in Smyth (ed.), *Postmodernism and Contemporary* Fiction, pp. 156–68.

Shklovsky, Victor (1965), 'Art as Technique', in Lee T. Lemon and Marion J. Reis (eds), *Russian Formalist Criticism: Four Essays*, Lincoln: Nebraska University Press, pp. 3–24.

Sierz, Aleks (2001), *In-Yer-Face Theatre: British Drama Today*, London: Faber.

Sinclair, Andrew (1995), *Arts and Cultures: The History of the 50 years of the Arts Council of Great Britain*, London: Sinclair-Stevenson.

Sinclair, Iain (1991), *Downriver*, London: Paladin.

—(ed.) (1996), *Conductors of Chaos: A Poetry Anthology*, London: Picador.

—(1997), *Lights Out for the Territory: 9 Excursions in the Secret History of London*, London: Granta.

Sinfield, Alan (1989), *Literature, Politics and Culture in Post-War Britain*, Oxford: Blackwell.

Smyth, Edmund J. (ed.) (1991), *Postmodernism and Contemporary Fiction*, London: B. T. Batsford.

Spencer, Luke (1994), *The Poetry of Tony Harrison*, Hemel Hempstead: Harvester Wheatsheaf.

Stevenson, Randall (1991), 'Postmodernism and Contemporary Fiction in Britain', in Smyth (ed.), *Postmodernism and Contemporary Fiction*, pp. 19–35.

—(2004), *The Last of England? The Oxford English Literary History, Volume 12: 1960–2000*, Oxford: Oxford University Press.

Suvin, Darko (1979), *Metamorphoses of Science Fiction: On the Poetics and History of a Literary Genre*, New Haven, CT: Yale University Press.

Swift, Graham (1983), *Waterland*, London: William Heinemann.

—(1989), letter to Barry Fishman, reproduced at http://www.scholars.nus.edu.sg/post/uk/gswift/gdletter.html

Taylor, D. J. (1989), *A Vain Conceit: British Fiction in the 1980s*, London: Bloomsbury.

—(1993), *After the War: The Novel and England since 1945*, London: Chatto and Windus.

Tennant, Emma (1989), *Two Women of London: The Strange Case of Ms Jekyll and Mrs Hyde*, London: Faber.

Tew, Philip (2004), *The Contemporary British Novel*, London: Continuum.

Thatcher, Margaret (1982), Speech to Conservative Party Conference, Brighton, 8 October, at http://www.margaretthatcher.org/speeches/displaydocument.asp?docid=10503 2

—(2003), 'Reflections on Liberty', in Pugliese (ed.), *The Political Legacy of Margaret Thatcher*, pp. 1–8.

Todd, Richard (1996), *Consuming Fictions: The Booker Prize and Fiction in Britain Today*, London: Bloomsbury.

—(2006), 'Literary Fiction and the Book Trade', in English (ed.), *A Concise Companion to Contemporary British Fiction*, pp. 19–38.

Toynbee, Polly (2007), 'Disaster in Iraq masks the truth: Blair's brand of social justice by stealth transformed Britain forever', *Guardian*, 11 May, *The Blair Years* supplement, 30.

—(2010), 'Tory cuts pave the way for a return to 80s dole queues', *Guardian*, 9 February.

Tredell, Nicolas (ed.) (2000), *The Fiction of Martin Amis: A Reader's Guide to Essential Criticism*, Cambridge: Icon.

Utley, T. E. (1991), 'Thatcherism: A Monstrous Invention', *Spectator*, 9 August, reprinted in Marsden-Smedley (ed.), *Britain in the Eighties*, pp. 146–9.

Wandor, Michelene (2000), 'Women Playwrights and Feminism in the 1970s', in Aston and Reinelt (eds), *The Cambridge Companion to Modern Women British Playwrights*, pp. 53–68.

Warner, Marina (1985), *Monuments and Maidens: The Allegory of the Female Form*, London: George Weidenfeld and Nicolson.

Waterstone, Tim (1993), 'The Other Side: Bookselling in Britain and the United States', in Peter Owen (ed.), *Publishing Now*, pp. 101–10.

Waugh, Patricia (1995), *Harvest of the Sixties: English Literature and its Background 1960 to 1990*, Oxford: Opus.

Williams, Raymond [1958] (1963), *Culture and Society 1780–1950*, Harmondsworth: Penguin.

—(1977), *Marxism and Literature*, Oxford: Oxford University Press.

Williamson, Judith (1987), *Consuming Passions: The Dynamics of Popular Culture*, London and New York: Marion Boyars.

Williamson, Kevin (2002), 'Under The Influence', in Phil Moores (ed.), *Alasdair Gray: Critical Appreciations and a Bibliography*, Boston Spa and London: The British Library, pp. 165–87.

Winterson, Jeanette (1987), *The Passion*, London: Bloomsbury.

—(1989), *Sexing the Cherry*, London: Bloomsbury.

—[1985] (1991), *Oranges are Not the Only Fruit*, London: Vintage.

—(1996), *Art (Objects)*, London: Vintage.

Witts, Richard (1998), *Artist Unknown: An Alternative History of the Arts Council*, London: Warner.

Wood, Michael (1998), *Children of Silence: Studies in Contemporary Fiction*, London: Pimlico.

—(2002), 'Enigmas and Homelands', in Leader (ed.), *On Modern British Fiction*, pp. 77–92.

Wright, Patrick (1985), *On Living in an Old Country*, London: Verso.

—(1991), *A Journey through Ruins: A Keyhole Portrait of British Postwar Life and Culture*, London: Radius.

York, Peter and Anne Barr (1982), *The Official Sloane Ranger Handbook: The First Guide to What Really Matters in Life*, London: Ebury.

York, Peter and Charles Jennings (1995), *Peter York's Eighties*, London: BBC.

Index